The Printer and the Prince

THE PRINTER
and
THE PRINCE

A Study of the Influence of Horace Greeley
Upon Abraham Lincoln as Candidate and President

JAMES H. TRIETSCH

EXPOSITION—UNIVERSITY BOOK

EXPOSITION PRESS • NEW YORK

FIRST EDITION

All rights reserved, including the right of
reproduction in whole or in part in any form
Copyright, 1955, by James H. Trietsch
Published by the Exposition Press Inc.
386 Fourth Avenue, New York 16, N.Y.
Designed by Morry M. Gropper
Manufactured in the United States of America
Consolidated Book Producers, Inc.

Library of Congress catalog card number: 54-13410

475

To
DR. JACK B. SCROGGS,
DR. FRANK H. GAFFORD,
and
MR. TERRELL W. OGG,
who have inspired me.

Preface

In a startlingly brief period of six years, from the date of its inception in 1854 to the national elections of November, 1860, the Republican Party experienced such a phenomenal growth and expansion that it was able to choose the sixteenth president of the United States.

One cannot overestimate the part which journalism played in this unusual growth of a new American political party, and among the journals which guided the development of the Republican machine and fostered its growth, none was more potent than the New York *Tribune,* edited by Horace Greeley. With its daily, its weekly, and its semiweekly editions, the *Tribune* spread its influence throughout the East and the Middle West, guiding the thoughts and opinions of farmers, of protectionists, of industrialists, of homestead advocates, and of those who favored internal improvements at federal government expense, in the direction of the Republican Party as a savior and as an instrument which would grant their political, social, and economic desires.

The Republican Party was Horace Greeley's dream come true. In 1856, he was instrumental in forcing the party's convention to choose John C. Fremont as a presidential candidate. When Fremont lost the election to James Buchanan, Greeley immediately began preparations for the campaign of 1860, telling his readers that the Republicans must choose a moderate candidate in order to win.

In 1860, Greeley proved instrumental in the national convention's choice of Abraham Lincoln as a presidential candidate. Greeley played an essential role in the campaign. Lincoln was elected, and civil war followed.

Fundamentally a pacifist, Horace Greeley was mentally overcome by this internal conflict, by the length of it and the bloody

cost of it. He endeavored to guide Lincoln into what he believed was a pathway to peace. But his advice was as erratic as
his mind was unstable; his influence upon Lincoln, who soon
fathomed Greeley's unreliability, was therefore negligible.

It is the purpose here to present the problem of Greeley's
efforts to influence Abraham Lincoln, with specific emphasis
upon his nomination, his election, his attitude toward secession
before his inauguration, and his presidential policies during the
four years that he served as chief executive in the White House.

Both primary and secondary sources have been used extensively. Although the research has been hampered by a lack of
access to the Greeley manuscripts and copies of the New York
Tribune (only in the New York Public Library and in the Library of Congress), the study involves a careful synthesis of secondary works, reinforced by heavy reliance upon the published
writings and correspondence of Lincoln and the memoirs, letters, anecdotes, and recollections of men and women of the time
who knew Greeley or Lincoln.

Although this study is by no means exhaustive, it has proved
substantially the premise that Abraham Lincoln entered the
White House totally unfamiliar with the problems which were
to face him, but before his death had grown in stature to a point
where no problem seemed too great or too grave for his understanding, sympathy, and solution. In this growth, Horace Greeley
played only a negative role. His badgering opposition to the
President, his erratic utterances in favor of either a vigorous war
or a sudden peace, helped guide Lincoln down a path of firm
resolve, wisdom, and stability. Therefore, despite the fact that
Horace Greeley did not directly influence Abraham Lincoln's
policies, the latter has been immortalized in history as a far
greater President than he might have been without Greeley's
almost constant personal and journalistic opposition.

J. H. T.

Contents

CHAPTER ONE

Measuring Greeley and Lincoln

In order to understand the significance of Horace Greeley and his New York *Daily Tribune* in the rise of Abraham Lincoln to political power, in order to comprehend the influence or the lack of influence which Greeley exercised over Lincoln and his presidential policies, it is essential to examine the characters, the temperaments, and the motivating forces in the lives of these two great Americans—the sixteenth president of the United States and the eccentric editor of the then nationally known New York *Tribune*. Consequently, Greeley and then Lincoln must be measured, side by side, in order that comparisons may be made.

First of all, Horace Greeley described himself often as "being in the position of the rich old fellow, who, having built a church entirely out of his own means, addressed his townsmen thus:

> I have built you a meeting-house,
> And bought you a bell;
> Now go to meeting
> Or go to Hell!" [1]

---

[1] The notes are found at the end of the book.

Of course, in this respect Greeley referred to his oracular news-paper, whose columns he expected the people to heed as though his own words were those of God. For it has also been said of Greeley, as Shakespeare wrote of an individual, "God made him, and therefore let him pass for a man." [2]

From 1840 to 1864, roughly, no more important journalist lived and thrived in the United States than Horace Greeley. During the nineteenth century there existed numerous novel forces which developed and influenced human welfare and hu-man opinions. Yet, in America, no more significant force may be found than that of popular journalism, and in this field of popular journalism, no name is more intimately a part of the new concepts and the new humane influences of the ante-bellum period than that of Horace Greeley. He literally exploded into life as an intense and a vitally passionate worker both with his hands and with his fire-filled brain. He personally trained him-self, on a farm, in school, as a printer, and as editor of the *Trib-une;* in fact, he worked ceaselessly until his fingers had grown too weary to work, until his brain was battered, bruised, and worn to shreds. Much like the rest of his generation, particularly in New England, work was all of life that interested him; work bore its own reward.[3]

All of his life he possessed extraordinarily sensitive nerves, was often filled with frantic fears, inward shrinkings, and sometimes hidden reluctances to act or to speak; sudden excessively loud noises frightened and disturbed him, and he admitted that he could look through a window at the steadily falling rain, look-ing and looking until nauseated. Furthermore, all of his life he feared the dark; and, as a trembling child, the stories told by adults of wolves and other "monsters" drove sleep from his eyes for endless hours. In his later years, the "wolfish doings of men" equally haunted him, leaving him frightened and awake. Never-theless, his physique proved to be generally fitted for the tre-mendous tasks he ever set before his face; he knew how to sur-mount obstacles, although his insatiable desire for success often made his approaches to problems quite unorthodox, to say the least.[4] Nevertheless, his face shone with the optimism he possessed, glowed with his faith in human beings—in general, if not in particular. Even after thirty years of fight-filled, war-wearying New York journalism, he remained a man of "benignant features" and "rustic candor," glorying vainly in what a contemporary described as a "fringe of sparse white whisker, which always leaves one doubting between an inverted halo and a tonsorial negligence." With his countenance and with his pen he expressed his reforming zeal, his indestructible optimism in "human progress and perfectibility." [5]

In politics, writes the biographer Bradford, he always evidenced a "definite" and an "energetic" theory as well as positive and forcefully expressed opinions; quite early, he devoted himself to the Protectionist cause and "supported it to the very end." Moreover, his outspoken opposition to slavery during the decade of the 1850's made more friends and more enemies than anything else, probably, in his entire journalistic career. The Civil War, however, was too much for him, because he was distracted between his love for humanity, his love of the Union, his hatred for slavery, his hatred of war, and his general disposition to dictate to everybody on everything. In a broad sense, Greeley was first "for letting the South go" without war, then for freeing the slaves more quickly and more forcefully than the President chose to do, and then for peace by foreign mediation.[6]

Unfortunately, perhaps, although he possessed the ability to say a great many witty and sarcastic things, Greeley had no real humor in himself, because he never permitted himself to accept the humorous, detached view of life; everything proved too intensely and immediately absorbing to him. He took not only his work but also himself quite seriously. However, he did employ his quick and apt wit, through which he was constantly able to give momentous occurrences a mocking or a satirical turn, in the somewhat exaggerated fashion of Mark Twain. His intellectual powers seem not to have been profoundly penetrating; nevertheless, his mind was, to the time of his somewhat sudden death, quick and agile. Furthermore, it was inexhaustibly fertile in arguments and debates, and he possessed an eighteenth-century faith in the logic and the perfection of human reason, particularly that of his own mobile mind. He loved to argue, he adored opposition, and he wished people to differ with him, because this furnished him with an opportunity to demonstrate his rational powers. Unfortunately, he was ever reluctant to abandon an opinion, for he hated, above everything else, to admit his error.[7]

Nevertheless, Greeley saw clearly enough to subscribe to this statement, to hold hauntingly to this hope:

> Fame is a vapor; popularity an accident; riches take wings; the only earthly certainty is oblivion; no man can foresee what a day may bring forth; while those who cheer today will often curse tomorrow; and yet I cherish the hope that the journal [the *Tribune*] . . . will live and flourish long after I have mouldered into forgotten dust. . . .[8]

It has been indicated already that Greeley opposed slavery; vigorously he fought the Kansas-Nebraska Act, and loudly he proclaimed the principle of equality among Americans. When he set down his recollections, he loved to quote Lincoln's words as a reflection of his own thoughts: "I am naturally anti-Slavery. If Slavery is not wrong, then nothing is wrong. I cannot remember when I did not so think and feel." [9] Lincoln thus forcibly gave expression to the general experience of American "free boys reared in Free States forty to sixty years ago"—Greeley was writing in 1868—while "the tradition and the impulse of the Revolutionary Age" still lingered "vivid and pervading." At least, Greeley thought such was the case for those boys who were "trained by intelligent Federal mothers." "In the South," however, he lamented, "it may have been otherwise." Nevertheless, "Southrons of greatness . . . of our country's *pure days,*—from George Washington and Thomas Jefferson down to Henry Clay, —at least theoretically" professed to be "Emancipationists." Unfortunately, though, complained the *Tribune's* supporting column of strength, in the South "the Revolutionary fires never burned so deeply or shone so brightly as in the North"; therefore, in the southern states, these "Revolutionary fires were very soon stifled and extinguished." [10]

Now, to understand in adequate measure why Greeley spoke so vehemently concerning slavery and the position of the South, to see why he sought so constantly to influence the policies of President Lincoln, one must delve deeply into the character and the composition of this man. As a contemporary of the mighty editor so quaintly stated, "The character of a man is derived from his *breed,* from his breeding, from his country, from his *time.*" Thus, Horace Greeley's poetry, his humanity, his tenderness—all those things that made him, at times, lovable and pleasing and even worshiped—he inherited from his tender Scottish mother. His "nice sense of honor," his Churchillian perseverance, his anxious honesty, his bulldog-like tenacity—these traits he inherited and had vocally instilled in him by his New England, old-English father. Furthermore, continues Parton, Greeley's childhood, spent in the rocky rises of Republican, Puritan New England, in a secluded rural section, tended to furnish him with his habits of shyness and fear in the New York crowds, his constant companionship with himself in his frequent moods of reflection, his readiness and his absolute independence of custom and of restriction, his rustic roughness and toughness.[11] In a real sense—more so than Lincoln—he was of the generation in which he lived; therefore, he "must share in the humanitarian spirit which yearned in the bosoms" of the "Saxon men" of his reforming age. In addition, he "escaped the schools," generally, as Parton so plaintively portrays it, and so "passed through childhood uncorrupted." However, if certain schools of the day corrupted certain youths—as schools may always have done—both Greeley and Lincoln escaped this form of human corruption; at any rate, Greeley, fortunately or unfortunately, became "his own man," not formed upon any pattern, not "trained up," as Parton puts it. Instead, Greeley "grew up," for "like a tree, he was left to seek the nourishment he needed and could appropriate." [12]

Perhaps it was for this reason that the influential editor "came close to Dr. Samuel Johnson's estimate of Oliver Goldsmith: 'No

man was more foolish when he had not a pen in his hand, or
more wise when he had.' " [13] As late as 1870, according to Joseph
Bucklin Bishop, his power, which, through his New York paper,
he wielded across the country, was not equaled "by any other
editor, either at that time or since." In truth, the *Tribune* was
a matchless moral force in the land because of the immense faith
of the plain people in the basic honesty of the editor. In fact,
Horace Greeley was the *Tribune* in the minds of thousands of
"everyday folk," and every word printed in that newspaper was
believed because of him. Just as to many Lincoln became the
symbol of America when he was assassinated, to many who read
his thousands of words Greeley symbolized, in essence, American
journalism.[14]

Perhaps some measure of his importance reached beyond
Greeley's vanity into his hopeful heart, for in 1860 in a letter
addressed to young men seeking to enter the arena of politics he
wrote these poignant words:

> The moral I would inculcate is a trite one, but none the
> less important. It is summed up in the Scriptural in-
> junction—"Put not your trust in princes." Men, even
> the best, are frail and mutable, while principle is sure
> and eternal. Be no man's man but Truth's and your
> country's. You will be sorely tempted at times to take
> this or that great man for your oracle and guide,—it is
> easy and tempting to lean, to follow, and to trust,—but
> it is safer and wiser to look ever through your own eyes,
> to tread your own path, to trust implicitly in God alone.
> The atmosphere is a little warmer inside some great
> man's castle, but the free air of Heaven is ever so much
> purer and much [*sic*] bracing.[15]

In general, this was Greeley's creed; if he did not always live by
it himself, at least he always preached it to others. He had ample
opportunity to learn its truth from experience, also; and he, like
Lincoln, learned from experiences—after experiences, and not before them. Consequently, the lessons he learned proved more
precious, if more costly.

A need still exists to show Greeley's mode of thinking, as reflected in his prose writings particularly; furthermore, those who write of Greeley's life and his work invariably minimize his interest in and his work in the fields of socialism, Grahamism, spiritualism, "teetotalism," Fourierism, and other equally vital isms. Almost no one has endeavored to reconcile Greeley's activity in these isms with his pragmatism in his approach to many other subjects; perhaps no reconciliation is necessary, if one sees the diversity of ideas and the radical range of thought in Greeley's mind. True, he was a man of "queer predilections, backings, fillings, and self-contradictory tangential excursions." [16]

With all of these contradictory tangents and turbulences to his credit, Greeley went beyond such trivia, succeeding as the editor of the *Tribune;* he may have failed as a politician—unlike Lincoln—but he did not fail as a journalist. Furthermore, his success was primarily due to his talents and to his professional experience, all of which he possessed in quantity by 1841—the year in which he commenced his colossal career at the helm of his newspaper. In addition, he furnished an immense impetus to the Free State movement; and, in turn, this impetus boosted the popularity of his *Tribune.*[17] His newspaper received a second boost through Greeley's own native intelligence, which, without self-imposed or externally created discipline, seemed quite adequately fitted for the northwestern section of the country. In other words, Greeley's brand of conservative thought—with its narrow moral code and its general opposition to woman suffrage, etc.—appealed to the readers of Ohio, Illinois, Indiana, and Michigan. But Greeley was recalcitrant, also, and this trait made him even more contradictory; he supported the protective tariff long after its original purpose had been accomplished, but he upheld the progressive doctrines of free education for the masses and freedom and opportunity for the immigrant Irish. Without doubt, he spoke for and was the child of his age.[18]

Consequently, as the child of his age, Greeley was politically conscious, without knowing quite why or how; and like the Whig Party, to which he, as a typical reforming conservative, had so long belonged, he initially refused—without quite knowing why or how—to take up the burning political issues of the day. In doing this, the Whig Party easily made way for its successor; and Greeley, with all of his political prescience, did not quite comprehend or realize that his party had been taken to the grave by Webster and Clay. As a result, for a long time he worked toward its dissolution unwittingly; then, when he did desire to assist in the formation of a new political party, he was skillfully held in check by one of history's wisest political bosses, Albany's Thurlow Weed, assisted by William H. Seward.[19] When Wisconsin Republicans laid most of their plans before Greeley early in 1854, he, because of his own political ambitions and because of Weed's half-promises, appeared unreceptive to the idea. However, in a letter of March 7, the editor did inform his friend Alvan E. Bovay that he would follow the latter's lead if the people were really ready for the establishment of a new political party; "we will try and do what we can," he promised.[20] "Remember," cautioned Greeley, "that editors can only follow where the people's heart is already prepared to go with them. They can direct and animate a healthy public indignation, but not create a soul beneath the ribs of death." [21] Perhaps Greeley believed this, and perhaps it is sometimes true; but it is safe to say that he did not endlessly practice it and that, in approaching Lincoln during the war, he apparently felt that he was endeavoring to create a soul of some sort beneath the ribs of death.

Still, Greeley followed some of his credos some of the time; and Bishop, working for the *Tribune* in 1870, recalled the "democratic policy" in the strange man's editorial office—a shabby room, shabbily furnished, containing an insufficient number of chairs and desks, sometimes an insufficiently large editorial staff. Even so, Bishop declares that a moral and an intellectual spirit pervaded that office—a spirit he had found nowhere else during his thirty-five years of journalistic experience.[22] Ill-kept and ill-furnished though this office was, it was the dream of every ambitious newspaperman to have a desk there some day, to write for the same page on which Horace Greeley wrote; to this end, the ambitious spent hours studying that editorial page and striving to copy and capture its style.[23] Moreover, into this romantic edi-

torial office drifted daily a deluge of reformers and intellectuals
—the former mainly leftovers of antislavery days, surviving abolitionists who wished editorial support for their various causes and
pecuniary aid for their material wants. As for the intellectuals,
they included among their number Edmund Clarence Stedman,
Richard H. Stoddard, Charles Dudley Warner, Thomas Bailey
Aldrich, Bret Harte, and Joaquin Miller. Bishop notes with interest that the two groups—intellectuals and reformers—refused
to mingle; however, Greeley was equally at home with both, was
equally sought out by both groups, responding with equal moods
of unpredictability to callers of both classes. And by far the
quaintest figure in the entire office at any time was the "great
editor," Horace Greeley—"careless and dishevelled in dress, as if
he had put on his clothes in the dark, with the round, rosy face
of a child, and a cherubic expression of simplicity and gentle-
ness." [24]

Numerous legends of the amazing eccentricities of this unusual man still exist, and most of them, strangely enough, are
reasonably authentic. Perhaps the oldest one of all is told by
Charles T. Congdon, who had gained considerable antislavery
fame in his *Tribune* editorials. Congdon relates the story of
Greeley finding a number of hand grenades hidden in the editorial room, placed there to be used in an emergency to fight
off the draft-rioters in 1863; when Greeley saw them, he screamed
and cursed in his high, squeaky voice, and then shouted in high-
pitched tones familiar to his associates, "Take 'em away! take
'em away! I don't want to kill anybody!" Furthermore, he would
not subside until the instruments of destruction were dutifully
removed from the room.[25]

During the war, the draft-rioters did virtually lay siege to
the *Tribune* building. On the first day, Greeley wrote steadily
until about noon, and then rose to go out for lunch. Oliver Johnson tried to detain him, but the editor shook off his protests,
donned his familiar white hat, and emerged from the building.
To the amazement of those inside the building, the crowd, as
by magic, opened an aisle through its midst, and the waving white
hat slowly disappeared. Greeley ate his lunch, then returned by

the same route through the midst of the quiet and docile crowd. Many have condemned Greeley as a coward; Bishop, however, upholds this true story as proof of the editor's real personal courage. Without doubt, this one anecdote exemplifies the true bravery of a man who usually possessed the courage to speak his own mind, even against the President, and who thus calmed and influenced many minds, including that of the President.[26] Furthermore, Congdon's narrative of how Greeley came to his office defying the rioting crowds is thoroughly confirmed by the private diary of Horace Greeley, as well as by other statements of reputable witnesses.[27] One of these was "Mr. Gibbons, a prominent abolitionist Quaker, who, as a devoted friend of Greeley's, cared for the editor during one of his serious illnesses"; in fact, Gibbons himself was almost attacked by the rioters in 1863, and he was always amazed at the courage with which Greeley faced them and at the way the crowds were muted by his bravery.[28]

Bishop relates one personal account demonstrating Greeley's ability to remain calm in the face of bitter opposition. One of the civic leaders of New York City, feeling that Greeley in his *Tribune* had aggravated the problem, entered the editorial office one day and exploded in curses and screams over Greeley's back, the latter being bent over a desk, engrossed in preparing a column for the presses. Greeley continued to write, apparently not heeding the party leader, whom his columns had not actively supported, until at length the angered man had exhausted his repertoire of recriminations; then, as the man was turning to leave, his wrath fully spent, the editor looked up from his work with his frequently seen childlike smile, remarking casually over his shoulder, "Don't go! don't go! come back and free your mind!" [29] And this was no isolated example of the editor's patience, for as a matter of course, when troublesome individuals entered his office with complaints, it was Greeley's habit to become absorbed with his work and not to look up at his antagonists. Moreover, those who were present and who knew Greeley well have declared repeatedly and emphatically that this method of forcing enemies to exhaust themselves and their anger upon an ignoring back proved invariably successful.[30]

Although generous to a fault in the field of monetary "handouts," Greeley proved equally ungenerous toward mistakes by his reporters. He could say what he chose in his editorials, twisting the truth to suit his whim of the moment, but he refused to permit his writers to make even one small mathematical error in their stories. In fact, Bishop declares that such errors in figures almost inevitably led to immediate dismissal of the guilty writer. As for Greeley himself, he had a phenomenal memory of dates and figures, when he wished to employ it; and he did almost all of his own writing, although his hand was virtually illegible. Bishop recalls the time that he declared, in reporting some election returns, that the Republican majority in a certain county was twelve thousand votes. When Greeley saw the story, he called Bishop to him, told him that "any fool should know that there were not even twelve thousand people in that county who were eligible to vote," and then gave him an illegible note of dismissal. Trembling and frightened at the man's wrath, Bishop carried the scribbled note to the managing editor who, unable to decipher the hieroglyphics, told Bishop to be more careful in the future and to continue working, remembering in reporting election returns that Greeley knew the voting strength of virtually every city, county, and state in the North and East. Bishop treasured this advice, and Greeley did not seem to remember that he ever had fired this faithful employee.[31] In fact, Greeley often dismissed his employees dozens of times, while they continued working for him; the handwriting of his dismissal notes was often so illegible that the dismissed persons took the notes to neighboring newspapers and used them as recommendations from Greeley. A more impracticable, whimsical, lovable man than Greeley never lived, writes Bishop; furthermore, American journalism has produced few, if any, superior editorial writers.[32]

Another contemporary of Greeley's insists that his breeding was remarkably fortunate, helping him much and hindering him little; the result was a man not perfect—indeed, "very imperfect, as all men are"—but a man who stood out as a "natural, peculiar, original, interesting" human being. He was a man

"dear to other men, a man to whom other men were dear"; and
his rarest, most divine gift was his ability to take a supreme interest in human welfare. Furthermore, Parton, filled with a deep
love and admiration for this unique and vacillating reformer,
writes that he, like few men, permitted himself "to go apart and
to ascend the height, there to survey the scene with serene, un-
selfish eye, and discover what those engaged in the struggle could
never see." Of course, exaggeration is evident and even paramount here; nevertheless, to certain contemporaries Greeley, like
Carlyle and Arnold, was not a genius, but a humanitarian, and
thus "liable to a certain class of mistakes" often not condemned
in lesser men.[33]

While engaging, at one period or another, in all of these
facets of nineteenth-century thought and expression, Greeley remained ambitious enough to hope that his *Tribune* would become, for his day and for posterity, the best newspaper that ever
existed—the leading paper of the United States. To this end,
Greeley worked; those who adored him said that he succeeded
by placing "the Right before the Popular, and the Just before
the Expedient," but those who condemned him declared that he
succeded only by employing the opposite formula. In actuality,
he used both formulas, or he could never have made the *Tribune*
the court of justice and injustice that it was. Of course, the
Greeley editorials were excluded from the slave states, and antislavery men insisted that this was because the editor upheld the
right point of view; of course, Greeley opposed the Mexican
War, and Lincoln and a number of Whigs were glad. However,
Greeley could not be satisfied with this response; he felt that
his fiery orations should be the gospel for all.[34]

Why did the *Tribune* so often swim with the current only
to change the direction of that current? Why was this newspaper
not always "catering to popular public opinion"? not always politically prudent and so often popularly prudish? The answer
must lie in the mind of the man who directed its course; Parton
insists that this man was the perfect example of a "Yankee,"
combining "French adroitness, German perseverance, and English pluck." Greeley was so tenacious that when his paper had

a purpose to proclaim, it was single in that purpose, although reading only on the surface of the columns did not always disclose the true single purpose hidden beneath the propaganda of the first several layers. This proved to be the case when Greeley secretly fought Seward's nomination for the Presidency in 1860, as well as when the *Tribune* supported Douglas's re-election to the United States Senate in 1858, so that the Democratic Party might be divided and the Republicans successful in the canvass of 1860. Greeley succeeded in these two single purposes. Sometimes he failed, however, as when he endeavored to elect Henry Clay to the presidency, and when he tried to force the Whig Party to adopt a policy and a political platform of "general beneficence." Nevertheless, although he sometimes failed, he wielded great power through his written words, principally because of his earnestness: he believed so profoundly in himself that he convinced others that he must be right. Then, too, one must not overlook the fertility in illustrations which he never ceased to employ; sometimes, as when he fought the institution of slavery, these illustrations were a bit absurd, but they worked very effectively, as did Lincoln's stories, to sell the public on a program and a policy. Some men even called him the "Franklin of the nineteenth century," because he said not many things but much.[35]

Almost singlehanded, he created modern popular journalism. He fought for issues rather than for personal monetary advancement. He chased ideas, and caught up with them; and this man who was always too frightened to play baseball, because of the speed with which the ball was thrown at him, took his very life in his own hands when he decided to pay Jefferson Davis's bail bond. He looked so peculiar that he made even Lincoln, whom we shall describe later, look debonair; and yet, so precocious was he that, at the age of three, he could read rapidly and, at the age of five, he had already read through the entire Bible. As a child, he was all brain, with a body so little that it scarcely counted in the figuring. As a man, he proved to be a political encyclopedia of dates and figures, entirely trustworthy, carelessly candid.[36] A brain, a sense of integrity, an overabundance of passion—these three things Greeley possessed. And what he had took him a long way—a very long way.[37]

Yet, along with his real integrity, Greeley played little games of revenge; and because Thurlow Weed and William H. Seward had prevented Greeley from organizing the Republican Party in New York State in 1854, and also from becoming either governor or lieutenant-governor of that state in that year, Greeley went to Chicago, as we shall see later, and defeated Seward for the Republican presidential nomination, thus actually helping to nominate Lincoln. As a result, Seward prevented the New York Legislature from sending Greeley to the United States Senate to fill out Seward's unexpired term when the latter became Secretary of State in Lincoln's administration. In the long run, Greeley discovered that his plans of retaliation did not gain for him the political office (any political office) that he sought so desperately.[38] However, his retaliatory rout of Seward in the convention at Chicago made history, and it was Greeley's first real step in influencing the destinies of Abraham Lincoln. Still, Greeley did not often seek vengeance, for his wars in behalf of liberal reforms, honest government, and efficient political economy proved him to be "rash but righteous." Finally, political defeat in 1872, when he "also ran" for the presidency, plus the sudden death of his wife and his hearing of a rumor that the managing staff wished to retire him from the newspaper to which he had given his whole life, wrote "30" (finis) to his story; and he too "went West," without, in life, receiving the loving cup he had so passionately wanted and so richly deserved.[39]

Yes, Greeley was an odd man; his oddities developed from his early, stony, New England days. Particularly is this true of his crude dress, which he refused to alter even after long years in New York, even after his mode of costuming himself had been ridiculed by the best citizens of the city. From the moment that he earned his first pennies to the day of his death, he spent almost no money on clothes; he always dressed roughly, uncouthly, ineptly. He could be seen on the streets or in his office, any day, in his "trailing coats and trailing trousers and clumsy boots"; his slouch hat and white overcoat were objects of everlasting caricature. He was clean but eccentric, thinking that such dress enhanced his democratic hold upon the affections of the public, but never feeling that his manner of attire was artificial. Furthermore, he trained his wife and his children in this same Scottish frugality of dress and habits; yet he loved them— that is, at least he loved his children; there is some question about the true affection that he may or may not have held for his wife. Probably, though, he loved his spouse and his offspring more completely and absolutely than his manner would ever indicate; certain it is, at any rate, that he especially adored his son Arthur—"Pickie," he called him—and that the death of this son, like the death of Lincoln's youngster in the White House, was "a prostrating blow." For even after the child's death, Greeley clung to his memory and loved him yet, with apparently pathetic, lingering fondness.[40]

The editor's wife was a schoolteacher when he met and married her—a woman "crazy for knowledge," as Greeley succinctly put it. Actually, she greatly influenced this man's career, for although the marriage may not have been wholly a happy one, Mrs. Greeley supervised with care her husband's needs, guided his quest for learning, and prolonged his life. Moreover, she sympathized with his dietary fancies and eccentricities; this made Greeley cheerful, although it drove away many mealtime guests. As she, like Greeley, desired to own a farm, they bought one. She insisted, though, that the farm must have on it a spring, a brook, and some woods; of course, her qualifications were met. But, to say the least, she, like her husband, lived oddly.[41]

Among Greeley's other oddities was the fact that, even as a boy, he had had no interest in play or in games; he declared to people repeatedly that he "had no taste for play." This may have been because of his fear which he often mentioned; yet, in the world of business and politics and journalism, he loved competition and repeatedly evidenced his unwavering personal courage. At any rate, one form of sport did appeal to him: he liked to fish. But as has been so cleverly remarked, "He fished, not for fun, but for fish." In addition, he liked to roam the woods, because there he found wild honey, "and wild honey was marketable." He sometimes liked to play checkers, it is said; however, he played so hard at the game that it became work to him. He traveled extensively, but it was clear that he was always in a hurry; and, either in traveling or at home, he had no taste whatever for ordinary social gatherings. Besides, when he was in company with others, his clothes were inappropriate and his manners brusque; usually he neither enjoyed himself nor conferred enjoyment.[42]

As we have indicated, Greeley, like Lincoln, had a taste for rural things; but in Greeley's eyes the crops and the insects and the manure loomed larger than the sunsets and the songs of birds and the smells of flowers. Always he remained an enormous, a voracious reader of books; but his preferences in reading, as in agriculture, were practical. Furthermore, he expressed a lifelong desire that education should be made very practical, that the schools should turn out artisans and farmers who would know their business and would enjoy it. Colleges seemed to him dangerous institutions and in great need of reform; he wrote, therefore, "We must have seminaries which not merely provide work [manual work] for their pupils, but require it inflexibly from all." [43]

It is doubtless understandable that this mysterious editor distrusted schools and mistrusted colleges, because his thinking was almost always that of the self-made, self-taught man; in other words, he thought constantly, but seldom with either logic or depth. Greeley acquired knowledge readily and widely, but without much system or exact organization. In fact, very much like Hitler, in Germany, and like Lincoln, in Illinois, Greeley possessed little training in the use and the organization of thought; consequently, he absorbed many facts, but he drew many fallacious conclusions.

Dangers are very inherent in this type of haphazard learning; Greeley and Lincoln both fell a prey to a number of them. Furthermore, Greeley lacked a natural mental control, proved to be erratic, was easily led and more easily misled. However, the greatest tragedy seems to have been that he was duped by himself more often than he was by others, and even more disastrously in many instances. In addition, not only did he not have mental control and discipline naturally, but it is also important that he never gained it through alarming experiences. Many have compared him with Benjamin Franklin; truly, in his printing aptitude he was much like this practical philosopher of the eighteenth century, but Franklin's common sense never failed him, and Greeley's often did.[44] Especially did his common sense forsake him when anyone approached him with the idea of a new reform; every practical and impractical reform interested him, because he could not leave "this dull old world alone." [45] He resented modern progress principally in but one important point—that of divorce. Prohibition, a reorganized educational program, peaceful emancipation of the slaves, improved conditions for labor, an improved status for the poor—all of these things made up his work of life. In his social and economic ideals, he anticipated the days of co-operatives, but he did not visualize the evils in men which developed both in the American Civil War and in the American labor movement. Schemers, declares Andrew D. White, took most of his time, most of his money, and most of his influence, but his fervor was earnestly sincere in desiring to lift the lowly, not above labor but above ignorance and want, to a position of mutual partnership "with Capital, which Labor will make fruitful and efficient." [46] To this dream of advancing the position of the laboring classes Greeley turned much of his own labor, but his exalted and unorganized thoughts led his ideals to heights which far exceeded the realms of practicality. Still, he dreamed.[47]

Margaret Fuller, who knew him well, was often critical of his dreams and of his philanthropy; "with the exception of my own mother," she wrote. "I think him the most disinterestedly generous person I have ever known." We have seen how he gave so generously, albeit sometimes roughly, of his money and his advice; he is sometimes well remembered for his gift of advice to the young males he saw starving in the East—"Go West, young man; go West!" [48] But this advising Greeley was not always cold, not always cryptic; he wrote an introduction to a book of Margaret Fuller's works, and he paid her his greatest honor and respect. He wrote pensively that she was more "uncomprehended" by the public than were any of her literary contemporaries; and what he said of her may also be said of him, who was at the same moment both idolized and shunned, reverenced and ridiculed, with conversation which charmed and manner which repelled. He, like her, "being dead, yet speaketh." [49]

In the long run, what Greeley said proved to be more important than what he did; his influence in words upon Lincoln, in both negative and positive reaction, proved more significant than his own actions, although they also were of paramount import, particularly at Chicago and at Washington. Yet there lies a link between what he wrote and what he did, that link being what he stood for and what he fought for; in that remains his most monumental achievement.[50] Few of us are creators, but all of us are critics; the first height is loftier, but the second is more readily appreciated by the world.[51] Both Lincoln and Greeley created something; hence, their contributions are permanent. While it is true that Horace Greeley is known to most people by one insignificant phrase—"Go West, young man; go West!" (Greeley meaning by the term "West" only Erie, Pennsylvania)—this New York editor should be known for his actual achievements. For example, Greeley in his newspaper initiated the idea of "stringer" correspondence; with other newspapers he inaugurated the locomotive-horseback-steamer relay to get news from the ships fresh in from Europe, faster than his competitor, James Gordon Bennett, of the New York *Herald*.[52] Out of this service grew the immense wire-service organization, the Associated Press. Furthermore, Greeley outdid Bennett's flair for sensationalism with a real newsworthy thoroughness and with various journalistic tricks and maneuvers; in addition, he outstripped the sensationalism of the Weed-Seward political combination with a Greeley thoroughness which amazed even the editor himself. Finally, before his death, he took a tremendous forward step at his newspaper desk when he hired Whitelaw Reid, the man who made of Greeley's "Old Rookery"—as they used to call the *Tribune* building—the modern New York *Herald Tribune* of today.[53]

Back to the nineteenth century we turn for a final contemporary view of Greeley, for an illustration that places him in a niche he deserves to occupy. Parton writes, from his vantage point of 1854, that, if Horace Greeley had been but a flower, nineteenth-century botanists would have called him a "single," and would have examined him with minute interest. Those scientists who study nature find scant pleasure in those plants—the pride of most gardens—that have all grown into flower or blossom, referring to them as "monsters." They are not beautiful to scientific eyes because of their lack of harmony, because nature has destroyed the geometrical proportions of the plant; the simpler, uncultivated "denizens of the woodside and the woodpath" more accurately fit the needs of the botanists who seek not uniform glory but singleness of structure.[54]

In addition to being a creator, Greeley was also a critic; and "a critic should be higher than those he criticizes, for a critic is a judge, and the judge is the highest official in the court." Greeley was. He began life as a working man; he rose from the ranks to become a working man for working men. In the editor's chair, on the lecturer's platform, in Congress, he tried to be true to his order; and the people were his order.[55]

Horace Greeley tried to be his own man—not a great man, not a model. Every sterling man is an original.[56] Parton declares —and Greeley would acquiesce—"if you like Horace Greeley, do as well in your work as he did in his; and, if you like him not, then do better!"[57]

Perhaps Abraham Lincoln determined to follow Greeley's and Parton's advice and do even a better job than Horace Greeley, at least in the province of politics. For when he was elected in November, 1860, the people asked what kind of President he would make. How would he handle the storm—the storm which was threatening to submerge and divide and destroy this nation? They knew "he had come up the hard way. But now, would he, or could any other man, be hard enough to meet this storm" and not be swept away by it? Born in the Kentucky wilderness in 1809, only two years before New England gave birth

to Horace Greeley, he had first glimpsed the light of day from
a one-room, clay-floor log cabin; this Abraham Lincoln had
grown up among pioneers who always said, "You never cuss a
good ax." He had worked diligently in fields and in woods, going
to school only a few months, borrowing books and burrowing
through them, endlessly studying books and people.[58] What little education he had was "picked up" along his rugged way; and
as a lawyer, a member of the Illinois Legislature, a congressman
during the Mexican War, he became no national figure. In 1858
the country first looked at him, first saw a shadow of him, when
he wrestled so rowdily and so royally with Senator Stephen A.
Douglas. Some, though not Greeley, thought he might make a
president, and two years later he was elected. By 1865, some of
the predictions had been justified; not only had he been elected,
but he had also made a president.[59]

By 1860, some of the people had heard of Lincoln's "matchless definition of the political injustice of slavery," applicable to
all nations and to all ages: "When the white man governs himself, that is self-government; but when he governs himself and
also governs another man, that is more than self-government—
that is despotism." [60] Some of the people had also heard Lincoln's irrefutable statement of the "natural right" of man "to
eat the bread, without leave of anybody else, which his own hand
earns"; and others had seen prophetic statesmanship in his declaration that the "Union cannot permanently endure half slave
and half free," issued a full four months before William H.
Seward proclaimed the "irrepressible conflict." Furthermore, some
knew—all were soon to learn—how he rose "from obscurity to
fame," "from ignorance to eloquence"—as had Greeley—"from
want to rulership." As he rose, as much as anyone could be he
remained uncontaminated by moral and political vices, undefiled
by heady yielding to political temptations, uneducated in the
schools of his day, "without family influence," lacking wealth
and prestige.[61]

Rendering his party every service it requested, by his talent
he helped Greeley when neither man held much respect for the
other, to lead that party from a state of despondency and in-

fantile immobility into stages of life and growth and energy and success. Meanwhile, at every stage of his own career, from nothingness to the head of a nation, he walked among his fellow men with such "irreproachable personal conduct that his very name grew into a proverb"—a proverb of integrity and of honesty that passed among the people, becoming eventually equivalent to the coin-current, a recognized token of social, political, and moral uprightness. Truly, this honor took time in coming; and when it came, it was not wholly deserved. Nevertheless, in his rise from nothingness to everything, through faith in God and in humanity, there lay a foundation for such acclaim. Yet he remained the "rail-splitter," six feet four inches in height, with a "spare but muscular" frame, uglier than friends like Nicolay would ever admit; quiet in demeanor he stood, erect in bearing.[62] His voice was pitched in a high tenor key like Greeley's, but his pronouncements came from a voice perhaps more clear and penetrating, less squeaky and excited, than that of the dynamic editor. His speeches he made short, filling them with pithy, epigrammatic sentences—sentences which presented the questions and the answers of the hour in new and in unwonted aspects, as in the Gettysburg Address.[63]

On the second day he was President, Lincoln made a cool, dry little speech to a visiting Pennsylvania delegation, saying he would like to spread the idea "that we may not, like Pharisees, set ourselves up to be better than other people"; as President, he would prefer them to feel that, "while we exercise our opinion . . . others have also rights to their exercises of opinions, and that we should endeavor to allow these rights, and act in such a manner as to create no bad feeling." Moreover, he chose to apply this principle rigidly in his own life and thoughts.[64] His second speech that same day included thanks to a Massachusetts delegation for its sanctioning of his inaugural address and for its assurance to him of its wholehearted and active support. He assured the delegation, furthermore, that, as President, he would hold national views; "I hope to be man enough not to know one citizen of the United States from another, nor one section from another," and his hope he realized in full measure. Both of these speeches had the "equilibrist air" of a man refusing to lose self-possession—refusing to be swept off his feet by hotheads—refusing to be "put in a hole" by certain shrewd schemers who were trying to outguess him.[65]

Continuing this policy, Lincoln carefully chose his Cabinet of advisors, trying to avoid the deals his managers had made for him, making the best of those he could not for the moment avoid, and balancing many fine points of divergence in geography, in politics, in economics, and in social thought. Then, when he was told regarding his Cabinet members, "They will eat you up," he replied, wisely, "They will be just as likely to eat each other up." [66] He employed cleverness, epigrammatic wisdom, very often tempering the tension of the storm and the falling rain of tears and blood with an easy humor.

Other impulses also motivated Lincoln's words and actions, impulses as noble as humor; in a letter for Secretary of State Seward to the governors of the North requesting more troops for a continuation of the war, Lincoln made this oath of determination: "I expect to maintain this contest until successful, or till I die, or am conquered, or my term expires, or Congress or the country forsake me." Often both Congress and the country forsook him; still, he continued the contest "until successful," and then he died.[67]

About July 9, 1862, Lincoln visited General George B. McClellan at Harrison's Landing on the James River; he held a sort of informal court of inquisition on the conduct of the campaign. Strangely, he did not ask for advice, as he had formerly done on military affairs with which he knew himself to be unfamiliar; his temper and his attitude were profoundly different from what they had been in his conference with his generals on March 7, 1862.[68]

The contrast between these two military conferences conducted by the President cannot be overemphasized, for during the four months intervening, Lincoln had passed through a transformation, or "something very near to that." Therefore, the month of June, 1862, is probably the actual turning point in his career; some change within him was coming rapidly forward, although just what the change was, and exactly how it was accomplished, prove to be matters only of conjecture, speculation, and assumption. At any rate, the interview with General Winfield Scott seems to have encompassed a crucial moment in Lincoln's period of adjustment both to the war and to his presidential task.[69] It is to be noted, moreover, that General Pope, "who accompanied him to West Point, was placed in high command immediately upon their return to Washington." When Lincoln visited McClellan at Harrison's Landing, all the timidity and hesitation that was so conspicuous in him four months before had entirely vanished.

There is much in his attitude toward life before this time that is problematical; from this time forward there is almost none. Through past, present, and future mistakes a great genius has found himself; and henceforward, through erroneous and irrefutable judgments alike, he will be master of his own house. From this point, Lincoln concluded that the desperate position in which he was now placed compelled him to shift the issue of the war and halt his hesitancy, making emancipation his avowed aim and purpose. The first basic step was another of his wise and soft-pedaled appeals to the border states. He proceeded to his Emancipation Proclamation, a step for which Greeley had been storming stoutly for some time in the *Tribune* pages.[70]

Lincoln was in a religious mood when he prepared his statement of emancipation; he worked on it diligently and lamented what he considered to be its lack of success.[71] During this period he spoke freely of religion to his friends and regularly attended the New York Avenue Presbyterian Church in Washington, D.C.[72] Meanwhile, Greeley was a weekly worshiper at the Universalist Church in New York City, where he constantly slept through the services and then freely applauded the liberal sermons of the minister. On the other hand, Lincoln wrote in a letter to General S. R. Curtis these well-prepared words:

> It is most cheering and encouraging for me to know that
> in the efforts which I have made and am making for
> the restoration of a righteous peace to our country, I

am upheld and sustained by the good wishes and prayers of God's people. No one is more deeply than myself
aware that without His favor our highest wisdom is but
as foolishness and that our most strenuous efforts would
avail nothing in the shadow of His displeasure. I am
conscious of no desire for my country's welfare that is
not in consonance with His will, and of no plan upon
which we may not ask His blessing. . . . If there be one
subject upon which all good men may unitedly agree,
it is imploring the gracious favor of the God of nations
upon the struggles our people are making for the preservation . . . of civil and religious liberty.[73]

Still, overtowering this and all other issues was the personality and the character of Lincoln—his acts, his decisions, and his
words. He proved to be spokesman and master mind of the war
in a more strict sense than any other person; yet he remarked
and wrote, in a letter made public in the spring of 1864, "I
have been controlled by events." "My policy is to have no policy," he had announced to a secretary in the spring of 1861.[74]
He swung out and came back with the numerous changing tides
of thought and feeling in the American people; on one issue,
however, he stood granite-hard, crystal-clear—that was the Union,
its preservation. On all other issues he would have compromised,
and so indicated to the public.[75]

Year after year, the two foremost American newspapers had
belittled and criticized Lincoln and his policy or his lack of
policy. The New York *Herald* and its publisher, James Gordon
Bennett, saw him as "too friendly with the antislavery crowd";
on the other hand, the New York *Tribune* and its editor, our
Lincoln influence, Horace Greeley, saw Lincoln as "too slow, too
hesitant, too 'vacillating,' too late with the Emancipation Proclamation, which should have been issued earlier, and too 'inde-
cisive' in his management of the war." Furthermore, many of the
leading men of Lincoln's own party in the Senate and in the
House of Representatives leaned toward this Greeley viewpoint,
or what was later termed "radicalism," as did at least one mem-

ber of the Cabinet, Salmon Portland Chase, the Secretary of the Treasury.[76] In fact, Chase carried on a "curious and furtive" procedure aimed at undermining Lincoln and getting himself nominated for the presidency in 1864.

Nevertheless, through trials and difficulties—even hours of agony—Lincoln moved, holding a depth of profound faith in the people. They could certainly be trusted. He told Dick Oglesby, of Illinois, that if in the long run a man did right by them, the people would know it and would do right by him. "Now he had been the first Laughing Man in the White House, yet also the most Solemn Man the Executive Mansion had ever known." To many "plain folk" over the land he had become a living reality during the bloody months of that terrible war—a man warm and keen and with humor and understanding. Many people dismissed his habit of joking and saw him actually as a tall, lean, melancholy prophet, doing probably as well as any other man could have done, maybe a lot better, in a tangle of fate and circumstances where it seemed at times the will of God was the most decisive factor.[77]

Nathaniel Hawthorne, the great nineteenth-century novelist, himself a bit eccentric and a New Englander with many ideas of social reform and with many socialistic tendencies similar to those espoused by Horace Greeley, watched Lincoln literally "handle a committee" who presented the White House with a new buggy whip from a Massachusetts factory. Of the war over which Lincoln presided, Hawthorne had written that he approved it, but he had subsequently added, in his whimsical way, "I don't quite see what we are fighting for." In his most somber syllables, he sketched Lincoln as the *"essential* representative of all Yankees"—this of a true Westerner! [78] Upon his arriving at high office, Hawthorne lightly concluded of Lincoln, "presumably, it was his first impulse to throw his legs on the counciltable, and tell the Cabinet Ministers a story." No words could tell how long and how awkward the President was—thought Hawthorne—"and yet it seemed as if I had been in the habit of seeing him daily, and had shaken hands with him a thousand times in some village street." Describing him further, he noted that "the whole face" was "as coarse a one as you would meet any-where in the length and breadth of the States; but, withal, it is redeemed, illuminated, softened, and brightened by a kindly though serious look out of his eyes, and an expression of homely sagacity, that seems *weighted* with rich results of village experience." [79]

Thus, it would appear that Hawthorne's own appraisal of Lincoln, after seeing him in the White House, proved to be very near that of Mrs. Hawthorne, who once wrote, in a letter, "I suspect the President is a jewel. I like him very well." [80] A jewel, indeed, he was—a diamond, polished and made beautiful by hard licks and by rubbing constantly against the elements, humanity, and disaster. A jewel he was, indeed, and a jewel made more noticeable, more picturesque, more beautiful, by his setting—at the head of and in the very center of the Union itself. For far had gone his homely remark that, in order to win the war for the Union, they must "keep pegging away." Far, too, among the people, his people, had traveled his statement, made to some who desired a favor at one of the governmental departments, "I have no influence with this administration." Once, also, a woman asked him to use his authority in her behalf at the War Department; and she quoted his reply thus: "It's of no use, madam, for me to go. They do things in their own way over there, and I don't amount to *pig tracks* in the War Department." [81]

He moved with events, once telling a New York citizen, "I do not lead; I only follow"; furthermore, he made it quite clear to the Prince de Joinville that he had no "policy" as such. "I pass my life preventing the storm from blowing down the tent, and I drive in the pegs as fast as they are pulled up." [82] Because he claimed that he pursued no policy, because he thought slowly and acted slowly but wisely, because he could control men and could compromise on certain issues, two opposite points of view often seemed to be held by him at the same time; thus, a St. Louis clergyman once mentioned a letter of Lincoln's concerning a case of disloyalty in Missouri, which had been read before a large assembly of churchmen, with both sides of the dispute claiming to have Lincoln's support. Lincoln, who perhaps supported neither side, hearing of this humorous incident, declared that it reminded him of an Illinois farmer he once knew who, with his son, was out in the woods one day looking for a lost sow. After an extended and fruitless search they at last arrived at a creek branch, where they discovered hog tracks as well as "signs of a snout rooting for some distance on both sides of the creek." After surveying the situation soberly for some moments, the old man remarked acidly to his boy: "Now, John, you take up on this side of the branch and I'll go up t'other, for I believe the old critter is on both sides." [83]

In the face of all criticism, Lincoln performed his staggering national assignment without "squealing," without murmuring. For in speech he liked to be short-spoken, once saying of another man, "He can compress the most words into the smallest ideas of any man I ever met"; and Nicolay heard him tell of a southwestern orator who "mounted the rostrum, threw back his head, shined his eyes, and left the consequences to God." He did not "care a cornhusk for the literary critics," ran one comment; but Lincoln was careful with his speech, although he never ceased to flavor it with his own brand of syrup. The Boston *Transcript* saw him as a man familiar with the "plain, homespun language . . . of the people, accustomed to talk with the folks." [84] The Chicago *Times,* however, spoke for a definite element in its opinion: "Such a garrulous old joker with his pen is our President. A very 'phunny' man is our President." [85]

Nevertheless, despite such damning criticisms, "his sober face, his solemn purposes and words," had gone out and made their impress here and there, and in his Annual Message to Congress in December, 1862, he almost apologized for his "undue earnestness," which led to his challenge:

> The dogmas of the quiet past are inadequate to the stormy present. The occasion is piled high with difficulty, and we must rise with the occasion. As our case is new, so we must think anew and act anew. We must disenthrall ourselves.[86]

And simultaneously with his challenges to the people, this sixteenth president of what he considered to be an indestructible
Union, in painful power, sounded the deep call:

> Fellow-citizens, we cannot escape history. We of this
> Congress and this administration will be remembered in
> spite of ourselves. No personal significance or insig-
> nificance can spare one or another of us. The fiery trial
> through which we pass will light us down, in honor or
> dishonor, to the latest generation. . . . The way is
> plain, peaceful, generous, just—a way which, if fol-
> lowed, the world will forever applaud, and God must
> forever bless.[87]

What was Lincoln's generous, just, plain, and peaceful plan
of procedure?—to free the slaves, adequately to compensate their
owners, to preserve the Union, to end the war. Furthermore, in
this aim Lincoln did not hesitate, as Greeley thought; instead,
he flowed toward its accomplishment with firmness and with
fervor.[88]

In a foreword to one of the numerous contemporary accounts
of Lincoln and his life, Ida M. Tarbell declares that, without
qualification, "the man [Lincoln] we get from the mass of reminiscences left of him is very much of a piece." Oftentimes, when
his contemporary reporters found themselves at a point in his
character which baffled them and halted them in a state of confusion—such as Lincoln's secretiveness and his periods of silence
and gloom—they sought in themselves, in their own imaginative
ideas, an explanation containing nineteenth-century logic and
lucidity. Thus, Nicolay and Hay—who thought that they knew
the true Lincoln very well—explain his periods of depression and
his frequent states of melancholy in terms largely of indigestion;
Herndon, on the other hand, refers this same characteristic of
depression to Lincoln's morbid belief in an irregular ancestry
and to his inability to forget a lost love. At times, both points
of view may seem perfectly legitimate to the ardent researcher;
nevertheless, neither explanation may be adequate or even correct in the remotest detail. The recollections of Lincoln that

come from contemporaries who had the opportunity to observe him closely over a considerable period, but who never followed the circuit or never campaigned with him—particularly those contemporaries who never had the misfortune to have Lincoln become a common, everyday, and useful factor in their lives—are especially noteworthy for their naïveté, for their "preciousness." [89] Henry B. Rankin's recollections of Lincoln are of that sort, precious. They come from a man possessing the unique opportunity of observing Lincoln through an ardent, active, youthful mind—from a man whose background, whose relationship, whose age, and whose nature make his remarks "special and different." Rankin was but a youth of less than twenty when, in 1856, he entered the law office of Herndon and Lincoln as an apprentice-student; Lincoln was already to this young man a romantic and inspiring character, for Rankin had learned from his parents—who knew by direct contact—of Lincoln's struggles toward success through the devastatingly thick walls of obscurity and poverty.[90] Yet, Rankin waited until he was eighty-six before he attempted to put into writing his recollections of Lincoln. This caused his thoughts and his words to lack the license of undisciplined youth, but to contain the seasoning of frontier maturity. Pledging himself to be as truthful as any man can be, Rankin set forth his ideas confirming other statements about the basic honesty of Lincoln.[91] It is the opinion of Rankin, furthermore, that in the Menard County Circuit Court in the state of Illinois, Lincoln really began his long task of fitting himself to serve the American democracy, to serve in and for that democracy. Here "he acquired a genuine fellow-feeling for, understanding of, and broad sympathy with his fellow men, whatever their social standing, their wealth or poverty, be they educated or ignorant, their creed or their birthplace." [92]

However, Horace Greeley ever stood somewhat aloof from Lincoln and from Lincoln's aims and ambitions, unless those aims and ambitions were directed and charted by the impulsive and the vigorously vacillating Greeley. In 1858, when Republicanism was catching on, as its time of triumph grew near, William H. Herndon, Lincoln's law partner, went East from Illinois,

hoping to enlist support for his partner's senatorial race against
Stephen A. Douglas—support from the powerful eastern leaders
of the Republican Party. In general, Herndon found these "great
men" friendly but immovable—some more friendly, others more
immovable. And Editor Horace Greeley, from his shabby editorial office, squeaked to him that "the Republican standard was
too high." "We want something practical," insisted Greeley; and
this, we may be quite certain, "stiffened Lincoln's back" when
Herndon reported it to him. For the young, gaunt, and tall determined and decisive lawyer from the West, being a man with a
cause, cared deeply for his future—even more deeply for his present. And, for that matter, Lincoln was fast becoming a really
shrewd manager in a political party which, he firmly believed,
stood for something.[93] Charnwood believes that Greeley's compromising answer to Herndon reveals the spirit of "flabbiness"
which the northern and northeastern Republicans were in danger of making a governing tradition. It seems to him that, in
Greeley's mind, the wrongfulness of any extension of slavery
might be loudly asserted in 1854, but, in 1858, when it no longer
looked as if so great an extension of it might be really imminent,
there was no harm in shifting toward some less provocative principle on which more people at the moment might agree.

Actually, Greeley's plan was this: successfully to combine the
divergent interests, ideas, and principles of the Northeast and
the Northwest, in order to make certain that the Republican
Party would win the all-important presidential election of 1860.
It was for this reason that Greeley supported Douglas, whom he
despised, and that he was unwilling to support Lincoln, whom
he never seemed thoroughly to trust, but whom, in 1860, he preferred for reasons of expediency to William H. Seward.[94] As for
Herndon's own account of his journey to see Greeley, we may
read of it in the published Herndon letters and papers. In discussing this man, who made of Lincoln an idol which he worshiped, Albert Beveridge writes that "Herndon was forty-seven
years of age when Lincoln was murdered. For fourteen years
after that event, he kept up his Lincoln researches, delivering
several lectures on phases of Lincoln's life, practicing law, and

keeping up a large general correspondence." Beveridge continues thus, revealing an important and a sometimes overlooked fact:

> Perhaps it is not unworthy of note that it was to Herndon, and not to Lincoln, that, for years before his nomination for the Presidency, such men as Parker, Sumner, Seward, Phillips, *Greeley*, and Garrison wrote. To be sure, the youthful and ardent Herndon always began the correspondence; yet, even so, it was to him and not to his partner that these brilliant men, molders of the public opinion of the time, looked for reports of conditions in Illinois. It is extremely curious that, judging from their letters to Herndon, these leaders seemed not to have realized that Lincoln amounted to anything during that period.[95]

Now, in order to learn from this reliable witness, Herndon, what he thought of the Greeley-Lincoln relationship prior to the days of the Republican Convention in Chicago in 1860, we need but quote from the correspondence of Herndon—first, a letter written to Weik, April 14, 1885, from Springfield, Illinois:

> I saw the "great abolitionist," I think in 1858, just a little while before the race of Douglas and Lincoln *actually* began; went to see them at the implied request of Lincoln, as I understood his *hints;* did not let the "great abolitionist" know who sent me nor whom I *impliedly* represented; saw Trumbull, Sumner, Greeley, Parker, Phillips, Garrison, *et al.;* stated to them what I wanted, i.e., what the great West wanted. Told them that Douglas could not be trusted, that Lincoln could, gave them facts upon facts, and opinion upon opinion. All went well, *except Greeley.* . . .[96]

From another letter—Herndon to Weik, December 1, 1885—we read a more complete statement elaborating the Herndon visit to the *Tribune* editor, and explaining how, at first, Greeley promised to co-operate with Herndon and to assist Lincoln, although in his heart Greeley did not intend that either the office of United States Senator or that of United States President should go to a man by the name of Abraham Lincoln:

> I then went to New York, saw Greeley, told him politely and cautiously my story, said to him that Douglas was a new convert, was not to be trusted, was conscienceless, and without political principles or honor, etc. I said to Greeley: "You do right in patting Douglas on the back, but wrong when you indirectly hit Lincoln, a true, real, and long-tried anti-slavery man, in order directly or indirectly to overthrow or kill Lincoln. Can you not assist Douglas and our cause by helping Douglas without stabbing Lincoln?" We had a long conversation, but this is the shell and substance of it. Greeley said to me, as I *inferred*, as I understood it, that he would most assuredly assist Douglas in all honorable ways; that he liked Lincoln, had confidence in him, and would not injure him; that he would somewhat change tactics and be careful in the future. . . . Greeley for some time acted up to the square thing. . . .[97]

It is fairly apparent, however, from Greeley's own letters to Schuyler Colfax and to others, from his own editorials, as well as from his private statements, that the editor neither liked Lincoln particularly nor had any real confidence in him. Furthermore, he scarcely knew him, having seen him but briefly in the Mexican War Congress, when they served together in the House of Representatives, and he continued to distrust him slightly. As for Lincoln and his western friends, including Herndon, they remained wary of Greeley, often having editorial difficulties with him.[98]

In fitting himself for his task, Lincoln faced many obstacles, and after he attained his exalted position, he faced even greater opposition. Men of the press like Horace Greeley wielded great power in the land, and Lincoln himself knew the formidable strength of the blessed support which propaganda afforded. His skillful usage of the Emancipation Proclamation proves this fact; propaganda was paramount in every phase of federal government maneuvering. For example, John Hay wrote in a letter to John G. Nicolay, from Stone River, South Carolina, April 8, 1863:

> DEAR NICO:
>   I arrived here tonight at the General's Headquarters and was very pleasantly received by both him and Halpine. They are both in fine health and spirits.[99]

At first glance, this seems like an innocent, even worthless quotation; however, investigation reveals its grave importance, discloses a hidden meaning in these few simple words written by Hay to his esteemed Lincolnian colleague. Thus Tyler Dennett concisely comments upon this portion of Hay's friendly epistle:

> Halpine, of whom Hay saw a good deal, deserves more than passing notice. He was an Irish journalist who had been private secretary to P. T. Barnum. Under the name of Miles O'Reilly he wrote humorous sketches for the New York *Tribune*. After the war he entered New York politics, becoming Registrar of the County and City on an anti-Tammany ticket. We are accustomed to think of government propaganda as having been developed during the World War [World War I]. From the Hay diary it would appear that throughout the Civil War it was not uncommon to place journalists in important military and political positions whence they could write for the papers with a view of directing public opinion.[100]

We may safely say that Lincoln and Greeley had one thing in common; both men apprehended the value of favorable propaganda, and both men fought, each in his own way, to find favor in the hearts and minds of the people. Lincoln was more successful at this endeavor than was Greeley, perhaps because Lincoln pursued his policy more gradually. Nevertheless, both men received an overabundance of criticism in their lifetimes, and death brought more fame to them than life ever had. In many things Greeley and Lincoln differed, but most of all they differed in their temperaments and in their ways of handling men. Horace Greeley was a public oracle, and he wished to become a public politician; Abraham Lincoln, on the other hand, was a true politician, and he instinctively avoided sounding oracular. Greeley, always a strenuous actor, looked at Lincoln's amiable, shrugging moods and thought him much too easygoing for leadership; and Lincoln, watching Greeley's brittle, hortatory air, thought him too tense to be trustworthy.[101]

In this appraisal, each man mistook one characteristic for the whole person; Greeley could be supple and compromising when he was sure of the road ahead, just as Lincoln could be hard as flint when he was also sure. The differences between the two men often occurred only in timing and in much-emphasized public utterances; however, such differences, trivial as they may seem to us now, proved sufficient in the hour of crisis to make each man wary of the other. Actually, the two men had much in common; they shared a point of view on the problem of slavery, avoiding the two extremes of "abolition" and "appeasement." Both men distrusted the eastern leaders of the Republican Party, and both desired the best possible way of life for the plain people—supporting homestead legislation and plans for improved labor conditions as the centers of population gradually shifted westward. Furthermore, both men themselves came from impoverished origins, struggling upward through many strata of society in order to reach their respective positions of leadership.[102] In common, they seemed to have dismally unhappy marriages, and reputations for being odd, quizzical, rustic characters, far out of conformity with most of the fashionable standards of the urban East. Also, each could easily be spotted in a crowd because of a homespun, familiar jocularity, a trait which pleased many but annoyed some; both men could be identified by their improvident natures, their frequent plunges into lonely, dismal despair, their yearning toward poetry, their insatiable reading, their accumulations of vast stores of folklore and legend and citation, their love of the just use of words, their emergence as unique craftsmen of prose in writing and in speaking, with sure rhythms of their own, with terse and totally unvarnished common speech.[103]

In fact, these two men actually thought and wrote so much alike that their words, but for mood and cadence, might even be interchangeable; and yet, they mutually looked the other way, repelling one another, as if they sensed the great measure of similarity in their concrete and in their ephemeral ideas, as if they perceived the vast difference of temperament between them. When they met, it was with reserve; and Greeley has insisted that he was one of the few men who never heard Lincoln tell a funny story. As for Lincoln, although he seldom heeded the advice of Horace Greeley, he kept a special pigeonhole in his desk for the latter's letters.[104]

As previously indicated, Lincoln possessed a powerful yearning toward poetry; he enjoyed reading it, whether it made him laugh or made him weep, and he even wrote some of his own. In a letter to Andrew Johnston, dated April 18, 1846, Lincoln reveals this little-known and seldom explored side of his character:

> Your letter, written some six weeks since, was received in due course, and also the paper with the parody. It is true, as suggested it might be, that I have never seen Poe's "Raven"; and I very well know that a parody is almost entirely dependent for its interest upon the reader's acquaintance with the original. Still there is enough in the Polecat, self-considered, to afford one several hearty laughs. I think four or five of the last stanzas are decidedly funny, particularly where Jeremiah "scrubbed and washed, and prayed and fasted." [105]

Although it is unfortunate that we do not have at hand this humorous parody, we may still savor the essence of Lincoln's humor from his words and may continue his letter, closing with a portion of his own poem:

> I have not your letter now before me; but, from memory, I think you ask me who is the author of the piece

I sent you and that you do so ask as to indicate a slight
suspicion that I myself am the author. Beyond all question I am not the author. I would give all I am worth,
and go in debt, to be able to write so fine a piece as I
think that is. Neither do I know who is the author. I
met it in a straggling form in a newspaper last summer
and I remember to have seen it once before, about fifteen years ago, and this is all I know about it. The piece
of poetry of my own which I alluded to, I was led to
write under the following circumstances. In the fall of
1844 [Lincoln was thirty-five then], thinking that I
might aid some to carry the State of Indiana for Mr.
Clay, I went into the neighborhood in that State in
which I was raised, where my mother and only sister
were buried, and from which I had been absent about
fifteen years. That part of the country is, within itself,
as unpoetical as any spot of the earth; but still, seeing
it and its objects and inhabitants, aroused feelings in
me which were certainly poetry; though whether my
expression of those feelings is poetry is quite another
question.[106]

No person would deny the emotional fervor, sway, and power
of Lincoln who has read his Gettysburg Address or his Second
Inaugural; both of these are virtually poetry, containing vivid
poetic passages. It is significant, therefore, to follow this letter
and to read Lincoln's rhyming poetry:

When I got to writing, the change of subjects divided
the thing into four little divisions or cantos, the first
only of which I send you now and may send the others
hereafter.

My childhood's home I see again,
    And sadden with the view;
And still, as memory crowds my brain,
    There's pleasure in it too.

O Memory! thou midway world
  'Twixt earth and paradise,
Where things decayed and loved ones lost
  In dreamy shadows rise,

And, freed from all that's earthly vile,
  Seem hallowed, pure, and bright,
Like scenes in some enchanted isle
  All bathed in liquid light.

As dusky mountains please the eye
  When twilight chases day;
As bugle-notes that, passing by,
  In distance die away;

As leaving some grand waterfall,
  We, lingering, list its roar—
So memory will hallow all
  We've known, but know no more.

Near twenty years have passed away
  Since here I bid farewell
To woods and fields, and scenes of play,
  And playmates loved so well.

Where many were, but few remain
  Of old familiar things;
But seeing them, to mind again
  The lost and absent brings.

The friends I left that parting day,
  How changed, as time has sped!
Young childhood grown, strong manhood gray,
  And half of all are dead.

I hear the loved survivors tell
  How nought from death could save,
Till every sound appears a knell,
  And every spot a grave.

I range the fields with pensive tread,
    And pace the hollow rooms,
And feel (companion of the dead)
    I'm living in the tombs.[107]

It appears here that Lincoln proved to be not only a statesman but also a poet; the reason that he was both lay in himself,
in his deep and emotional comprehension of the inestimable
value of human beings and of things. Lord Charnwood correctly
wrote that "many great deeds" were accomplished during the
American Civil War, but that by far the greatest of these accomplishments was the "keeping of the North together" in an
enterprise "so arduous, and an enterprise for objects so confusedly
related as the Union and freedom." Abraham Lincoln did this;
"nobody else could have done it." And to do it, he bore "on his
sole shoulders" such an immense and measureless weight of care
and pain "as few other men have borne." [108] Then, when the
war was all over, it seemed to the people that he had, all along,
been thinking their real thoughts for them because they had
been too preoccupied or too benumbed by fear and sorrow to
think for themselves; still, they knew that it seemed this way
because he had fearlessly thought for himself. He had been able
to save the nation, when the war was over, partly because he
saw that unity was not to be sought by the "way of base concession"; and he had been able to free the slaves partly because
he refused to hasten to this object at the sacrifice of what he
thought and knew to be an even larger purpose. Paradoxically,
this most unrelenting enemy to the project of the Confederacy
was the one man in America who had quite purged "his heart
and mind from hatred or even anger towards his fellow-country-
men of the South." [109] Eventually that fact came to be seen in
the South, too, and generations in America "are likely to remember it when all other features of his statecraft have grown indis-
tinct." Why? "Perhaps because not many conquerors, and certainly few successful statesmen, have escaped the tendency of
power"—a tendency which hardens or at least narrows human

sympathies. In this man Lincoln there stood forth a "natural wealth of tender compassion"; and, as the war dragged on and on from month to month and from year to year, this compassion "became richer and more tender, while in the stress of deadly conflict he developed an astounding strength." [110]

He accepted those institutions to which he was born, "and he enjoyed them"; furthermore, his own "intense experience of the weakness of democracy did not sour him" on the essential goodness, righteousness, and even superiority of that way of government. Yet, "if he reflected much on forms of government, it was with a dominant interest in something beyond them"—something more permanent.[111] For "he was a citizen of that far country where there is neither aristocrat nor democrat."

No political theory, therefore, stands out from his words, nor do his actions reveal such a specific theory; instead, both his words and his actions evidence "a most unusual sense of the possible dignity of common men and common things." Thus, his humor rioted in comparisons "between potent personages and Jim Jett's brother or old Judge Brown's drunken coachman, for the reason for which the rarely jesting Wordsworth found a hero in the 'Leech-Gatherer' or in Nelson," and a villain "in Napoleon or in Peter Bell." Lincoln could use and respect, he could pardon and overrule, his far more accomplished associates, "because he stood up to them with no more fear or cringing, with no more dislike or envy or disrespect than he had felt when he stood up long before to Jack Armstrong." [112] Moreover, he "*faced* the difficulties and terrors of his high office with that same mind with which he had paid his way as a poor man," with little business success, seeking to learn law, and with the same mind in which he had "navigated a boat in rapids or in floods." For whether those floods were water or war, Lincoln met them with equal courage, with humble but hearty faith.[113]

If he really possessed in himself a theory of democracy, as such, it was contained in this condensed note, which he wrote perhaps as an autograph, just a year or two before his accession to the presidency:

> As I would not be a slave, so I would not be a master.
> This expresses my idea of democracy. Whatever differs
> from this, to the extent of the difference, is no democ-
> racy.
>
> A. LINCOLN [114]

This makes us feel very warmly attracted to Abraham Lincoln and to his simple doctrines; but what of Greeley? We remember that he had arrived in New York, a "greenhorn from
Vermont farms," an ambitious young egotist who had picked
up the trade of printing and who entered the big city "a stick
and bundle over his shoulder, ten dollars in his pocket; twenty
years old." His first work was on a job no other printer in the
city would take, "setting the type on a 32mo New Testament
with Greek references and supplementary remarks." After this,
he edited the *New Yorker,* the *Jeffersonian,* the *Log Cabin,* and,
in 1841, inaugurated his penny morning paper, the New York
Tribune, which for twenty-one years was at the forefront in reporting, if not advocating, "every reform, radical idea, and ism
that came to view." His *Tribune* writers included Charles A.
Dana, George William Curtis, William Henry Fry, Bayard Taylor, Margaret Fuller, George Ripley, Count Gurowski, Henry J.
Raymond, and a host of other notables, radicals, and reformers. Of course, Greeley himself received all sorts of epithets, had
them hurled at his head, through the door of his editorial office, and directly into his face. "I have been branded aristocrat,
communist, infidel, hypocrite, demagogue, disunionist, traitor,
corruptionist, and so forth," Greeley once declared in urging a
friend not to class him also as a poet, despite the fact that he
had poetic leanings, although he would scarcely admit that he
leaned in such a direction.[115] He remained always close to work-
ingmen's movements, as we have seen, close enough to see the
need for them, not close enough to see the real problems of
labor; of course, for a long time he followed in the fading and
faltering footsteps of the French utopian socialist Fourier. In
fact, in the very first year of the *Tribune,* Greeley wrote, "We
have written something and shall yet write more, much more,

in illustration and advocacy of the great social revolution which our age is destined to commence . . . in rendering all useful labor at once more attractive and honorable, and banishing want and all consequent degradation from the globe." [116]

Thus we see very clearly that this editor thought of himself as one of the sponsors of the new Utopia; however, he was never a man of small or narrow ambitions. "Mr. Greeley," commented one of his staff men, John Russell Young, "would be the greatest journalist in America if he did not aim to be one of the leading politicians of America." This is certainly true, and it is concomitantly true that this man of great hopes and dreams sacrificed a large portion of his journalistic success and esteem and power in a vain effort to become a politician. In fact, he often refused, long before his own political ambitions had matured to giant proportions, to print important speeches of Democrats as news, saying he would do so when Democratic newspapers "begin printing equally important addresses of Republicans." Such words and actions seemed natural to this man whose personal ways, plain and queer, and whose abrupt manners and peculiar clothes made him a half-myth that the country talked about constantly.[117] In a sense, though, he embodied the vague, grandiose ambitions and hopes "of Americans from coast to coast," and his history tells the overseas world, looking on, that it may yet copy American democracy and be redeemed.

But Greeley wished to do more than to tell Americans and the "overseas world" of the heritage of the United States; he himself wished to accomplish the world's redemption. Next to writing for the public, Greeley enjoyed lecturing to it; he often took "the platform." Henry Ward Beecher asked him what he considered "success" in a lecture, and he answered, "Where more folks stay in than go out." He was the first president of Typographical Union No. 6, in New York, although he later fought the union when it ordered a strike on the *Tribune* to stop the publication of an advertisement for printers by a rival paper. Also paradoxically, though a member of the Universalist Church, which taught that there was no hell, Greeley, when he was once asked to subscribe to a fund that would save sinners from going to hell, told the solicitor: "I won't give you a cent. There don't half enough go there now." [118] Thus he implied that he would like for all of his opponents—"sinners"—to go to hell.

He owned a farm at Chappaqua, thirty-three miles from New York, and liked to call himself a farmer; his farmer readers knew well enough that Greeley could not run the country and a farm both. And he did try to run the country, especially for the Whigs and then for the Republicans, hoping he could send all Democrats to where he said more sinners should go. But once, in making a political denial, he declared that: "I never said all Democrats were saloon-keepers. What I said was that all saloon-keepers were Democrats." And, though this statement may not have been popular in certain quarters, thousands of "self-made" men echoed his statement throughout the corridors of the nineteenth century that, "of all horned cattle, the most helpless in a printing office is a college graduate." Greeley was just such a self-made man; and Junius Henri Browne, of many years' service under the editor, noted him "a character combining numerous antagonisms, wayward, moody, undisciplined." [119] His friends could not be certain of him, for he could not be certain of himself; he was not only unlike other men—"he was often unlike himself." General rules "failed to apply to him," for he applied himself to every individual eccentricity.

James R. Gilmore quoted Greeley as saying, in late 1861:

> We are all going to the devil . . . all owing to stupidity at Washington. . . . It pains, it grieves me to think of it. For you know it is said that but for my action in the convention, Lincoln would not have been nominated. It was a mistake—the biggest mistake of my life.[120]

CHAPTER TWO

From the "Tribune" to the Tremont

As the year of 1860 dawned upon a somewhat dazed America, William H. Seward stood forth as the leading Republican figure in American political thought. In the eyes of the new and rapidly advancing party, Seward seemed to be the man destined to capture the Republican nomination in May, and appeared to be the man who should succeed James Buchanan in the White House, March 4, 1861. In the Senate, where Seward held the respect of the Democrats and the admiration of the Republicans, he had gained pre-eminence because his body and his brain moved together, functioned quickly and surely. He was known in the exalted chamber for his bouncing air, his irrepressible talk, and his hoarse voice which could capitalize upon the qualities of brusqueness and cordiality. Hearty he was, and confidential; ideas, phrases, repartee—these darted out of the man's mind and mouth in incessant streams, accompanied by original gestures and by winning ways. To sidetrack such an individual, backed by the seemingly indestructible power of America's foremost political boss, Thurlow Weed—a man respected by both houses of the Congress, a man idolized by the people of the North, a man whose press support and monetary sponsorship loomed larger than many western and northwestern Republicans appeared to know—to sidetrack such a man was Horace Greeley's avowed purpose. If it seemed impossible to other men, the New York editor, swallower of so many visionary schemes, thought it a necessary task and one simple of accomplishment. However, Horace Greeley knew that, in order to accomplish this end, he must use care, deceit, and caution; he must find another candidate whom he could present to his vast reading public and to his lecture-tour audiences as a more acceptable, a more desirable, a winning candidate. And Abraham Lincoln did not fit into Greeley's plans.[1]

On the eve of 1860, Lincoln and Greeley passed each other by as though they were total strangers or sworn enemies. They were neither. From the Congress of 1848 they remembered each other well; but to Greeley, Lincoln had been only a tall, quiet, unimpressive man, not aspiring to leadership, the only Whig congressman from Illinois. To Lincoln, moreover, Greeley was the author of a willful attack upon his integrity in regard to the mileage rates congressmen charged to their expense accounts. Each man had seen the other at a distinct disadvantage in Washington; after 1848, both men had soared in the skies of achievement and had grown to new heights in their respective fields.[2]

Furthermore, in the Congress of 1848, Greeley, it seemed to Lincoln, had deliberately antagonized him, arrogantly misquoted him, purposely belittled him. This may be gleaned from a letter which Lincoln saw fit to write to Greeley, calling the latter a friend but writing to him in the same tone of disgusted pity he used in numerous letters addressed to the editor in the following years:

FRIEND GREELEY:

In the *Tribune* of yesterday I discovered a little editorial paragraph in relation to Colonel Wentworth of Illinois, in which, in relation to the boundary of Texas, you say: "All Whigs and many Democrats having ever contended it stopped at the Nueces." Now this is a mistake which I dislike to see go uncorrected in a leading

Whig paper. Since I have been here [in Congress], I know a large majority of such Whigs of the House of Representatives as have spoken on the question have not taken that position. Their position, and in my opinion the true position, is that the boundary of Texas extended just so far as the American settlements taking part in her revolution extended. . . . Will you look at this? . . . If the degree of arrogance is not too great, may I ask you to examine what I said on this very point in the printed speech I send you. . . .[3]

Apparently in 1848 Lincoln possessed a certain measure of respect for Greeley, as this letter would indicate. However, Lincoln seemed to doubt Greeley's wisdom, even if he did not doubt his magnanimity and his character; since he understood men, he fathomed Greeley's weaknesses and inconsistencies. Even the little children who romped about the future president understood his human approachableness; Greeley, so much like a child in so many respects, did not. It was not Greeley but one of Lincoln's own sons who shouted too loudly: "Old Abe came out of the wilderness, out of the wilderness," and, when reproved for his vociferousness by a Greeley-like individual, the son retorted fearlessly: "Oh, Pop doesn't mind—he never minds anything." In this he was wrong, because Lincoln "minded" Greeley, minded his erratic bursts of friendship and volleys of hatred, minded him and would not trust his future to the editor's shaky hands. Nevertheless, in the words of his boy one catches a glimpse of Lincoln as he was to almost everyone—a man unheroically casting no shadow of awe. "For those who look for habiliments of the hero he is not to be envisaged"; Greeley looked for such trappings, and he found them not, for Lincoln lacked them.[4] Lincoln's consistency and his lack of ambivalence irritated Greeley as much as Greeley's inconsistency and erratic qualities rubbed against Lincoln's grain.[5] However, the future president—according to a letter he wrote in 1858—felt that Greeley's essential honesty could not be doubted. "I do not know how you estimate Greeley," he wrote to Charles L. Wilson, June 1, 1858, "but

I consider him incapable of corruption or falsehood." [6] Could it be possible that Lincoln had, in ten brief years, forgotten Greeley's fallacious editorial in regard to the Illinoisian's stand on the Texas boundary controversy? It is more sensible to suppose that the prospective president wished to gain Greeley's *Tribune* support in his plans for future offices, without committing himself in any way to Greeley's wavering personality.

Yet, in regard to his future plans, Lincoln in this same letter declared emphatically that he had no intention of opposing Seward for the presidency in 1860.

> As to myself, let me pledge you my word that neither I,
> nor any friend so far as I know, has been setting stake
> against Governor Seward. No combination has been
> made with me, or proposed to me, in relation to the
> next Presidential candidate. . . . I am not directly or
> indirectly committed to anyone, nor has anyone made
> any advance to me upon the subject. . . .[7]

Lincoln further states that he has no desire to cause any division within the new political party and that he hopes the primary object of every leading Republican will be to erase the marks of suspicion created by the various disputes among party leaders.[8]

It seems apparent from this that Greeley and Lincoln had no intimate acquaintance with each other and with their respective problems; Lincoln was totally unaware of Greeley's 1854 severance of connections with the tremendously important political firm composed of himself and Thurlow Weed and William H. Seward. Lincoln was also ignorant of the fact that Greeley had already determined to prevent Seward from being nominated at Chicago in 1860; and Greeley and Lincoln were both unaware of the vital part which Lincoln was to play in this drama.

Nevertheless, Lincoln occasionally wrote to Greeley, particularly after 1858, when William H. Herndon, Lincoln's law partner, had gone to the East and visited Greeley. There is evidence that John G. Nicolay, Lincoln's private secretary, knew Greeley quite well and probably thought no more highly of him, in the long run, than did Lincoln himself. However, on November 8, 1858, just at the time that Lincoln had been defeated for the Senate by Stephen A. Douglas, just at the time that Lincoln was casting about for support for a new political office, he wrote to Greeley concerning his friend Nicolay:

> This will introduce our mutual friend John G. Nicolay, who resides here—He wishes an arrangement to correspond for your paper—He is entirely trustworthy; and, so far as I am capable of judging, altogether competent for such a situation—I hope you will conceive it your interest to engage him. . . .[9]

Apparently Nicolay became an ambassador of good will in a very informal sense between Lincoln and Greeley, Lincoln proposing the measure in order to win Greeley's editorial support after the latter had favored Douglas in the Illinois senatorial campaign.

Meanwhile, in the year of 1859, Lincoln's home state of Illinois became the first state in the nation in the monetary value of agriculture and of agricultural products; the following summer a man with a telescope looked at 146 reaping machines from one vantage point in Lincoln's rapidly advancing home state. This seems to be vitally significant, particularly when one also notes that in the same year the first oil well came into existence in Pennsylvania, the mass production of iron and steel was initiated in Pennsylvania, and the railroads of the North began a steady program of interior progress. Greeley decided that it was time to push not only a moderate Republican candidate for 1860, but also a candidate who would help him to inaugurate his program of political economy.[10] Greeley could truthfully declare that, in 1860, hardly a single reaper could be seen south of the Ohio, while north of it the machines for reaping, and for everything else, stood out at every turn of the road. Even the moderate Lincoln, at his Cooper Institute Address, February 27, 1860, concurred with Greeley when he declared that the South was lagging so far behind in production that it would be foolish

for it, as a section, to secede, calling the North a "murderer."
Horace Greeley was in the New York audience that February
night, and he saw the new rising star from the West, heard him
speak eloquently. However, not Greeley but the bearded, elderly
William Cullen Bryant, ex-Democratic editor of the New York
Evening Post, introduced the speaker. Greeley, in his own urgent
manner, secured the manuscript of the speech for printing in
his newspaper the following day. Lincoln visited the offices of
the *Tribune* that night in order to check the accuracy of the
galleys, and as he bent over them, serenely working, oblivious
of his noisy surroundings, he was closer perhaps than he would
ever be again to the true heart, the life, the sounds of Horace
Greeley.[11]

Originally Lincoln had been invited to speak at Plymouth
Church, in Brooklyn, in February, 1860, but financial or other
difficulties arose, and the engagement was taken over by the
Young Men's Central Republican Union of New York City,
which had already determined upon a series of political addresses, into which schedule Lincoln was fitted. It was not until
he reached New York that Lincoln became fully aware of the
change in arrangements; and when he faced his New York audience he discovered, as he had suspected, that it was filled with
the elite, the cultured, the wealthy of America's greatest metropolis. "Horace Greeley and David Dudley Field escorted Lincoln
to the platform," where William Cullen Bryant introduced him.
The speech he delivered "is now acknowledged one of the greatest efforts of his life" and won a great measure of instant recognition for him in the East, where he needed it so desperately.
"It is supposed to have been largely instrumental in securing
his nomination for the Presidency." [12] However, many authorities concur in the belief that Lincoln's managers, with their bargaining ability, and Horace Greeley, with his vengeful tenacity,
also played major roles.

Nevertheless, it is quite plausible to agree with the author
who insists that "Lincoln's speech in response to the invitation
from the Young Men's Central Republican Union of New York
City, at Cooper Institute, February 27, 1860, before a brilliant

and intellectual audience, was a marked and, if we could trace all the threads of politics, perhaps a momentous event." [13] His text was the understanding of those who framed the Constitution as to the power of the federal government to control slavery in the territories. Apparently at this time no better or more powerful presentation of the subject had been made in the East; therefore, the speech deserved Greely's praise as "the very best political address to which I ever listened—and I have heard some of Webster's grandest." [14]

Lincoln concluded by saying, "Let us have faith that right makes might, and in that faith let us to the end dare to do our duty as we understand it"—words which were to mean more and more to Lincoln during the next four years.[15] Unquestionably, this speech proved the most effective piece of work Lincoln performed that entire critical winter. It is significant to note, also, that he had accepted the invitation only after he was promised that he could make a political speech; when he arrived in New York, learned of the change of plans in the meeting place, and discovered what a distinguished audience he would have and what a great opportunity had been afforded him—an opportunity to address Greeley—he spent the two and a half days which he had in the city before the speech was to be given revising his material and familiarizing himself with it. Furthermore, in order that he might be certain that he was heard everywhere in the room, he arranged with a friend, Mason Brayman, who had come to New York with him, to sit in the back of the hall, and, in case he did not speak loud enough, to raise his high hat on a cane.

Before he began, no one present—especially Greeley—thought that he would do more than interest his audience, perhaps presenting some sound, albeit often heard, arguments; many in the audience later confessed that they frankly feared that his queer manners and quaint form of speech would amuse the people so much that they would fail to catch the weight of his logic. But to the surprise of all, Lincoln impressed his audience from the beginning by his dignity and, most amazing of all, by his seriousness. "His manner was, to a New York audience, a very strange one, but it was captivating," wrote one of the men present. "He held the vast meeting spellbound, and as one by one his oddly expressed but trenchant and convincing arguments confirmed the soundness of his political conclusions, the house broke out in wild and prolonged enthusiasm." [16]

Without doubt, Greeley suddenly saw Lincoln in a new light as he applauded and cheered with the rest of the vast audience. Although he still did not think of Lincoln as a presidential possibility, Greeley did think of him now as an excellent lecturer and public speaker, as a politician and a magnetic producer of crowds. This may be seen from a letter which Greeley addressed to an Ohio associate on March 4, 1860, after having been asked to address a gathering in that state:

> I do not feel able to promise *now* to go to Ohio at the time you mention. After the Conventions, it may be possible for me to consent to do so. But I cannot make any such engagement now. My judgment is that . . . Abraham Lincoln will not only make a more effective speech than I could, but draw a larger audience. Think of that. . . .[17]

"Think of that!" Imagine the egocentric Greeley admitting such a thing, that Lincoln could make a more effective speech and could draw a larger audience! However, Greeley thought within himself, although he did not write it down, that Lincoln had the time to spare for such a speech. On the other hand, Greeley was needed in Chicago; there he must defeat William H. Seward for the presidential nomination.

This wide-eyed, beaming Greeley was disarming—a deceptive personality. Looking benevolent and radiant, he bore an air of childlike simplicity; but now he was engaged in a terribly dangerous and tremendously forceful political maneuver—a maneuver which some have termed "devious" and others "plain dishonest." In order to accomplish his ultimate aim, Greeley involved himself with both Lincoln and Stephen A. Douglas, although neither man was certain that he understood the editor's masterful motives. His purpose was plain: to prepare the way for a Republican sweep of the national elections of 1860.[18]

Nothing appears to have been obscure in Greeley's general thinking about this problem. He reasoned, first, that the present popular base of his party was far too narrow and therefore must be broadened; and, secondly, that the base of the Democratic Party had been stretched so wide in order to please the involved divergent elements in the party that it was strained in the middle and must be there cracked and broken in two. Greeley summed up his strategy neatly in this way: attach to yourself the maximum number of allies, and then divide and conquer. Thus his reasoning was simple and rather straightforward and direct; the complexity lay in his tactics. He functioned as an independent and as a political power in his own right after he severed his connections with Seward and Weed. However, the public did not realize that he was independent, and Weed and Seward doubted his real intentions. Furthermore, Greeley was not one who treasured his associates above his aims; he did not care in the least what trusting Republican leaders he injured.[19] With malicious pleasure, Greeley began to shake up the party organization, sidetracking those men, like Seward, who felt that they had the strongest hold upon the party machinery.

Privately, Greeley dealt with certain Democrats in Congress, working to widen the rift in the party, so that the hot tempers and feverish anxieties of the national election year would bring about an open split within Democratic ranks. Furthermore, in order to achieve his goal, the editor dealt with the most powerful Democrat in the land, with the man whom the Republicans feared more than any other—Stephen A. Douglas. Through his editorials and his contacts, Greeley helped widen the split between Douglas and President James Buchanan over the Kansas problem and the Lecompton Constitution; at the same time, the editor chuckled quietly to his congressional and journalistic friend, Schuyler Colfax: "Douglas has broken the back of the Democratic Party. It will hold Douglas responsible for the loss of Kansas and will never forgive him—never!" Consequently, Greeley worked to widen and deepen this breach, to exploit it with all of his vast public-opinion-making power. To do this, he had to support Douglas in his bid to return to the United States Senate in 1858; he had to encourage Douglas, the leading Democrat of the West, and had to make the "little giant" tread upon the toes of the South, which he felt ruled the party. He frankly told Colfax that, by lending Douglas the columns of his *Tribune,* he would aid the Republican cause of 1860. "Everything I have done to favor Douglas since 1857," Greeley gloated to his Indiana friend, "is treasured up in the South and used to diffuse and deepen the impression that he is a disguised Abolitionist and virtual ally of the Black Republicans." [20]

Since in Greeley's private opinion Douglas was a "low and dangerous demagogue," he felt that it was a fair game if he could bestow upon him the political kiss of death, a kiss he used upon Seward and tried to use upon Lincoln. To those Republicans who did not know Greeley's secret purpose and the way in which the editor played his cards, the Douglas-Greeley association appeared to be an over-flirtation; some Republican leaders went so far as to expect Greeley to support Douglas for the presidency. Because of this misunderstanding, Greeley tried to set forth his long-range plan in general terms to William H. Herndon, to other Illinois Republican leaders, and to Joseph Medill of the Chicago *Tribune.* He told these men that he wished to re-elect Douglas to the Senate, to antagonize the South, to divide the Democratic Party, and to prevent Douglas from ascending to the presidency in two years. He advised the Illinois leaders of his party not to put up an opponent for Douglas in order to make certain that the latter retained his seat in the Senate. However, the Republican leaders of Illinois had already chosen the "shambling, story-telling, rustic Springfield lawyer," Lincoln, to oppose Douglas; and they were in no mood to take dictation from an eastern busybody who sent his newspaper into the West and there gave New York advice by the column-full to Illinois farmers. "Keep Lincoln on the shelf," Greeley's *Tribune* told the Illinois subscribers. Medill, Herndon, and the downstate Lincolnites were furious at this meddlesome editor who had the audacity to tell them that the Republican standard was too high and that something more practical was needed.[21]

"We want to be our own masters," Herndon wrote hotly to Greeley on April 8, 1858; and this sentiment Greeley discovered to be unchanged in 1860, when he traveled to Chicago and there found the masterful Illinois men demanding Lincoln and nothing else.[22] On the other hand, Greeley was to go to Chicago with the determination that the nominee must be anyone but Seward, whose backer was that "oily" Thurlow Weed. "I was a packhorse for Weed and Seward for the first half of my career," Greeley wrote to Justin S. Morrill, March 12, 1872; "I revolted at last and was not ruined." [23]

When Greeley had come to New York City, in 1841, he had been without friends; soon, though, ambitious as he was, he formed a political triumvirate with Thurlow Weed, the powerful boss of New York State politics and editor of the Albany *Evening Journal,* and with William H. Seward, Weed's puppet, first in the governor's chair, and later in the United States Senate. During the 1850's, both Weed and Seward found themselves unwilling to abandon the already nationally dead Whig Party, while Greeley insisted on joining the newly formed Republican organization. This led to the disruption of the political firm of Weed-Seward-Greeley. Actually, a fundamental political difference estranged the two senior partners from the junior member, Greeley; the surprising fact is not that the association collapsed but that it held together as many years as it did. Greeley's political outlook was dangerously emotional—a blend of his political ideals and his own personal ambitions. He insisted that a political party was of value only when it advanced the progressive aims of the people; moreover, he eagerly desired a public office from which he could direct his idealistic reforms and administer his progressive aims to the people. On the other hand, Weed and Seward were more practical; their position depended not upon a mass of newspaper subscribers but upon a smoothly functioning, well-oiled political machine which could not be retooled over night. In 1854, Greeley saw his dreams coming to fruition in the antislavery movement. Weed saw Seward's future only in terms of the state party, which he controlled, and which was his virtually by absolute ownership.[24]

From the beginning of the partnership and even after its dissolution, Greeley admired Weed more than he did Seward; Greeley and Weed had been in business ventures together, and Greeley respected Weed's ability as a politician, envied his versatile supervision over men, groups, and interests. "Weed is confident, and I have great faith in his knowledge and sagacity," Greeley once wrote.[25] Consequently, it tortured Greeley to part with Weed and to oppose him at Chicago in 1860; but, as has been indicated, Greeley treasured his purposes above his friends.

In the early days of the partnership, Greeley expected the Albany journalist to enter into numerous reforms with him, and, in 1843 and 1846, Weed was tempted to do so. Weed had even become interested in the labor-union movement, obtaining for the Typographical Union a state charter which made the society a benevolent organization. With age and maturity, however, the Albany journalist put idealism behind him, becoming a powerful political boss with monetary and economic considerations foremost in his mind; and his sway over political and economic matters ranged from Albany to Washington. Few men in history have rivaled his string of political marionettes. As John L. Schoolcraft wrote truthfully of Weed in 1853, "You see the golden dollars in the distance, and the energy of your mind is to enter for the race." [26]

The significant political partnership began when Weed, in his earlier and more benevolent era, went to New York City to engage Greeley as Seward's press agent, as a man who could sell the Whig economic policies and party principles to the working classes, who respected Greeley's generous viewpoint. All went well until Greeley suddenly found himself no longer content with his inferior status and wished to become a policy-forming executive within the powerful political firm. "I'm quite enough accused of being under Albany influence," Greeley growled; and Weed and Seward recognized this defection and wholesale dissatisfaction in 1846, when Greeley advocated Negro suffrage and direct appeals to laborers. He revealed his personal aspirations at the same time, also hinting that an elective office would be most appreciated—anything from the governor's chair down to a mere seat in the party councils. Furthermore, although it was not in Greeley's nature to ask outright that his political thirst be quenched, both Weed and Seward knew of the editor's attack of politicophilia; they were not, however, disposed to satisfy his political desires except in so far as was necessary to keep him playing their game.

By 1848, Greeley felt that he was a co-equal member of the triumvirate; moreover, he insisted that the Whig Party might be killing itself by not taking a stand against the extension of slavery and by nominating Zachary Taylor, a man Greeley thought inferior to himself.[27] However, Greeley was silenced for the moment, and he remained reluctantly within the ranks of the Whig Party and the political firm until 1854, at which time Weed refused to let him join the Republican Party, refused to let him organize a Republican unit in New York State, and refused to proffer him the political office he desired—that of lieutenant-governor. Furthermore, Weed, after half promising, as Greeley thought, the office to him, saw that Greeley's enemy, Henry J. Raymond, editor of the New York *Times,* received the office of lieutenant-governor. Greeley supported the ticket and the Whig organization until after the November elections of 1854. Then, on November 11, he wrote a letter to Seward (not made public until 1860) in which he withdrew himself from the partnership.

In reality, Weed and Greeley came to the parting of the ways when the *Tribune* outgrew its swaddling clothes, when Greeley became too personally ambitious for political power, and when Weed found in Henry J. Raymond and in his *Times* a mouthpiece and a political organ of propaganda better suited to the rigid needs of the Albany machine. Raymond, much better than Greeley, appreciated Weed's true position, his conservative political views, his lobbying activities, and his forms of contact and persuasion with men of all political ideals, views, and factions. Raymond also understood the basic source of Weed's

strength—control of the New York Legislature. It mattered little who sat in the governor's mansion so long as he was practical
in his political persuasions, for while Weed controlled the legislature he possessed all the state and national strings he could
possibly afford to pull anyway. Raymond accepted this situation;
Seward accepted it. Greeley could not. His prestige rested upon
moral foundations, with a structure of section-wide, almost
nation-wide, propaganda. Weed's practical politics and maneu-
verings had constructed a barrier to Greeley's dream of obtaining
elective office. For these reasons, Greeley developed one of his
many hatreds—a hatred for professional politicians. For these
reasons, the Weed-Seward-Greeley partnership could have lasted
little longer than it did. Greeley's character and ambitions made
him turn from Weed and Seward; that same character and those
same ambitions, and the hate they engendered, drove Greeley
to Chicago, in May, 1860, and made him vote at last for Lincoln, helping to bring about the presidential nomination of the
"rail-splitter." [28]

Because of his acquired hatred of political bosses and of professional politicians, Greeley basically began to dislike political
parties. He believed that they should be broken up approxi-
mately every twelve years in order to prevent corruption from
infiltrating the leaders and then directing the operations of the
parties along selfish channels. As usual, though, Greeley proved
inconsistent, tending to censure the Democratic and to excuse
the Republican land speculators in 1860, for example. And,
at this time, Greeley saw the necessity of a political party to im-
plement his political and economic philosophy as a machine
by which he could set at work his economic program for freeing
the slaves, restricting international trade, and bringing a period
of independent prosperity to the nation he loved. He did not believe in "flinging stones at one's own crockery", and, possessing a
poorly disciplined and an exasperatingly stubborn mind, he set
his politico-economic course and would not alter it short of
catastrophe. Greeley was stubborn, slow to alter his course, quick
to excuse himself, ready to blame his poor judgment upon some-

one else. These facts are demonstrated by his association with Weed and Seward, in his support of John C. Fremont as the Republican candidate in 1856, in his attitude toward Lincoln before the latter's nomination, when he was nominated, during the campaign, and during Lincoln's presidency. So also are these facts evident in Greeley's contribution to the causes of the Civil War, when he preached peaceable secession because he "knew" that the South would never fight. When he looked about for a candidate to support in 1860, he wished someone with an agrarian background, but with progressive ideas, because he applauded the new farm machinery inventions but feared that the small farmers would never be able to afford them, because he believed in little, self-owned plots of land (he suggested 160 acres in his homestead propaganda and in his farm lectures) in order to prevent the destruction of individual initiative, while admiring the huge farms where modern machinery could be employed. In searching for a candidate, he desired one who had owned slaves or at least appreciated the slavery problem, but who had freed those slaves—a moderate man. Yet he was generally ranked with the violent abolitionists because of his stand on emancipation.[29]

From the Lincoln-Douglas debates of 1858 Greeley had learned that, in order to win with the type of conservative platform necessary to unite the divergent elements of the Republican Party, his 1860 candidate should not be an eastern man, who would be distrusted both by the South and by the West. He must be a moderate man, a Westerner, a "new face." This description precisely fitted the man whom Greeley had, without success, invited to visit him in his hotel room in Bloomington while conducting his 1858–59 winter lecture tour through the old Northwest. Lincoln, doubtless hurt by Greeley's attitude toward him in the recently concluded campaign against Senator Douglas, refused the invitation of a man upon whom he had laid partial blame for his defeat. Had Lincoln accepted the invitation, had the two men sat down in the same room together that day and talked over their mutual problems, Greeley might have seen in the rustic lawyer his 1860 ideal. Instead, the editor spent an additional year searching for his ideal candidate, finally choosing Edward Bates of Missouri unequivocally.[30]

At heart, Greeley resented Seward and sought to be his personal political assassin. Seward at times sensed this animosity in the then coolly calculating editor; as early as 1858, the senator endeavored indirectly to patch and sew up the wound of late 1854. Somehow, though, Seward's indirect efforts always went astray. And once while the senator was trying to reach Greeley with a letter in which he gave the editor ample praise, the *Tribune's* top man was writing acidly to Schuyler Colfax, "[Seward is a] good fellow at heart, only he is a bad one to belong to. I have been there." [31]

Yet it seemed that Greeley's antipathy to Seward, because of the former's secrecy in his intriguing, had not and would not—even could not—hurt Seward's chances to gain the presidential nomination. When the year of 1860 opened, the primacy of William H. Seward had been universally conceded. He was the first choice not only of New York and New England but also of Michigan, Wisconsin, and Minnesota. His enthusiastic reception on returning from Europe, and the general praise for his politic senatorial speech of late February, 1860, had strengthened the confidence of Weed and of the other Seward managers. Cool, calculating, and realistically informed, Thurlow Weed believed his nomination as good as already accomplished. Even Greeley, hostile as he was, and growing more so by the day, wrote from Davenport, Iowa, in January of the fateful year, that Seward enjoyed the preference of the Northwest. Furthermore, his claims to the nomination on the grounds of governmental experience, his long term of service to the "free soil" cause, and his tested ability seemed to outweigh those of any other Republican contender.

Nevertheless, the field was crowded with possible candidates, for the relatively new party had appealed so strongly to the idealistic young men of the day and had drawn so heavily upon the best of the Whig and the free-soil Democratic talent that it was rich in ability. In the Northwest, wrote Greeley reluctantly, many wished Lincoln's name on the ticket; but everywhere the merits of Edward Bates, of William L. Dayton, of John C. Fremont, and even of Simon Cameron were canvassed.[32]

The *Tribune*'s and hence Greeley's favorite at Chicago was neither Abraham Lincoln nor William H. Seward, but Edward Bates, the elderly Whig gentleman from Missouri who had recently manumitted his slaves. Actually, if one may believe Greeley's own erratic statements, the charges of sectionalism against the Republican Party finally brought Greeley to choosing Bates. As long as this accusation could plausibly be maintained, it represented the source for disunion and disunion sentiment, the excuse for southern secession, if the Republicans should win the presidential election of 1860, as Greeley intended that they should. He thought that if these charges of sectionalism went unchallenged they would split the Republican vote in the North, endangering the chances for a national victory. The nucleus of the "Know Nothing" Party flourished in the so-called border states, and Greeley wished to make a concession, in the form of a candidate, to this section and to the remaining elements of the Whig and Know Nothing parties in order to prevent a Republican defeat in November. In short, his method of divesting his party of its sectional character was unusual but logical: he wished to introduce antislavery sentiment below the Ohio River in the border states, thinking that his "economic nationalism" would turn the trick. He wished to delay his drive for emancipation until slavery was prohibited from national territories, and until the "slave culture" in the northern tier of southern states was changed to one of diversified industry and small farms. Greeley did not know how long such an evolutionary process would take, but he felt it could be accomplished in a relatively brief period of time.[33]

As a part of his economic and political program, Greeley could use Bates to much better advantage than he could Lincoln. Therefore, he was a very strong advocate of Bates in 1859 and early 1860. Although the bucolic-looking editor declared privately that "it was anything to beat Seward," he gave as his public reasons for supporting Bates the facts that, as a former slaveholder and former Whig, the Missourian was thoroughly conservative and could thus pull votes out of the southern and border states, polling a sizable number of ballots in "every slave state." And, if elected, Bates could rally all that was left of the Whig Party membership within the slave states around the Republican banner, thus resisting secession and rebellion. Furthermore, Bates was, to Greeley, the only Republican whose election "would not *suffice as a pretext for Civil War.*" Thus, he seemed the "one most likely to repress the threatened insurrection, or, at the worst, to crush it." Greeley, who also thought Bates's qualifications sufficient to place him ahead of Seward when the time for nominating candidates arrived, later admitted cautiously but firmly, "I did not hesitate to avow my preference [for Bates], though I may have withheld some of my reasons for it." [34]

As a part of his freedom-with-Bates program, Greeley wished to effect emancipation for the Negroes first in Missouri, Kentucky, Delaware, and Maryland; and his hopes ran high when the so-called Emancipationists carried the St. Louis elections in 1857 and again in 1859. True, this Emancipationist Party, led by Frank Blair and B. Gratz Brown, did triumph in the St. Louis elections, but as usual Greeley overlooked one important factor: the animosity toward the "blacks" so evident in this triumphant Blair party.[35] These victories, appearing as good omens to the economic emancipationist, caused him to think that the Republican Party could gain strength and solidarity from the small farmers of the South as well as from the artisan, the nonslaveholding, and the "poor white" groups by appealing solely to their material interests—in short, by offering them the Greeley platter of economic nationalism, served up with factories and farms and excellent jobs and reasonable prices, all in the proper proportions.

Consequently, in the *Tribune* Greeley upheld in lofty admiration William Gregg's Graniteville textile experiment, and at the same time deplored the annual southern commercial conventions, which were dominated, he maintained, by the slaveholding, cotton-planting aristocracy—a minority of a minority. He felt in all honesty of purpose that 80 per cent of the southern people were in the classes of artisans, farmers, poor whites, and non-slaveholders; and he assured himself and his readers that these eight tenths of the southern populace would profit from a tariff and would, if they could, come into the Republican fold. The remaining 20 per cent of the people controlled the 80 per cent, produced the politicians, yammered about secession, and controlled the presses, pouring out propaganda about southern states' rights.[36] Therefore, the Republicans' immediate aim in 1860 should be to launch an administration which "shall do all in its power to confine Slavery within the limits of the existing Slave States." Slavery was local. Freedom was national. The territories were the public property of the federal government and should be reserved to free labor. His party's mission was not sectional in scope, he hammered out in the headlines of the *Tribune,* but the southern people were unenlightened in general and must be enlightened by the gleam of a Republican victory.[37] Greeley thundered that what he called the "sham democracy"—the Democratic Party—would split in 1860. Why? Because the Douglasites stood behind their hero and demanded popular sovereignty in the territories, because the followers of Buchanan were for permitting those who owned slaves to inhabit federal territories with their property to enjoy protection through the decision of the Supreme Court, and because the Calhounites demanded the passage of an "explicit and formal Slave Code for the territories" by Congress. Thus, the Democratic Party would ultimately split into three distinct segments, declared Greeley; yet the country would not be safe under the governing hand of any of the three groups, because not one of the three actually prohibited the spread of slavery into the federal territories. The only escape was for the Republican Party to nominate Edward Bates, a national conservative, whom the people could elect, and in whom they could place their confidence and their trust.[38]

It is significant that Bates was backed by Frank Blair and his conservative Missouri followers, and by Horace Greeley, who, in general terms, even in 1860 should be considered "a radical." Greeley became firmly attached to Bates after talking with him in 1859; it seemed to him that the Missouri jurist had impressed

him more than any man since he had withdrawn from the partnership with Seward and Weed in 1854. The views of Bates on
internal improvements pleased the *Tribune* editor immensely.
Therefore, he informed his vast reading public that Bates, as a
true conservative, could draw all of the old-line Whig and
"American" votes into the Republican columns in November,
1860. In actuality, Greeley, who, as we have seen, had been for
some years a veteran antislavery man, was becoming frightened
at the danger of disunion sentiment, although he did not feel
that it was appreciably deep in southern hearts. Yet he wished
to put forth a candidate who could quell cries of disunion, but
who would also be a weak man, since the editor himself dreamed
of being a "king-maker"—another Weed.

Hence, he wrote to his friend Schuyler Colfax about Bates
first, asking Colfax to consult with Frank Blair. Colfax, founder of
the Indiana Republican Party and former New Yorker, had been
elected to Congress on the anti-Nebraska, temperance, "American" party ticket in 1854. Like Bates, he opposed northern and
southern sectionalism and favored internal improvements at
federal government expense. Adopting Greeley's suggestion, Colfax consulted Blair, and then wrote to the *Tribune* editor that
Bates, "if brought out right," could easily carry the state of
Missouri. Colfax further stated that the Missouri gentleman
could carry Lincoln's home state, "he being quite strong in southern Illinois, where our cause is weak." And the letter concluded
on the encouraging note that "Winter Davis says he can carry
Maryland and Delaware, if we do not repel them by too strong
a platform." [39]

Colfax represented Indiana sentiment correctly in backing a
conservative like Edward Bates in his paper, the South Bend *St.
Joseph Valley Register,* for the Hoosier State had never been
rabid against slavery, since the lower counties had been settled
by southerners. In fact, in 1856, Indiana refused to support the
antislavery Republican candidate John C. Fremont, and by 1859
public opinion in Indiana had not altered at all. In general,
the people were indifferent to slavery, and the Democrats mo-
nopolized state politics. Nevertheless, Indiana was a worthy prize,

ranking third among the states of the Northwest in convention
and in electoral votes; like Pennsylvania and Illinois, it was considered indispensable for the success of either party in 1860.[40]
As a consequence, the Bates forces worked with extreme diligence
in Indiana, many of the Hoosier leaders, wanting nothing of
Seward, throwing their support behind Bates. However, Bates's
chances were irreparably weakened by an interparty split, and
the Indiana delegation sent to Chicago was uninstructed. Nevertheless, a schism in Democratic ranks somewhat offset this
Greeley misfortune. But Colfax felt that a conservative candidate, running on a conservative platform, could carry the
state for the Republicans; consequently, at Chicago, when Greeley saw that Bates was not in the running, he turned to Lincoln
as the type of conservative he needed for Indiana and certain
other pivotal states like Illinois. Although an article from Greeley's *Tribune* printed in pamphlet form favoring Bates for numerous reasons was distributed to the Indianapolis convention
when the delegates were being chosen for the Chicago conclave,
the anti-nativist Germans, under Theodore Hielscher, prevented
the Bates men from sending a delegation to Chicago instructed
to vote for the Missourian. And Greeley, in 1859, found himself
weakened in his northwestern position, lagging behind the offensive tactics of Seward there.[41]

Returning for a moment to Greeley's publicly avowed program of 1860, one finds that, in addition to a policy of conservatism, two essential factors, plain to see when looked for
but often obscured by Greeley's deceptive tactics, are very apparent. Most noticeable in his private correspondence but also
evident in his editorials, these factors were the editor's intense
desire to put into effect his beliefs concerning a system of political economy, and his great conceit. "I want to succeed this time,"
he wrote, poignantly; "yet I know the country is not Anti-Slavery. It will only swallow a little Anti-Slavery in a great deal of
sweetening. An Anti-Slavery man *per se* cannot be elected." However, Greeley voiced cautiously the belief that a "Tariff, River-
and-Harbor, Pacific Railroad, Free-Homestead man, *may* succeed,
although he is Anti-Slavery." Furthermore, Greeley whispered

around that "I mean to have as good a candidate as the majority will elect. And, if the people are to rule, I think this is the way."[42] Greeley substantially declared that the people should follow the dictates of his wisdom, which, he implied, was complete; moreover, it was, he felt, his duty under God to show the people the way to defeat what he termed the "slave-drivers" of the South. Of course, salvation generally requires an author (Greeley) and an agent (Bates), for Bates was the editor's moderate man—in other words, the "antislavery" ideal with a "great deal of sweetening."

Although Bates had been retired from national politics since 1836, Greeley considered that he was still well known; in addition, he forgot that one of the qualifications for his conservative candidate was a "new face," and that Bates had a very old one. However, having been formally out of national politics for twenty-four years, the Missouri jurist had not been embroiled in the slavery controversy; being a conservative, he would draw southern and border-state votes, perhaps even from slaveholders, although he himself had freed his slaves and now opposed the Kansas-Nebraska Act. He condemned the Dred Scott Decision and denounced the Lecompton Constitution. Thus, the Missourian should be accepted by the straight-laced, Sewardite Republicans. More important still in the mind of the editor, he knew that Bates agreed with him substantially on his ideas concerning political economy. Even as early as the winter of 1858, immediately after Lincoln ignored Greeley's invitation to talk with him, Bates was prepared as a possible choice for the nomination by the *Tribune* columns, in which Bates apologized and atoned for his support of Millard Fillmore and the old-line Whigs in the election of 1856.[43]

By February, 1859, Greeley appears to have been serious about pushing Bates as a full-fledged contender for the nomination. A letter written by Bates to the New York Whigs in which he advocated a protective tariff, internal improvements at federal government expense, and a nonaggressive foreign policy was deliberately forced out into the open by one of Greeley's sound-and-fury editorials. Then, the Missourian declared himself politically unaffiliated, as the Whigs "had ceased to exist as an organized and militant body." This was insufficient ammunition for Greeley's cannon-like columns, and he deplored the excessively weak stand which Bates had taken, urging him, by way of Colfax, to broaden his program to include slavery restriction in the areas where it now existed. At the same time, in the *Tribune,* he interpreted Bates's pronouncements to mean what they did not declare at all—that is, that slavery was a moral wrong, but that the eradication of the morally indiscreet practice was a state and not a national problem. Furthermore, in his 1859 cross-country tour, Greeley spoke for Bates in Kansas; and Charles A. Dana, his assistant editor, who for once totally agreed with his chief, supported Bates in the *Tribune* columns while his superior was traveling to California, giving exceptional coverage to Bates's rise from virtual obscurity.

Greeley himself, however, clever as he was, had not yet promised Bates his unqualified personal support. In October, 1859, he half promised Bates this personal endorsement if the latter would agree to uphold the principle of slavery restriction. Then, in November, the *Tribune* carried an interview, supposedly authentic, in which Bates admitted that Congress had jurisdiction in the territories, and in which the principle of the restriction of slavery was inferred but not actually admitted. From this point onward, Greeley appeared at least satisfied, if not exultant, over Bates and, fearing that the precious applecart might be upset, informed his emissary Colfax that he should tell Bates to make no more public statements until he was nominated.[44]

Greeley's extended winter lecture tour of 1859–60, including all of the Northwest but Minnesota, convinced him that he must inevitably back Bates to the hilt. For he discovered two inescapable factors, made two unavoidable observations—first, that Douglas was tremendously popular in Democratic circles, and, secondly, that Seward, in every northwestern section, was preposterously popular in Republican circles. The first observation elated Greeley; the second appalled him beyond words. Since 1857, he had employed every ounce of his journalistic skill to create an impassable gulf between Douglas and the Democratic

administration forces; and, on this lecture tour, seeing how amazingly popular Douglas had become in the Northwest, he worked
ceaselessly to widen the ever-growing wedge of divergence. He
wrote editorial letters back to the *Tribune,* in which he prophesied the nomination of Douglas at Charleston in the spring of
1860, although in his heart he secretly doubted that such an
eventuality could ever come to pass. He hoped beyond all hope
that his propaganda would injure Douglas so that he would be
"read out" of the old Democratic Party permanently.

Nevertheless, he knew that Douglas's popularity in the Northwest would help a conservative like Bates and hinder a "radical"
like Seward; yet this was not enough, because the danger of
Seward's pre-eminence loomed daily and even hourly greater.[45]
In such a situation, Bates seemed to be the best contender against
Seward, because it could be said—and Greeley said it—that Bates
could win in 1860 with the votes that Fillmore had drawn away
from Fremont in 1856. Therefore, the *Tribune* turned all of its
power out in a campaign for Bates, openly suggesting that Seward and Salmon P. Chase were too radical to draw enough votes
to carry the crucial states of New Jersey, Pennsylvania, and Illinois. Moreover, it would be utterly inconceivable to anyone in
a slave state that Bates could be the cause of disunion, that his
election would precipitate a crisis or a war against slavery—so
Greeley reasoned. And all practical emancipationists, ordinary
abolitionists, and old-line Whigs would virtually be compelled
to support him, Greeley told his readers. Furthermore, Bates,
more than any other contender, stood staunchly with the "tariff"
men, with the "river-and-harbor" men, and with those who favored the construction of a Pacific railroad. From February 20,
1860, with the editor having returned from his informative winter lecture tour, the *Tribune,* in its daily, its weekly, and its
semiweekly forms, sponsored Bates's candidacy, although it published letters which favored all contenders, and despite the fact
that Greeley admitted, out of the corner of his mouth, that
he would support the candidate chosen at Chicago.[46]

Lincoln knew that Bates carried real weight with those men
who saw in him an opportunity for a compromise between the

radical antislavery elements of the party and the conservative elements formerly aligned with Whigs and free-soil Democrats. Because Bates was ostensibly a southern man with antislavery principles potent enough to make him free his own slaves, he did appear to be a dangerous contender, as the Chicago convention approached. Lincoln realized this sadly, possibly regretting the fact that he had not made greater efforts to conciliate Greeley, whom he saw throwing every inch of *Tribune* space possible in Bates's direction for the public and private anti-Seward reasons already mentioned. And, although Lincoln grew daily more concerned, he could find no means, through Nicolay or any other man, of effecting a *rapprochement* with Greeley.[47]

However, Lincoln found an unexpected ally in the circumstances surrounding the conventions of the other major parties, circumstances which, in a great measure, Greeley had foreseen and privately foretold, but which injured rather than abetted his own presidential choice. In May, 1860, the old-line Whigs and the remaining Know Nothings met together in what was now called the Constitutional Union Party and nominated for president John Bell of Tennessee and for vice-president the noted orator Edward Everett of Massachusetts. Actually, this action was water on the Bates fire, because the Constitutional Union Party set forth the type of conservative platform on which Bates must run, and the Constitutional Union candidates, Bell and Everett, talked like Bates and stood for those things dear to the Missourian's heart. Hence, if the Republicans nominated Bates, the people would have no real choice between his principles and those of Bell and Everett.

If this action poured water on the Bates fire initially, a regular deluge of rain was in the offing. In late April, 1860, the Democrats met in Charleston, promptly splitting into two distinct factions, as Greeley had predicted, with lines being drawn between the Douglasites and the "regulars," and with no agreement found upon a platform which would satisfy both segments of the diversified party. Consequently, the Democrats broke up their own convention, the Douglasites adjourning to meet in Baltimore in June to nominate their man and Herschel V. Johnson of Georgia, and the regulars meeting finally in Richmond and in Baltimore, then nominating John C. Breckenridge of Kentucky and Joseph Lane of Oregon. Of course, both of these Democratic nominating conventions met after the Republicans had made their selections at Chicago, on May 18; but what the two segments did was not unexpected, and the actions served to annihilate most of the Bates followers and most of the hopes of Greeley. Nevertheless, the *Tribune* editor, sincere in his anti-Seward stand, continued his pro-Bates badgering from the time that the Democrats first met in April until time for the Republicans to meet in Chicago, constantly warning his readers that the Democrats might reunite, and "sticking" with flypaper consistency to his conservative horse, Edward Bates of Missouri.[48]

As the Chicago convention loomed daily nearer, Greeley proclaimed flatly that the Republicans had better nominate a *true* conservative, a man who could draw a large popular majority and a large electorial majority. If, he declared, the Republican candidate received an electoral majority but a popular minority of the votes, this would furnish the southern "fire-eaters" with an excellent excuse for precipitating secession and for initiating a civil war. Furthermore, when Greeley saw that the Democrats had split and that this action enhanced Seward's chances of receiving the nomination, he endeavored to serve himself and indirectly Lincoln, too, by having the convention date moved up to early May. In this he failed. Feverishly, through sleepless nights, he worried about his problem, knowing that Weed could now insist, because of the Democratic division, that Seward could win the election on straight Republican votes. And the *Tribune* editor feared that, if Seward were nominated, and if he won the election, Weed's Albany machine would be greatly strengthened, and an element of corruption would be introduced into the first Republican administration that would ensure that administration of failure, of disgrace, and of a very brief tenure of office. Moreover, Greeley knew that if Seward were elected, he would have no voice in the government; and Greeley wanted a voice in the government, wanted a man new to politics on a national scale, a western or semi-southern "greenhorn" to whom he could dictate and whom he could dominate through the power of the press. When in partnership with Seward, the latter had never treated him as an equal, had never asked his or anyone's advice, save that of Weed. But Bates would be different; even Lincoln, who was spoken of for the candidacy in Illinois, might this time bend to the Greeley will and influence.[49]

Consequently, as early as late 1857, the *Tribune* had implied in its columns and on its editorial pages that New York politics needed overhauling, that Weed's political methods left something to be desired in the field of ethical practice. By 1860, the columns of this Republican mouthpiece openly expressed the conviction that if Seward were nominated and elected, through Weed's tactics of corruption and unsavory bargaining, the entire party would be disgraced. Such comments fell into the waiting hands of western Republicans who favored Lincoln; he was set forth as the ideal of honesty, the poor but truthful rail-splitter, the direct and dynamic counterpart of Weed and of Seward. In fact, the entire *Tribune* staff concurred in Greeley's opinion of the New York party boss and his puppet; and James S. Pike expressed the combined sentiment of the paper's editorial staff when he wrote, "I never knew the time when Seward did not vote on the stealing side." Such vitriolic denunciations appeared daily in the *Tribune* and in the private letters written by Greeley and his staff to politicians throughout the North and in Washington. This fever pitch of criticism and hatred gathered momentum as the date for the convention rapidly approached.[50]

As the *Tribune* thus continued to pound out its punches against Seward and for Bates, with Lincoln caught in the middle, receiving no positive support in any direction from the paper, the people who read Horace Greeley and believed that his word was gospel asked who Edward Bates was. This they had asked in 1859; this they asked again in 1860. And, when they found out who he was, as already described, they asked why Greeley would back this Missouri patriarch who was more a relic than a rallying leader, who had actually fought in the War of 1812, who was the father of seventeen children—a Jeffersonian of Virginia, transplanted to Missouri soil, where he had made a for-

tune, become a conservative Whig, freed his slaves, and emerged
as a gracious and warmhearted champion of western growth,
expansion, development, and internal improvement. As has
been emphasized, and as Lincoln's managers continually repeated in southern Illinois, Bates had retired from national
politics twenty-four years before; with the exception of the free-
soil Missourians who revered him and admired him, Bates was
an utterly unknown factor to all Republican elements everywhere.

Joseph Medill of the Chicago *Tribune,* who backed Lincoln,
emphasizing that the latter had emerged from the Lincoln-Douglas debates and campaign trail a national figure and a Republican hero, called Greeley's appendage Bates a "fossil of the
Silurian age." Greeley himself, who could not quite find it in his
heart to approve Lincoln, admitted that his contender was "old-
fogyish," that he had not yet really joined the Republican Party,
that, ensconced among his books and horses, he was nothing
more or less than a vestigial Whig, a preposterous affront to the
abolitionist wing of Greeley's own party, the wing to which
many thought that he belonged. Yet, cried Greeley, this man
could prevent a frontal crisis between the two sections of the
country by carrying the wavering border states—those states over
which Lincoln spent so many costly hours in later months—into
the free-soil column and into the Republican camp. Besides,
thought Greeley, what if Bates were not a dynamic figure, a
national leader? Since the days of Andrew Jackson there had
not been a strong man in the White House, and never would
there be one in that state mansion again. Congress now ruled
the country; and Bates, not Lincoln or Seward, possessed the
most perfect qualifications to fit him for from four to eight years'
residence in the monumental dwelling place on Pennsylvania
Avenue.[51]

In all men's hearts there reign together evil motives beside
good ones; Greeley opposed Seward for selfish reasons, but also
for practical political ones. For example, Greeley truly believed
that Seward possessed less chance of winning the election than
did most of the other prospective candidates. However, Greeley

still preferred Seward to a Democratic administration. There-fore, in mid-April, because the Seward boom was so strong and because it seemed to be an absolute certainty that the New Yorker should be nominated, Greeley ceased his editorial opposition to Seward and to the Albany machine, fearing that, in further damning the character of the senator, he might jeopardize his chances in November, were he, as it seemed that he would be, nominated. It was at this juncture, also, that Weed and Seward made several unsuccessful attempts to regain Greeley's support; they still doubted the intensity of his bitterness, and strove to placate him without making him any promises or too many overt overtures of peace. They failed in every attempt. And, as Greeley himself declared, he "carried none of New York's dirty linen to the Chicago laundry." [52]

Greeley made it plain to his associates—and it should have been equally clear to Weed and Seward—that he supported Bates because the Missouri patriarch was a type diametrically in op-position to Seward. Bates would not be a leader; yet he could be a symbol of American unity—North and South. Venerable, humane, conservative, he could figuratively, and from that point literally, unite and save the nation in an hour when it desper-ately needed union and salvation. Born in Washington's admin-istration, meeting Jefferson as a youth, Bates epitomized the American heritage. Lincoln also epitomized something Amer-ican, "log-cabinish," to many people, but not to Greeley. Lincoln was almost as untenable, in early May, as was Seward.

CHAPTER THREE

A Negative Delegate and a Positive Platform

In mid-May, 1860, 466 delegates to the Republican National Convention, plus thousands of newspaper correspondents, party leaders, and observers and cheerers, convened in Chicago. The Republican Convention met in a building especially constructed for its use—the Wigwam, a two-story wooden building erected at Lake and Market streets by enthusiastic Chicago Republicans. The construction of the Wigwam was scarcely completed when the convention assembled on May 16. The city's forty-two hotels found themselves taxed to their limits. Some were in a festive mood; drinking and "singing songs not found in hymn books" had begun on the trains before delegates and "boosters" arrived, and in the city it was observed by a correspondent that "the Republicans are imbibing the spirit as well as the substance of the old Democratic party." [1]

The complexion of the convention was most heterogeneous—an indication that the Republican Party of 1860 comprised a multiplicity of diverse groups brought together by common anti-Democratic feelings. Former Whigs were there, such as Caleb B. Smith of Indiana and Judge David Davis of Illinois, one of Lincoln's prime political pushers. There were erstwhile free-soil

Democrats like Preston King of New York and David Wilmot of Pennsylvania; German leaders like Carl Schurz of Wisconsin and Gustave Koerner of Illinois; abolitionists like Joshua R. Giddings of Ohio; conservative Union-lovers like the Blairs; political reformers, the most notable and noticeable being Horace Greeley; protective-tariff devotees like Thomas H. Dudley of New Jersey; antislavery men from the border slave states, such as George D. Blakey of Kentucky; finally, a "bogus" Texas delegation, recruited from determined Seward enthusiasts in a Michigan town, pretending to represent the Lone Star State.[2]

The first real cloud to cast a shadow on Thurlow Weed's fair hopes for William H. Seward's nomination was the arrival of Horace Greeley on the Chicago scene. Having been defeated for a delegate's place from New York by Weed's clever ingenuity, Greeley appeared with a "proxy" from the far-off and recently admitted state of Oregon. It should be said that the public, knowing that Greeley had been supporting Edward Bates, did not understand this maneuver, because everyone believed the Weed-Seward-Greeley partnership still to be intact. For a long time now—six years—Greeley had nursed in silence his grievances against Weed and Seward—that is, he had been unable openly to retaliate. On November 11, 1854, he had announced his enmity to Seward; and on May 13, 1860, no longer behind an editorial desk, he personally announced to the world his desire that Seward should be defeated for the nomination at any cost. Therefore, on his otherwise cherubic face, fringed with its motley gray beard, he wore a look of grim determination. His long linen duster streaming behind him—some wag pinned a Seward ribbon on it—he strode from one delegation to another denouncing Seward, sowing dissension among the loyal and doubts among the wavering. "He was a 'd—d old ass,' said the Irrepressibles; he was a tower of strength, thought Seward's opponents. He was a thorn in the flesh of Thurlow Weed."[3]

It was a mushrooming prairie city to which Greeley and these other notable and less notable men came—a city proud of its record of having just attained a population of 110,000, and of having just slaughtered 6,000 hogs in one day. No effort was spared in staging a carnival for the candidate drummers; the looming wooden Wigwam had been principally built and decorated by the Republican women of Chicago, and it demonstrated this fact on every inch of its surface. Furthermore, the plain clapboard fronts of the unpretentious business buildings had been transformed into scenes of gaiety and razzle-dazzle. Weed arrived, heading a Seward entourage which filled thirteen railroad cars, and which contained a brass band and a special cheering section led by the leather-lunged prize fighter, Tom Hyer. More than one thousand saloons stood open and beckoning to the president-makers; and most of the delegates felt that these sources of attraction offset the stench of the near-by stockyards, the piles of filthy garbage in the side streets, and the millions of healthy and diseased rats which scurried back and forth beneath the wooden planking of the pavements.

Perhaps forty thousand visitors infested the city, including an innumerable host of professional gamblers in their best form, prostitutes in their most appealing attire, and pickpockets in their attitude of innocence. These types particularly swelled the contingent of political bargainers and managers. The mayor was forced to stage a police raid on the famed red-light district, in which many delegates were picked up, including three indulgent men from Ohio found in one of the "fancier establishments." [4]

In this hurly-burly at Chicago from May 13 to May 16 and during the three days of the convention itself from May 16 to May 18, two figures were particularly prominent from every vantage point, except perhaps in the red-light district; those two figures were Tom Hyer, who managed the open-air Seward demonstrations, and Horace Greeley, who was conducting his independent anti-Seward campaign. Greeley, in his fervor, talked incessantly in his annoying, squeaky voice. It was only necessary for someone to say, in a rough but friendly way, "There's old Greeley," and all within hearing distance would group themselves about him. Not infrequently, the two or three to whom he began speaking "increased until that which had started as a conversation ended as a speech"—and an anti-Seward speech at that. [5]

Lincoln had many friends among the Chicago delegates,

though Greeley did not prove at first to be one of them; they were enthusiastic, straightforward, aggressive, unpurchasable. Sustained by an immense, omnipresent external pressure, powerfully strengthened by the Chicago *Tribune,* with its forceful editor, Dr. Charles H. Ray, "the ablest and most accomplished journalist of the West," with whom was associated the strongly pro-Lincoln voice of Joseph Medill, the Lincoln delegates pressed directly and incessantly for their man. Greeley saw immediately, as he should have seen long before, that there existed not the ghost of a chance for nominating "Judge" Edward Bates of Missouri; but he admitted this to no one, not even to himself. Instead, he "clung to Bates with unyielding pertinacity"; and his addresses in behalf of his favorite to the various state delegations were, to quote a man who was there and heard them, "marvels of diplomacy and political sagacity." When it was necessary, Greeley praised Seward's ability, but at the same time he sowed seeds of doubt and discord by pointing out how unwise it would be to nominate such a radical leader, a man who could poll no votes south of the Ohio River. Gradually, slowly, surely, effectively, he was killing Seward's nomination.[6]

In a letter to Lincoln at Springfield, written by Jesse K. Dubois from Chicago shortly after the latter had arrived there to work for the rail-splitter, one catches a glimpse, firsthand, of the Lincoln men at work and of Greeley's determined stand and its irritating effects:

> We are here [at Chicago] in great confusion. Things this evening look as favorable as we had any right to expect. Indiana is very willing to go for you, although a portion are for Bates. General Steele is taking them in charge. Eight of the Ohio men are urging you on with great vigor. Gov. Corwin is for McLean, we hope to in the end get them all. Penn. says Cameron or nobody, but that starch must be taken out of them. Horace Greeley is working for Bates. Judge Davis is furious, never saw him work so hard and so quiet in all my life.[7]

Abraham Lincoln was a born bargainer. But with the bar-

gains which led to his nomination at Chicago, in 1860, Lincoln
had nothing directly to do. In answer to an inquiry, he had
wired his backers: "I authorize no bargains and will be bound
by none." But his wily backers spat into the cuspidors and went
on with their bargaining, fighting ferociously for the votes of
Indiana and Pennsylvania. Greeley knew what was happening,
too, even if Lincoln did not; and Greeley wisely wrote, "Indiana
is our right tower of strength"—meaning that, for Bates or for
Lincoln, Indiana was safe from Seward's hands, free from Weed's
greedy grasp.[8]

Weed disgustedly concurred in the remark of one observer
that the most unique delegation sent to the convention was that
from the state of Oregon, at least three of whose five delegates—
Horace Greeley, Eli Thayer, and Franklin Johnson—were not
residents of that state. The time required to travel from Oregon
to Chicago, in 1860, necessitated the enlistment of the services
of eastern Republicans as "proxies." And Greeley, the most active of these "proxies," declared later—perhaps truthfully, although there is reasonable doubt of it—that "I intended to stay
away from Chicago, till I received my most unexpected appointment from Oregon; then it seemed that I could not [stay away]
without [evidencing] absolute cowardice." [9]

Greeley arrived in Chicago three days before the deliberations began, spending his time, as we have seen, in trying to win
the doubtful states either to Bates or away from Seward. Bates
had remained in St. Louis, and Seward stayed at his home in
Auburn, New York, for, according to custom and ritual, the candidates were not to appear at the convention itself. Seward prepared to receive, "with graceful surprise," the news of his nomination; meanwhile, Weed was confidently roaring into the
Windy City to stir up some wind of his own, surrounded by the
band which was to play the triumphal march for the Seward-
Weed success. The Albany political lieutenants, like homing
pigeons, headed for the nearest of the one thousand bars, there
to influence delegates by one drink or another. According to custom, Lincoln also remained at home, in Springfield; Norman B.
Judd and others assisted the politically skillful David Davis in

doing Lincoln's work for him, and in doing it amazingly well.

However, despite the feverish preconvention activities of Greeley and of the Lincoln managers, when the delegations assembled in the Wigwam on May 16, Seward entered the arena still the strongest candidate, still almost guaranteed the nomination on an early ballot. Therefore, it cannot be doubted, with all due praise to Lincoln's managers, that Horace Greeley wielded a considerable amount of influence before the convention had gone into history, and that Seward's defeat, in part, is directly attributable to the presence and the actions of Horace Greeley.[10]

Greeley himself felt that the New York lieutenants of Weed used harmful tactics in their vigorous efforts to nominate Seward, and he remarked this here and there as he traveled among the knots of men in Chicago. Moreover, he wrote back to New York, that the "noisy barroom denunciations of the anti-Seward men from this State as ingrates and traitors; claims for Gov. Seward not only of the exclusive leadership but even of the authorship of the Republican party; public boasts that ever so much money could be raised to carry Seward's election, and none at all for anybody else . . . these were the weapons only of the lowest stratum of New York politicians," but these words and actions, concluded Greeley, had a most "damaging effect." [11]

Contrariwise, the Lincoln managers tried to make friends in all of the delegations, enemies in none, urging Lincoln upon all as at least a "second choice." Greeley worked as cautiously, and his tactics, like those of Judge David Davis and others, proved more effective than Weed's worldly wisdom.[12] However, James Watson Webb, of the New York City *Courier and Enquirer,* Henry J. Raymond, of the New York *Times,* and other newspaper supporters of Seward worked constantly to counteract Greeley's prestige and his telling logic by representing the editor as a disappointed New York office-seeker. In order to prove this, the letter which Greeley had written to Seward late in 1854 was referred to but not produced; neither the followers of Greeley nor the supporters of Seward openly attacked each other, for both sides thought of the November canvass and did not wish to injure party morale.

Unfortunately for Seward, this halfhearted warfare on both sides seemed to profit Greeley and to weaken the position of the New York senator. Greeley walked from group to group, telling them what he had told his assistant editor, Charles A. Dana, back in New York—that to nominate Seward would be re-enacting the old Whig error of running Henry Clay every four years. Dana, as violently opposed to Seward as was his superior, favored Salmon P. Chase, of Ohio, who was now fighting for support among the men to whom Greeley was talking. But Chase, Greeley told Dana and these men, was "as radical as Seward"; the party needed a moderate man, one who could, on a broadly conservative platform, unite all dissident elements of the new party, drawing in the shattered pieces of the old ones. In March, 1860, the editor had penned an editorial entitled "The Presidency," in which he had punctured the Seward balloon in a spot that had never been repaired even by the capable Weed. For Greeley had given praise to Seward as "our veteran leader," as "an able, patriotic Statesman," but one who had sustained "honorable wounds" due to "prejudices and incessant misrepresentations." Greeley continued, "Is the Republican party strong enough to elect a Seward or a Chase?" "Could either of them carry Pennsylvania, New Jersey, Indiana, or Illinois?" "If yes, then the only question is which of the two foremost Republicans shall be our standard-bearer?" The editor had concluded by saying that "we have our opinion, but we will leave decision to the convention and the delegates from the doubtful states." [13]

Greeley, however, as one may see from the way in which he spent his days and nights in Chicago, had no intention of leaving the decision to the convention. He based his policy upon the "doubtful states"; he used this phrase as a fulcrum in every place where he accosted delegates. And, as he hurried from one knot of men to another, he recalled that he had written to James S. Pike, in Washington, that he did not intend to trouble himself by coming to this convention; yet, now, as he wandered through every one of the forty-two hotels and as many of the streets as were available, he was the most looked at, the most listened to, and the most talked of man in all Chicago.

On the other hand, Weed, at his headquarters in the Richmond House, remained cool, affable, confident, letting the bargain-seekers and the office-hunters come to him. He sensed the powerful position he expected to hold as distributor of patronage for the next national administration. New York's big delegation was firmly under his thumb. He had learned from past experience how to act and think; he had already influenced and chiefly brought about the nomination of William Henry Harrison in 1840, of General Zachary Taylor in 1848, of Winfield Scott in 1852, and of John C. Fremont in 1856. His leadership broadened in Chicago, where he was certain that he would nominate for president the man whose political career for thirty years he had fashioned according to his own pattern. "I love my tyrant," Seward had written to Weed, after the former's first election as governor of New York in 1838; and the love was still lavished upon Weed in the same unbounded way. Weed had made him New York's governor and United States senator; why could not Weed make him a Republican president, through his skillful convention manipulations at which he was so adept, in spite of that "blundering, foolish Greeley"? Seward, even more confident of his success than was Weed, ready to affect surprise at news of his nomination, permitted his Auburn neighbors to drag a cannon upon his lawn and to load it in preparation for a mighty salute as signal that the nomination was his.[14]

Carl Schurz, who favored the New York senator's nomination, declared that he was chilled at the rashness of Weed's commitments, which Seward, if elected, could not possibly carry out without dishonor to himself and disgrace to the party. William Cullen Bryant telegraphed his paper, the New York *Evening Post,* that he was horribly shocked by the freedom with which Weed boasted of a campaign "barrel" of from $400,000 to $500,-000 that only the Seward managers could raise. "A reproach" and "a byword" were what the Weed tactics were dubbed by others; it is not difficult to imagine what capital Greeley gained from all of these scandals. They merely confirmed what he had been telling his western readers for months; now, they saw and believed Greeley, and then listened to what he had to say. How-

ever, to Weed it was as simple as this: dollars would elect his
candidate, but they would be available to no one else. But to
the *Tribune* editor, with his trailing linen duster, who found
headquarters out of the question (they would be like a prison
cell to him), who shared a room in the Tremont Hotel with two
other delegates from the state of Oregon, who had reserved no
accommodations with lights and liquors as had Weed, the tactics
of the latter furnished ammunition for a ready gun. Because
he had no thorough plans for his campaign, and because he had
no headquarters, Greeley continued to make his rounds, urging
that the nominee be chosen on the basis of probable election,
and not upon the hope of the corrupt corporation dollars which
Weed alone could promise.[15]

As the champagne flowed faster from the Richmond House,
and as the cigars and dollar promises left that hotel more and
more rapidly as the hours passed, Judge David Davis, in his
quiet, efficient manner, opened up the Lincoln headquarters in
the Tremont Hotel, where Greeley had his accommodations—or,
rather, his shared room. The formal Bates headquarters were
also in the Tremont; but, as we have already seen, Greeley had
no headquarters of his own, and he worked independently for
Bates, not subject to any organization or rules of planning.
Greeley communicated with William Cullen Bryant, who, serious
and subdued, exposed Weed's cash handouts and thus assisted
Greeley accidentally, for the editor of the *Evening Post,* unlike
the *Tribune* monitor, was building up Lincoln. Henry J. Raymond, from his *Times,* cool and well-dressed, in pushing the
Seward machine a little too haphazardly also unintentionally
supplied fodder for Greeley's fire. Colonel James Watson Webb,
of the *Courier and Enquirer,* also for Seward, also trying to place
a damper on Greeley, stood out in the crowds, strutting and indestructible, although his candidate was not. Murat Halstead,
of the Cincinnati *Commercial,* sketched all of the performers,
especially the bustling Greeley; and Joseph Medill, of the Chicago *Tribune,* backing Lincoln against all odds, cursed the New
York *Tribune's* editor for getting in the way of Lincoln's bosses
and for not helping Davis in this hour of crisis. But Greeley, for

once, knew what he was doing, as a political prime mover, as a man for whom Oregon had obligingly made a place; and Lincoln, in the end, was grateful for Greeley's one moment of astuteness, for his one instant of brilliance.[16]

More than thirty thousand straggling, steadfast strangers had crowded into the growing prairie city in upper Illinois with but one thought in mind—that of shouting until they were entirely hoarse for their winning horse, their rail-splitting candidate, gaunt and gangling Abe Lincoln. Seward's gaudily dressed, beaver-hatted, highly epauletted marching bands of representatives, parading the streets and stepping jauntily to the rhythm of loud brasses and rolling drums, seemed strangely out of place; and, anyway, the Lincolnites had the sidewalks and the lungs. "Lincoln could have a parade, too, if like Seward we had five thousand dollars to spend on one," declared the Chicago *Tribune*'s editor, Dr. Charles H. Ray, "but we haven't five thousand dollars for all our expenses!" [17]

Greeley had no cash balance, either, since he was a generous man, giving away most of his earnings, sometimes before he earned them. However, he had a purpose, expressed in the phrase "any candidate but Seward." And his purpose gave him persuasive powers. To Addison Proctor, Kansas delegate, Greeley looked like a "well-to-do dairy farmer fresh from his clover fields. He seemed to find a place in our hearts at once." Proctor continued, " 'To name Seward is to invite defeat,' Greeley told the Kansas men. 'What do you think of Abraham Lincoln?' one of them asked him in return." In Proctor's words, Greeley summed up Lincoln this way, in a few brief words: "Lincoln has a host of friends out here who see in him something that the rest of us have not yet seen. The trouble with Lincoln is that he has had no experience in national affairs. Facing a crisis, Lincoln is too risky an undertaking." [18]

A New York *Times* dispatch declared of Greeley's actions and advice: "Mr. Greeley has made a great sensation here. He is surrounded by a crowd wherever he goes, who besiege him for a speech." [19] Greeley could not help being noticed, and he thoroughly enjoyed the attention which he received. Furthermore,

although he could not see the immediate results of his anti-Seward
campaign, he hoped that something would come of it—hope
buried in pessimism until the very end.[20] Meanwhile, Murat
Halstead, editor of the Cincinnati *Commercial,* telegraphed his
paper wittily:

> The principal lions are Horace Greeley and Francis P.
> Blair. The way Greeley is stared at as he shuttles about,
> looking as innocent as ever, is itself a sight. Wherever
> he appears there is a crowd gaping at him, and if he
> stops to talk a minute with someone who wishes to
> consult him as the oracle, the crowd becomes as dense
> as possible; there is the most eager desire to hear the
> words of wisdom that are supposed to fall on such oc-
> casions.[21]

On Tuesday night, May 15, the eve of the assembling of the
convention in the Wigwam, Greeley wired the *Tribune* that the
Seward forces were strengthening; but the *Tribune* convention
reporter, with eyes and ears more alert than those of his editor,
disagreed, prophesying, in his report, a steadily mounting and
rapidly increasing undercurrent in favor of Lincoln. Henry J.
Raymond, still firmly loyal to Seward, grew hourly more appre-
hensive; he wired his paper, on the night of May 15, "The convention is perfectly willing to accept Mr. Seward's platform . . .
but it is not willing to accept Mr. Seward." [22]

On Wednesday, May 16, 1860, the assembly convened in the
giant Wigwam. The first day's proceedings involved the routine
matters of convention organization. It was now quite apparent,
too, that Greeley's judgment, made in his March editorial, had
proved true, and that the decision of which candidate should be
nominated would finally rest with the three so-called doubtful
states of Indiana, New Jersey, and Pennsylvania. Greeley feared,
however, that there was not the remotest chance that any of the
three would follow his overt suggestions and support Bates. At
the close of the second day, the platform having been drawn
up and accepted, the Seward forces loudly and vociferously demanded that the first ballot be taken. The clerks looked in vain

for the tally sheets, while tension mounted; at length, one Lincoln man cried, "Let's have supper," and the meeting was quickly dismissed by the Lincoln forces. It is generally conceded that the "lost" tally sheets decided the fate of a presidential candidate; the Seward forces led in strength on the evening of May 17, and during that night the managers of Lincoln traded Seward out of many votes and blocks of votes.[23]

"Make no contracts that bind me!" Lincoln wired his managers early in the course of the proceedings. "Hell!" exclaimed Norman Judd that night, "we're here to nominate him, and he's in Springfield." Thus, Lincoln was bound—bound by many promises, many bargains, and many contracts. And while the Greeley-Lincoln forces worked to defeat Seward that night, the *Times* correspondent wired his paper that Seward had not yet been nominated and might not be after all. But, as he worked, Greeley gave up hope.[24]

"Old Abe seems to be the coming man," the New York *Tribune* correspondent wired his paper, still in direct disagreement with his pessimistic chief. In the Weed headquarters, meanwhile, Seward's nomination was still regarded as an absolute certainty, and the night was spent in "confidence and enthusiasm," with no dark thoughts recurring to the disappearance of the ballot sheets. But it was a hectic night for Seward's opponents, and for no one more than Greeley, who canvassed the Ohio delegation at 11 P.M., finding them hopelessly split in three directions—some leaning toward Salmon P. Chase, some toward John McLean, and the rest toward Benjamin Wade. Depressed, he sought comfort among the Daytonites of New Jersey, who rallied around their favorite son no longer but who now stood ready to bolt for a sure winner. Misunderstanding their willingness to combine and move for one sure candidate, Greeley, in utter dejection, sent his now famous 11:40 telegram to the *Tribune:* "My conclusion from all that I can gather to-night is that the opposition to Governor Seward cannot concentrate on any candidate and that he will be nominated!" [25]

This may have been the true situation at midnight, but it was far from the picture which greeted the world at sunup, May

18. The poet Bourdillion's line "The night has a thousand eyes" is truest of that night just prior to the day of the three roll calls, when the sixteenth president of the United States met his destiny. Eager, sleepless eyes searched through that night to break the Seward ranks, to puncture holes in the dikes and let in a flood of Lincoln votes. Greeley, after sending his hysterical and disparaging telegram to his paper at twenty minutes before midnight, then hurried to the hotel room of his New York friend, David Dudley Field, and, throwing himself down on the bed, cried, "It's all over! All is lost!"

But Field shouted, "No, all is not lost! Let us up and at 'em! We can win! Let each of us visit every doubtful delegation." Furthermore, Field informed the prostrated Greeley that, at the very instant he had entered the room, Norman Judd and David Davis were at work on Pennsylvania, while other Lincoln managers were bringing Indiana into line. Field had a fatherly talk with Greeley, explaining to him that Lincoln alone could overcome Seward's strength and sending him to work in the New England delegations for Lincoln. By morning, Field and Blair could report to each other, "The work is done. Lincoln will win!" [26]

Meanwhile, James Watson Webb and Henry J. Raymond had wired their respective papers the sure success of Seward; for, after the costly demonstrations which Weed and his cohorts had provided the delegates and the populace, the Sewardites doubted not one instant that victory would be theirs. Greeley, too, as we have seen, had expected to see Seward nominated on May 18, before and even after his discussion with David Dudley Field. And, when one of the Seward men asked his opinion for a satisfactory vice-presidential candidate to place on the ticket with the New York senator, Greeley, with his watch pointing to midnight and his heart confirming the time, retorted, sadly, "Oh, never mind; fix up the whole ticket to suit yourselves." [27]

Weed would doubtless have put his candidate over the finish line, too, had he not ever been such an egoist, swelled up by past successes, and had he not so vastly overestimated the result of his demonstration on that "beautiful Thursday night," May

17. While Weed let his cronies engage in elaborate demonstrations for the masses, the Lincoln men worked without halting to eat or sleep; [28] and, as Greeley and Field, after their conversation recorded above, descended into the lobby of the Tremont House, they encountered the gargantuan form of Judge David Davis. As they passed, Joseph Medill called to Davis and asked him how matters stood; joyously, the skillful manager, able friend of Lincoln, replied that the Pennsylvania delegation had been won over, "by paying the price . . . by assuring their ill-reputed idol a Cabinet post." The rumor of this deal sent Greeley and Field out into the night, where they exhorted the Missouri delegates to "stick together" for Bates until the last possible moment; then Greeley would give the signal for a simultaneous block transfer of the Bates votes to Lincoln. During the wee hours of the morning, Greeley, gradually beginning to see the light, worked in the Vermont and New Hampshire delegations, begging them to switch to Lincoln, while his assistant and correspondent, James S. Pike, persuaded Maine to vote for Lincoln on the second ballot if Seward did not receive the nomination on the first.[29]

On the third day of the convention, May 18, Friday—a spring Friday similar to the one on which Lincoln was fatally shot—the ballots were finally taken. William Maxwell Evarts, brilliant young New York lawyer, nominated William H. Seward; a number of other candidates were nominated and seconded. Then Norman Judd, of Illinois, nominated Abraham Lincoln. Columbus Delano, of Ohio, rose up from his seat, stood tall upon a chair, and shouted so that the Wigwam rafters sang, "On behalf of a portion of the delegates from Ohio, I rise to second the nomination of a man who can split rails and maul Democrats—Abraham Lincoln." [30] Although the original shout, when Judd first nominated the prairie state lawyer, had not equaled the cries of "bravo" when Seward's name had been read to the immense audience, now, with the seconding statement from this Ohio Lincoln-chaser, the building was shaken to its foundations by the screams, and the Lincoln nomination began to roll. Three ballots were taken, but after the second one the opposition to

Lincoln had virtually evaporated. And, before the chairman, George Ashmun, could even report the already known results of the third ballot, William Maxwell Evarts withdrew his nomination of Seward, and the third ballot results were never formally reported.

The evaporation of Lincoln opposition after the second ballot was principally due to the manner in which Greeley held together the forty-eight delegates pledged to Edward Bates. For Greeley possessed enough political knowledge to realize that if, on the second ballot, Seward gained any of the Bates delegates, it would make the Seward candidacy "look like a band wagon," and enough delegates from other favorite sons would probably jump on the band wagon to nominate the esteemed senator from New York State. Therefore, Greeley held tightly to his forty-eight men, keeping them in check, except for thirteen whom he gladly and personally released to Lincoln on the second ballot, in order to make his candidacy and his nomination develop a band-wagon effect.

The convention readily understood Greeley's strategy, and when Lincoln was declared nominated, scores of delegates crowded around the *Tribune* editor, cheering him as if he, not Lincoln, were the candidate of the party. And his face has appropriately been described as one big, radiant sunburst of smiles. From that moment onward, he was heralded as the one man principally responsible for the defeat of Seward and Weed. George William Curtis, John D. de Freese, and others who were present insisted, until the day of their death, that Greeley more than any other one man defeated Seward and handed the nomination to Lincoln.[31]

Other eyewitness accounts of the procedure declare that, when Lincoln's name was placed in nomination, the building resounded, for Judge David Davis had packed the galleries with leather-lunged Illinois hog-callers. After the first ballot, Greeley bustled about the hall, keeping the Bates men together, arguing with them and persuading those who would vote for Seward not to do so. Then, as the second ballot was taken, carefully screening his brood, the editor permitted thirteen of the forty-eight charges to swell Lincoln's total. Pennsylvania, Indiana, New Hampshire, and Vermont all joined the Lincoln deputation on the second ballot, so that, with the Bates men Greeley released, Lincoln and Seward stood almost side by side in total votes. Finally, Weed really needed Greeley—needed him more than he had ever needed him in all of their long association. Weed proposed a deal, quickly, feverishly; those present saw it happen. It was too late! Greeley repulsed his enemy's advances, and on the third ballot the Bates men—thirty-five of them, including Greeley—went over to Lincoln at last. Lincoln was nominated! [32] And largely to Greeley and his clever manipulations could go the credit.

As the excited Lincoln fans gathered about Greeley and shook his hand, laughing with him, returning his smiles, he recalled the agonizing hours of the preceding night, remembering with pathos the midnight hour when he had sent that telegram to his paper saying that Seward would undoubtedly be nominated. He recalled, too, that he, normally an early retirer, had been too much aroused to sleep. He thought of his work during the small hours of the morning when the Lincoln men had clinched the doubtful states—those doubtful states that he had editorialized into fame—for their candidate. He reveled in the way that he had held the Bates men together until the swing to Lincoln was irresistible, and he gloried in the fact that he had been presented an opportunity to refuse a deal from Thurlow Weed. [33]

Then it was time to choose a candidate for vice-president, and Hannibal Hamlin of Maine received the nod. It has even been alleged that Greeley, in his hour of triumph, suggested Hamlin's name himself; certain it is that Lincoln did not. And then the convention was over, Greeley's influence and his persistence were not easily forgotten; the Sewardites were quick to lay the full blame upon him for the defeat of their hero. "Yesterday was a sad day to many in Chicago," one of these disappointed Seward idolaters wrote wistfully, on May 19; "when it

became evident that Seward was to be sacrificed, tears flowed
like water among the vast throng. . . . The white-livered old
cuss [Greeley] was jubilant. To his venom the result was attributable." Such ran the exaggerated expressions of those who wept
and wept alone at Seward's temporary political eclipse.[34]

In his own autobiographical work, Greeley declares that when
he went to Chicago in May, 1860, he found that New York,
Michigan, and most of Massachusetts backed Seward, but that a
surprisingly large number of the delegates present thought that
the New Yorker's nomination would be disastrous to the future of
the party. Greeley admits that he spread this idea, trying to convince everyone of the unadvisability of selecting a man thought
to be excessively radical by southern and border-state peoples.
However, the editor insists that he did much less to discredit
Seward than is popularly supposed and alleged—that is, in his
day. However, the views of his contemporaries have more clearly
coincided with the proofs of research than have the halfhearted
apologies of Greeley himself. For instance, Greeley declares that
he spent the last ten or more critical hours before the balloting
started in helping to frame the platform—the platform being
the work of the second day of the convention! Yet Greeley does
not deny his activities after midnight and into the morning of
May 18, nor does he discuss these escapades. He does declare,
though, that the efforts to concentrate the anti-Seward vote on
one candidate in the first balloting failed; Greeley admits that,
at this point, he still expected Seward eventually to win.[35]

One may not positively conjecture as to how much Horace
Greeley fought against William H. Seward for personal animosity and how much for the actual benefit of the Republican Party.
Greeley alone knew, and he did not say. He even deprecated his
popular acclaim as the cause of Seward's downfall. He was probably, at least possibly, loyal in his heart to Edward Bates, and
his third-ballot vote for Bates seems to bear this out. Certainly,
as he later often admitted, he was more satisfied with Seward's
defeat than he was with Lincoln's nomination. Greeley still believed that a part of the South could be won over to the Repub-

lican Party—at least that part which had been powerfully in the Whig camp for many years. However, Greeley did not believe that Lincoln was the man who could conciliate the South; he was too ignorant of national politics.[36]

Delegates to the Chicago convention and visitors there have stated that it was not so much Seward who was defeated as it was Weed and the others who lobbied, bullied, bought, and hurrahed for the New Yorker, and who, it was definitely feared, would represent him in the government, in the new Republican administration, were Seward to be elected. Seward looked upon this as his last chance at the presidency, and he thought that he held a party claim superior to all other men's; therefore, he was intensely bitter over his defeat. Weed, Seward, and the sardonic Henry J. Raymond believed Greeley to be the bitterest dregs in the distasteful medicine of failure.[37]

Doubtless Thurlow Weed, the man whom Greeley still somehow admired and almost respected, proved to be the person most bitter about the whole Chicago affair in the long run, but also the one more willing to philosophize upon the matter than was Seward. In later years, when both men had grown less vividly conscious of what had occurred in the Chicago convention, Greeley wrote those significant lines concerning his one-time friend and partner:

> Mr. Thurlow Weed was of coarser mold and fiber [than were most men who occupied a similar political position]—tall, robust, dark-featured, shrewd, resolute, and not over-scrupulous—keen-sighted, though not far-seeing. Writing slowly and with difficulty, he was for twenty years the most sententious and pungent writer of editorial paragraphs on the American press. In pecuniary matters, he was generous to a fault while poor; he is said to be less so since he became rich; but I am no longer in a position to know. I cannot doubt, however, that if he had never seen Wall Street or Washington, had never heard of the Stock Board, or had lived in

some yet undiscovered country, where legislation is
neither bought and sold [sic], his life would have been
more blameless, useful and happy.[38]

Thus, one may see that Greeley still appreciated Weed's
talents, even though he did not necessarily approve of the use
to which the Albany journalist-politician put them. Furthermore, as intimated earlier, Greeley probably suggested the name
of Hannibal Hamlin, of Maine, for the office of vice-president.
G. H. Stewart, together with Don C. Seitz, feels that, from a
firsthand study of the matter, Greeley did this as a means of
offering a sop—possibly a sardonic and a sarcastic one—to the disgruntled supporters of Seward, who saw the nomination pass
to Lincoln under their very noses. Certainly Hamlin was not
Lincoln's choice, but he may have been Greeley's, because the
latter, having told the Seward men the previous night to make
up the ticket to suit themselves, now decided that he had the
power to make up a ticket which at least pleased him from a
negative point of view.[39]

As has been indicated, no words seemed suitable for the supporters of Seward to use as epithets upon the barnacled back of
Horace Greeley. For example, Henry J. Raymond, after visiting
Seward at his New York home, wrote bitterly from Auburn in
the following manner:

> The main work of the Chicago convention was the de-
> feat of Governor Seward . . . and in that endeavor Mr.
> Greeley labored harder and did tenfold more than the
> whole family of Blairs, together with all the guberna-
> torial candidates to whom he modestly hands over the
> honors of the effective campaign.[40]

In fact, Henry J. Raymond continued his bitter denunciations
of Greeley, making references to the letter of 1854, until that
letter was published in the eastern press. Weed expressed sincere
regret that the letter had to be revealed; "it jars harshly upon
cherished memories. It destroys ideals of disinterestedness and

generosity which relieve political life from so much that is selfish, sordid, and rapacious." [41]

Weed's comments sounded so good, coming from the most notorious buyer and seller of men, legislation, privileges, and legislatures for both personal and party gain, that Greeley found himself retorting rapidly:

> The most careful scavenger of private letters or the most sneaking eavesdropper that ever listened to private conversation, cannot allege a single reason for personal hostility on my part against Mr. Seward. I have never received from him anything but exceeding kindness and courtesy in a manner which made them still more obliging; and I should regard the loss of his friendship as a very serious loss. Notwithstanding this, I could not support him for President. I like Mr. Seward personally, but I love the party and its principles more. [42]

Greeley gloated privately, "Do you see how the heathen rage? . . . how the whole weight of their wrath is poured out on my head?" Furthermore, he upbraided Schuyler Colfax for not walking directly into the jaws of the lion as did he, writing in a complaining tone:

> My share of the load was unreasonably heavy, considering where I live, and the power of the soreheads to damage me. . . . I don't think *you* wanted to come face to face with Weed in a case wherein his heart was so set on a triumph. . . . I ought not to have been obliged to expose myself to the deadliest resentment of all the Seward crowd as I did. But what I must do, I will, regardless of the consequences. [43]

Although Greeley had actually been outmaneuvered by the Lincoln forces, and knew it, Chicago was not without compensations. His personal acclaim could not have been greater; he was stared at, pointed out, booed, or greeted as the savior of his party. His mind "had been long before deliberately made up."

The nomination of Seward "would be unadvisable and unsafe"; in defeating Seward—even in striving for Lincoln—he had not utterly failed, but had achieved his primary purpose. His trip to Chicago proved a profitable one.[44]

Thus, although he had considered Edward Bates a wiser choice, the *Tribune* editor accepted the verdict of his fellow delegates at Chicago almost with alacrity. Actually, the ticket was cut to his pattern of expediency for the "doubtful free states"; and Lincoln, he finally admitted, was known generally to be a conservative, as well as a valid Republican, and his Chicago strength had come from the northern commonwealths which had voted for James Buchanan in 1856—Indiana, Illinois, Pennsylvania, and New Jersey. Greeley *knew* that Lincoln would be victorious. He declared that the refusal of the convention to nominate a "renowned radical" would keep from the "Southern hotheads a bludgeon with which to beat the masses of the South into a state of secession." Moreover, Lincoln's platform called for economic measures which would, in the long run, insisted Greeley, bring about peaceable emancipation. Thus, feeling that the southern non-slaveholders, imbued with a Jacksonian love of the Union, would fight for a separate government only if convinced by their aristocratic overlords that their rights were being confiscated by the federal government, Greeley thought that the threats of disunion were merely the mouthings of political charlatans. Consequently, he leaned heavily upon his nominee, Lincoln, and upon Lincoln's platform.[45]

As an observant young Springfield lawyer, Shelby M. Cullom, later wrote, "The Republican platform of 1860 stood in sharp contrast to that of 1856." While more conservative in phrasing, "it was far more boldly constructive in content." Already, Republican action in Congress and in the various state conventions had dictated a number of the planks: free homesteads, tariff revision, internal improvements, a Pacific railroad, a daily overland mail, the immediate entry of Kansas into the federal union. The subcommittee which put these political and economic doctrines into form included Austin Blair, Carl Schurz, John A.

Kasson, and Horace Greeley. The latter, especially concerned over the homestead resolution, later boasted that he had written it exactly to his liking. Moreover, the entire platform, the work of the second day in convention, bore the heavy marks of Greeley's hearty hand.[46]

In fact, because Greeley served on the resolutions committee, and because the document which that committee produced bears the strong marks of his influence, his most effective work at Chicago may have been his framing of the platform upon which Lincoln must run. The *Tribune* editor privately admitted that he had "labored long and earnestly" to divest this party pronouncement of all features "needlessly offensive or irritating" to the South. Specifically, Greeley claimed credit for having blocked "the requirement that Congress shall positively prohibit Slavery in every Territory whether there be or be not a possibility of its going thither." [47] Thus, he tried to placate both sides of the sectional conflict.

In the Chicago platform, the Democrats were berated for not having admitted Kansas as a free state, for disregarding the political mandate of the inhabitants. And Greeley, both in backing Bates and in forming this conservative platform, wished to draw as much free-state support away from Douglas as possible. He could best accomplish this, he thought, by removing the charge of sectionalism both from his candidate and from his platform. To insist upon a congressional edict against slavery within territories where the institution was economically infeasible anyway seemed senseless provocation; the Kansas troubles had taught him that, were the administration in Washington opposed to the extension of slavery, there would be in the future no difficulty in ushering into the Union those territories with climate and soil similar to that of Kansas. They could be brought in as free states without further pouring salt into the open territorial wounds. Such was Greeley's frame of mind as he approached the problem of framing the Chicago platform.[48]

On the other hand, Greeley still maintained that Congress possessed the right to outlaw slavery in any territory, "when-

ever," according to the Chicago platform, "such legislation is
necessary . . ." [49]

In addition to this stand, other parts of the platform begged
for the foreign vote by denouncing the rabid nativists and by
making due obeisance to the federal Constitution, the Union,
and the Declaration of Independence. Here, Greeley ran afoul
of that messiah of the abolitionists, Joshua R. Giddings, who,
venerable with age, rose haughtily from his chair and stalked toward the Wigwam door because the *Tribune* editor had made
mere mention of "Thomas Jefferson's great document" without
quoting the section on the fundamental equality of all men, as
Giddings demanded. Catcalls and cheers gave way to orations on
the disputed point, and finally "the old man," backed firmly
by the Sewardites, had to be satisfied, and one radical plank
was nicely nailed into the conservative Republican platform.
This accomplished, attention was then turned toward the vastly
more important economic resolutions: homesteads, tariff, and
internal improvements.[50]

After twenty years of agitation, Greeley stood at the threshold
of his greatest public achievement, the homestead law. Such legislation had been gaining favor, especially in the West, since
the Panic of 1857, and Greeley believed that it could not be denied the frontiersmen even if the Republicans lost the elections
of 1860. This consideration was partially responsible for the editor's letters to the *Tribune,* in the winter of 1859, in which he
prophesied the nomination of Douglas by the Democrats, for
the "little giant" had long been an advocate of free land. The
demand for a quarter section to be given any man who would
till the soil was the keystone of Greeley's theory of labor reform
and was the logical culmination of the *Tribune*'s antislavery
crusade.

Therefore, Greeley sponsored the homestead plank in the
platform of 1860, writing that plank to satisfy his own personal
philosophy. The second point on Greeley's economic agenda was
a protective tariff, a measure to satisfy the New Jersey and other
eastern Republicans, and a measure which fitted into his scheme

of economic nationalism and restricted foreign trade in order that the United States might become self-supporting. Because of this policy, Greeley disliked the South, where foreign trade was essential to survival; consequently, when he wrote this plank into the platform, he upheld certain Republican ideals without even remembering that he had planned a program of southern conciliation.

Likewise, Greeley's third influential measure in Lincoln's 1860 platform proved to be a northern and a Republican program—internal improvements, specifically a railroad to the Pacific. Congress should offer a contract to a company which would guarantee to complete the railroad within ten years, Greeley thought; all groups of capitalists interested should bid for the coveted prize, with the honor and profits going to the company which asked for the least government assistance, with this governmental assistance to be paid the company in government bonds, in land grants, and in timber rights. Furthermore, as to the route of the railroad, Greeley found himself partial to the central route, through Kansas and the newly discovered gold fields around Pike's Peak, which he had visited amidst much fanfare, as he crossed the Rocky Mountains in his spectacular journey of 1859.[51] In his book describing this trip, Greeley writes that, in 1860, many considered the prospect of a speedily constructed Pacific railroad to be "a humbug—the fantasy of demagogues and visionaries." Some men on the platform committee with Greeley held the same ideas; however, Greeley informed them that, in the year of 1857 alone, 22,990 persons had arrived in San Francisco by the water route, and 16,902 persons had departed by the same way. Moreover, there was a heavy overland immigration each year in both directions, east and west. Much gold could be shipped to the East, and many supplies sold to the West, with the cost of movement greatly reduced by a transcontinental railway. In addition, the disreputable living conditions in Kansas, Utah, and the Rocky Mountains might be improved, and the mail service stimulated, with the cost of transporting military supplies vastly reduced.[52]

Greeley quoted these "facts of life" to his committee members; and after having won a substantial victory in his homestead plank and in his protective tariff resolution, he scored another triumph in the internal-improvements section of the platform. Greeley was, however, not wholly victorious, nor was he wholly frank. He was in Chicago, and he had many subscribers in and around the metropolis—for that was what the prairie city was fast becoming. Consequently, he did not strain for his railroad as hard as he might have, because he desired its eastern terminus to be, not Chicago, but St. Louis—Blair town. For, if that city teemed with free laborers, brought there by the railroad, Frank Blair and Missouri emancipation would be upheld.[53]

Nevertheless, it may be stated that Greeley cast two profound influences upon Abraham Lincoln at Chicago: one was Greeley's part in preparing the platform—particularly the economic measures dealing with internal improvements, the tariff, and free homesteads—the other, the nomination of Lincoln itself.

Without patronage to give or even to promise, without actual power to help or to harm people in or out of public life and office, without excessive harsh criticism of Seward or of any other Chicago candidate, without the promise of one dollar, without any actual trading or bargaining—but with an earnest, crusading, persuasive, determined spirit only—Horace Greeley led in the directing of a convention of almost five hundred delegates from a nominee who entered the convention with the support of the majority of delegates and of newspaper correspondents and editors. Perhaps over and above his plans and his platform program for a protective tariff, for a homestead law, for internal improvements at government expense, and for the construction of a Pacific railroad, Horace Greeley did a far more practical and worth-while thing in opposing Seward and in aiding Lincoln. He declared, "If ever in my life I discharged a public duty . . . I did so at Chicago. . . ." "I did not, and I do not, believe it [would have been] advisable [to choose Seward as] the Republican candidate for President." [54]

Alvin E. Bovay, pioneer Republican, Greeley's friend since anti-rent days, wrote to the editor jubilantly:

> It seems to be the style just now to discuss the sayings and doings of Horace Greeley. . . . If it was through your efforts that William H. Seward was defeated, so much more glory and honor to you. It saved the Republican party and the country. . . .[55]

In addition, James Parton told Greeley, "I believe that you are the most popular man in the Northern States." But, of course, this was not true; Greeley was extremely unpopular in many quarters, for Seward had a host of supporters. The closest Seward advisers and supporters never forgave Greeley, who insisted that these men exaggerated the role he had played in the dethronement of their lord. Vitriolic Henry J. Raymond, however, wrote concerning Greeley that he "awards to others the credit which belongs transcendently to himself." [56]

Thurlow Weed, still smarting at the insult, after the convention, after the Wigwam tears, wrote to his puppet Seward: "Greeley was malignant. He misled many fair minded men. He was not scrupulous. He said to some that you could not carry New York and that twenty of our delegates were against you." [57]

Other factors than Greeley, however, also influenced Seward's failure: the availability of Lincoln, which proved attractive to a convention of heterogeneous elements; the choice of Lincoln on the second ballot by the doubtful states of Pennsylvania, Indiana, and New Jersey—those states whose electoral votes Buchanan had captured in 1856. In the end, it seems that this was the decisive factor, just as Greeley had predicted that it would be; as Henry Lane and Andrew Curtin led their delegations over to the Lincoln banner, the nomination of the man from Illinois was clinched. Then, too, another factor is here apparent: Lincoln's nomination meant the initiation of a real movement to promote Republicanism in the area now known as the Middle West, and it also marked the beginning of an alliance between the protectionists of Pennsylvania and New Jersey and the homesteaders of Illinois and the rest of the old Northwest. Such an alliance was absolutely essential to Republican success; and Greeley, by promoting in the platform a policy favoring both pro-

tection and homesteads, helped to unite the party, to secure
Lincoln's nomination, and to bring about his subsequent election.[58]

Although aware of the accusations of corruption hurled
against the Albany machine, although aware of the other very
significant factors which led to Seward's defeat, Weed and his
Chicago cohorts chose to exaggerate Greeley's influence at the
convention. They found this to be the most feasible tactic for
maintaining control of the party in the state of New York and
for assuring themselves of a lion's share of the patronage from
the Lincoln Administration. In reality, at Chicago Greeley
played the role of Brutus more than that of Judas.[59]

Yet, in spite of the measure of influence which Horace Greeley
exercised upon the nomination of Lincoln and upon the platform upon which Lincoln stood, the editor's opinion of this
man soon to be president passed through a course that seems
both tortuous and peculiar. In 1858, the year of the Lincoln-
Douglas debates, Greeley strove for the acceptance of Douglas as
the Republican as well as the Democratic candidate for the
United States Senate. In 1859, Greeley turned from Seward and
Chase to Edward Bates, not Lincoln, as his "moderate" candidate for the presidency. And, finally, in May, 1860, Greeley
landed at Chicago, doing everything in his power to defeat Seward and to nominate first Bates, and then Lincoln. What is more,
even after he decided to accept Lincoln, Greeley continued to
work for and to cast his Oregon vote for Bates, posing the while,
in the unknowing public's eye, as the ardent admirer of Seward. Now, after much study, it appears clearly certain that Greeley's opinion of Lincoln—at least, his publicly expressed opinion—passed through these tortuous stages as a result of Greeley's
political and economic ideas and ideals—postulates which are
most candidly viewed in the editor's handiwork woven into the
1860 Republican platform. When at last Greeley saw that Lincoln, as a moderate, as a Westerner, and as a "new face," could
fit into his national program, which involved gradual emancipation and internal social and economic improvements, the
candidate from Illinois was boosted for the nomination, can-

vassed for in the election, and pushed forward toward the White House. Unfortunately, a bitter wrangle ensued between Greeley and his associates and Seward and his admirers; and Lincoln's consideration for the advice of Thurlow Weed proved to be partially responsible for Greeley's persistent attacks upon Lincoln himself during the four years and one month which the tall, lean man from Illinois spent in the White House.[60]

Without any doubt, Greeley played one of the major roles in the nominating of Lincoln; and, as the months slowly passed, dripping with northern and southern blood, Greeley, ever the pacifist at heart, regretted more each day that he had placed his hand upon Lincoln's shoulder, that he had urged him on in the direction of Washington.

CHAPTER FOUR

Visions of Victory

Horace Greeley had, by 1860, made his New York *Tribune* a national institution. Animated by enthusiasms which tended toward fanaticism, and marred by personal eccentricities which laid him open to ridicule, this Yankee printer had risen from stark poverty to an enviable position of national power and influence. Moreover, as a supporter of the Whig and later of the Republican Party, he had demonstrated, in areas widely distant from his sanctum, the tremendous force of political journalism. With defects of character that were to grow with the years, he evidenced the finer idealism of an ardent nature in efforts to improve the lot of the workingman and in campaigns to free the slaves. As one who had always given generous, multi-column support to movements for political education and advancement, as one who had championed every progressive social experiment in America for more than twenty years, Horace Greeley faced with vigor the 1860 task of electing a Republican president, of bringing to the American people the candidate whom he had—at least negatively—helped to name.[1]

Many prominent leaders within Republican ranks realized that Greeley possessed the power to make or to mar Lincoln as a candidate; after hearing of his defeat in his bid for the presidential nomination, William H. Seward, in his Auburn (New York) home, penned a private note to Thurlow Weed, in Davenport, Iowa, in which he concurred in Weed's statements that Greeley had been chiefly responsible for his failure, and in which he declared that he had even foreseen his defeat when he learned of Greeley's presence at the Chicago convention. He feared for the party's future, particularly if that future lay in the hands of the editor of the *Tribune,* and he suggested that he would like to withdraw into political retirement when his senatorial term ended on March 4, 1861. Guessing that the Republican leadership for the campaign would surely pass into Greeley's editorial hands, Seward informed Weed that the latter could find asylum in Europe for six months while Greeley allowed the party to drift to disaster. At that point, after the elections were lost, Weed might return to the United States and reassume leadership of the party; after all, the organization was new, and one more lost election would not matter greatly, especially since Seward was not the candidate. With another lost election in his files, the *Tribune* editor would be thoroughly discredited as a political leader, and that upstart from the West, Abraham Lincoln, would be a hindrance to eastern Republicans no more.[2]

Greeley, sensing the important place he must fill in the presidential campaign, not knowing of Seward's underhanded remarks concerning his ability, stepped immediately into stride and pressed forward for victory. Describing the canvass a few years later, the editor declared that the issues over which the candidates battled shaped themselves into sharply defined lines of conflict. The Breckinridge Democrats—those of the South—insisted that the election of 1856 had been won by a policy of amiable ambiguity and friendly double-dealing on the planks of the platform, a document which meant one thing to the South and something else to the North; consequently, cried the Southerners, this misunderstanding must not recur in 1860. Greeley helped to state this southern position in his *Tribune,* hoping that by doing so he might prevent any *rapprochement* between northern and southern Democrats.[3] The Douglas group, Greeley

felt, were virtually as frank and equally as firm when they declared that they would win the election on the "principle of
popular sovereignty" or not at all. Although the South warned the
Douglas Democrats that their united party alone held the Union
together, and that, if the Democrats lost the election, the Union
would be broken, Greeley did not emphasize this point, for he
doubted the sincerity of southern threats.

At the beginning of the campaign, Greeley printed in his
Tribune these words of his candidate, Lincoln:

> Slavery can only exist by virtue of municipal law; and
> there is no law for it in the Territories, and no power
> to enact one. Congress can establish or legalize Slavery
> nowhere, but is bound to prohibit it in or exclude it
> from any and every Federal Territory, whenever and
> wherever there shall be necessity for such exclusion or
> prohibition.[4]

Douglas stood firmly upon his principle of popular sovereignty, as Greeley reported it to his readers—that each territory,
by virtue of the vote of its white inhabitants, is its own judge
as to whether it shall be "free" or "slave." John C. Breckinridge
said, in effect, that any citizen might migrate to a federal territory, taking his "property"—his slaves—with him, and that property must be protected there, if need be, by the Congress of the
United States. Stephen A. Douglas began a series of debates in
an effort to refute this Breckinridge principle; and he drew large
audiences, even in the southern areas which he visited. On the
other hand, the Breckinridge forces determined that they would
divide the Democratic vote in every free state in which they
possessed any strength to do so.

Greeley told his readers that the Democratic division was
based upon principle and that no agreement could be reached,
even though the Douglasites offered to form a "fusion ticket"
with the Breckinridge and Bell electors in a number of pivotal
states. "Nowhere in the Slave States would the Breckinridge
men consent to any compromise, partnership, coalition, or
arrangement, with the partisans of Douglas, though aware that

their antagonism would probably give several important States to the Bell-Everett Ticket," thus offering Lincoln ample opportunity for success. Greeley hastened to show the voters of the North how "selfish" and how "antagonistic" the South could be; and he tried to tell the South that, if his candidate won the election, the southern peoples would have nothing to fear, no reasons for secession.[5]

Furthermore, the *Tribune* told its readers that the Douglas men were willing to waive prestige and to form fusion tickets with the Bell and Breckinridge forces, such as the New York anti-Republican ticket, which was to contain ten electors for John Bell, seven for John C. Breckinridge, and the residue for Douglas. This, Greeley declared, was corrupt bargaining by which Douglas intended to elect himself; in fact, Greeley so publicized these stories that Douglas was injured, especially in the East and in the old Northwest, more than he was helped. In addition, Greeley told his audiences that Douglas, in "representing the mean," the average, a point of compromise, could hardly serve the nation to advantage in this hour of decision. In an argument of principle, the "tendency" is ever "away from the mean," and Lincoln stood for a principle diametrically in opposition to that of the South. Moreover, just as Douglas was weak, because he stood for negative compromise, Greeley decided that the Bell Unionists were weaker, because they stood upon a platform which pledged wholehearted allegiance to the "Union, the Constitution, and the enforcement of the Laws," and because the old Webster-Clay ideals of compromise, held up by this party, had soured upon the minds of southern slaveholders—the so-called Calhounists.[6]

While Greeley busied himself with his pen and on the stump attacking the other three parties in the field, he realized with horror that the elections of early 1860 were by no means favorable to the Republicans, who won in New Hampshire but were defeated in Rhode Island and scarcely re-elected the Republican governor in Connecticut. Democratic harmony at Charleston, or any accord occurring between the Democratic meeting at that city in April and the November elections, would have rendered inevitable a Democratic victory once more. It was only this Democratic split, Greeley predicted, which would allow Maine and Vermont, in September, and Pennsylvania and Indiana, in October, to join the Republican ranks. In addition, throughout the entire campaign, the state of New York would prove to be the arena of intense struggle, the actual deciding factor, because of the pro-southern mercantile interests which were so dominant in America's greatest metropolis.[7]

To Lincoln's opponents, New York State appeared to be the one and only place for accomplishing his certain defeat. If the Empire State's thirty-five electoral votes could be kept from the Republican standard-bearer, he would be deprived of a majority in the electoral college, even if he carried every other northern state. In such an eventuality, the presidential contest would be thrown into Congress, where the Democrats believed they had a chance to win. This could be said of no other state.

Realizing this, Lincoln worriedly wrote not to Greeley but to Thurlow Weed:

> I think there will be the most extraordinary effort ever made to carry New York for Douglas. You and all others who write me from your State think the effort cannot succeed, and I hope you are right. Still it will require close watching and great efforts on the other side.[8]

For a period following the Chicago convention, the New York Republicans were sharply divided into two hostile groups—the Weed-Seward faction and the anti-Weed or former free-soil Democratic faction led by William Cullen Bryant.[9] Horace Greeley co-operated with the latter wing of the party. Consequently, the pro-Seward editor of the New York *Times,* Henry J. Raymond, charged that Greeley was the principal cause for Seward's failure to receive the nomination and that the public should know the truth about Greeley's political and moral life. Raymond referred to the aforementioned letter of November 11, 1854, and Greeley hotly demanded that it be published in the press, as we have indicated. Seward reluctantly released the letter, with Weed protesting that the whole matter should have been forgotten for the sake of the campaign; both sides claimed that public response indicated that they had the support of the people. Lincoln, hearing of the incident, despaired of carrying New York. He probably blamed Greeley for the whole affair, but he urged that both factions co-operate. Although the bitter quarrel which ensued was not immediately quelled by Lincoln's indirect pleas, at length the wrangling temporarily subsided, when an enormous Lincoln-Hamlin ratification meeting was held at Cooper Institute on June 7. The "angel" of the Weed organization, Richard M. Blatchford, of course, presided, but rousing cheers were given in turn for Seward and for Greeley. In late August, the Republicans met in convention at Syracuse and reiterated that the hatchet had been buried for the duration of the campaign. Both factions were given representation in the state organization, and both sides agreed to wage a vigorous campaign so that Lincoln might be elected.[10]

According to one who took part in the campaign of that eventful year, who witnessed Greeley in action and heard Lincoln's noncommittal silence, all of the candidates for president were men of ability and character. Lincoln had recently won national renown by his powerful debates with Stephen A. Douglas, by many speeches in Illinois, and by profoundly thoughtful addresses in other states, such as his memorable Cooper Union declaration. Douglas was wonderfully popular with the Democratic masses of the North, a fact which Greeley knew and deprecated; like Lincoln, he had long struggled to win position and fame by virtue of his talents and energies alone. As the campaign progressed, and as Greeley again realized what a superb debater and what an amazing organizer Douglas was, the *Tribune* editor feared for the future. Also, as the days dragged by, John C. Breckinridge proved himself to be a "man of brilliant parts, and one of the most pleasing of public speakers." Furthermore, the remaining opponent to Lincoln, John Bell, stood forth, as time passed, as an excellent statesman of many years' experience in public life and political combat, as a man

justly entitled "to the general respect of the people." Consequently, Greeley found himself supporting the political novice
of the four candidates.[11]

As a result, the editor searched about for some exceptional
anti-administration campaign fodder. He found it in the demands of Westerners for a homestead bill and in the platform
plank he had written into the Republican platform, a plank
promising homestead action for the farmers of the West. Feeling that the passage of a homestead act would culminate in the
establishment of small farms throughout the free states, that this
would bring about the practical restriction of slavery within
the bounds which now held it, that eventually, when thus restricted, it could be eradicated by an educational, industrial, and
agricultural process, the editor of the *Tribune* pressed Congress
to pass a homestead act during the course of the last term before the 1860 elections.[12]

Mere platform sponsorship of such a measure, to be passed
by Congress some time in the future, was insufficient. If a homestead bill could be passed by both houses immediately, Greeley
felt sure that the President, James Buchanan, would veto it, thus
clarifying this first-class campaign issue. All was done to the
editor's satisfaction. Galusha Grow, congressman from Pennsylvania, secured House approval of his homestead measure in
March, 1860; however, southern opposition to the parceling of
the western prairies into small farms was much stronger in the
Senate, where Tennessee hillman Andrew Johnson had a difficult time obtaining even a semblance of the House version. Then
a conference committee of the two houses brought forth a virtual acceptance of the "watered down" Senate measure. This bill
was passed in June, 1860; and, as Greeley desired, Buchanan
vetoed it. This was all that the editor's heart could wish, and
Lincoln read how Greeley called the President a "tired old aristocrat" who would not even feed the crumbs of the Senate's "half-
loaf" bill to the masses. It was, hence, very dangerous to elevate
to the office of president of the United States a man who had
never associated with the poor; Lincoln, on the other hand, had
been, and still was, poor himself, and thus he favored a land

policy which would benefit the masses. Had he been president, he would have accepted even these crumbs for the sake of the people, but Buchanan would not. Would Breckinridge or Douglas be any different in their policies? [13]

In addition, Greeley's *Tribune* charged that "the [homestead] bill which he [Buchanan] vetoed . . . was not the Republican or House Free Homestead Bill, but that of the Senate, which nearly every Republican voted against" on its first passage, "and only acquiesced in at the last moment, in deference to the tens of thousands in Iowa, Minnesota, Kansas, etc., who are liable to be ejected" from their "rude homes at any moment," because "in the pecuniary condition of the Northwest, it is morally impossible that they should pay $1¼ per acre for the quarter-section each [the prevailing price of land] which is or contains their all." With this question Greeley closed this editorial: "Does anybody suppose that Abraham Lincoln would ever veto such a bill?" [14]

In this manner, Greeley indeed touched the popular heart in the Northwest, which had not yet fully recovered from the baneful effects of the Panic of 1857. Thousands of pioneers had no money to pay for land which they had bought under the then existing pre-emption law, and many blamed the "pre-emption land system" for "hard times." As if to make matters worse and to play further into Greeley's hands, Buchanan had, by proclamation, opened the lands to public sale. Immediately the cry was set up that the administration was deliberately endeavoring to injure the Northwest. Greeley, highly influential in that region, led in this outcry; in Minnesota, for instance, his weekly edition had a larger circulation than did any local sheet, and this weekly edition bombarded the Democrats for their anti-northwestern land policy. The editor continued to emphasize that persistent opposition by the Democratic Party and a majority of the Democrats themselves to a free homestead law, plus the erratic policy pursued by the Buchanan administration relating to the sale of lands, proved that salvation for the Northwest lay alone within the fold of the Republican Party—the party "which saves the people from the spoliation of their homes." [15]

Privately, Greeley wrote that the "Free Land or Homestead Bill is our tower of strength in the Northwest." But he realized that protection by a tariff for American industry loomed in the minds of the people as perhaps a dangerous course to follow; it was relatively simple to stir up popular support for homestead legislation, and it was easy to present Lincoln as the candidate of the poor but honest masses. However, it was a far different matter to obtain popular support for a protective tariff policy in 1860. Many of the free-soil elements of the party were still clinging to the Democratic ideal that free trade always benefited the consumer; hence, Greeley in his campaign speeches and editorials had to steer a middle course in order to satisfy these recalcitrants, while at the same time attracting Pennsylvania and New Jersey tariff enthusiasts. To lure these divergent elements under the Republican banner, Greeley had worded the protection plank of the Chicago platform with great moderation; he followed this by a cautious editorial policy, urging his friends in Congress not "to drive the wedge butt-end foremost, nor lose all in attempting to grasp too much." By these warnings, he insisted that the people would tolerate tariffs on iron, fabrics, and luxuries, but not on coal or, for that matter, on any other commodity which might be convincingly paraded in the Democratic press as an unnecessary burden upon the laborer.[16]

Lincoln appreciated these sincere campaign editorials and speeches, but he was not certain at what moment Greeley might alter his tactics. The editor's attitude in 1858, when Lincoln had opposed Douglas in the senatorial contest in Illinois, had taught Lincoln to beware of the press in general and of Greeley in particular. However, shortly after his nomination, Lincoln saw that not only the strongest men of his party were supporting him but also that they were working in almost every northern state, in a fair state of harmony but without the proper organizational guidance. Such organization as there was functioned splendidly, but there was not enough to carry the full load of such a campaign. Most of the Republicans, at the outset, agreed with Greeley's *Tribune* that "the election of Mr. Lincoln, though it could not be accomplished without work, was eminently a thing that could be done," and they set themselves vigorously about the task of accomplishing it. True, the widest party rift came to light in New York State, as we have indicated; however, the June 7 Republican rally at Cooper Institute did much to heal these wounds temporarily and on the surface. Meanwhile, as the party was composed largely of young men who felt that the cause was worthy of their best efforts, great zest and ingenuity were thrown into the campaigning. Arrangements were immediately made for a systematic stumping of the entire northern section of the country, with Greeley regretting that more attention could not be paid to the dissatisfied South. Nevertheless, the speakers engaged to do this unceremonious stumping proved to be generally of the highest order, despite the fact that most of them were despised by slaveholders who called the party, from the beginning, a sectional one. These stumpers included, among others, William H. Seward, Salmon P. Chase, Charles Sumner, Cassius M. Clay, Thaddeus Stevens, and, of course, the dynamic but erratic Horace Greeley. Many of these speeches were of more than usual dramatic interest; and Lincoln, in Springfield, feared most of all what Greeley might utter in his haste to win a few votes.[17]

Truly, Greeley, in deciding what to say, was faced with many problems. He insisted that Seward had been defeated for the nomination only because he was a radical, while Lincoln was a true conservative. This belied the true situation, but the editor devoutly hoped that the states of the South and of the border region would respond to talk of Lincoln's conservatism. When he was asked cryptically about Lincoln's "radical 'House Divided' " speech, Greeley squirmed and replied that the nominee had stated only that slavery should not be extended; "this would place it where Washington, Jefferson, and Madison placed it— in the way of ultimate extinction by the operation of natural causes, and in the peaceful legislation of the people of the states where it exists. . . . Such is the orderly and conservative policy of Abraham Lincoln and of the Republican party." [18]

Greeley's exceptionally favorable editorial treatment of Lincoln must have seemed a bit sudden to the readers of the *Trib-*

une, for, until the nomination was over, it had not even considered him as a serious contender for the presidency. At one point before the Chicago convention had begun its deliberations, Greeley had privately adjudged Lincoln's capabilities as suiting him for becoming a possible, even a logical, choice for the vice-presidential nomination, but this suggestion, or preference—if it could be called that—had never received any editorial backing, or even any public mention, because the *Tribune* waved its banners for Bates, and the ticket should not contain more than one former Whig. Furthermore, despite Greeley's recognition of Lincoln's forensic abilities as early as the Lincoln-Douglas debates, and despite the fact that Lincoln's Cooper Institute speech had drawn more *Tribune* applause than was normally accorded such efforts, Greeley had never publicly supported Lincoln in any way prior to the beginning of the presidential campaign.[19]

Now, of a sudden, the *Tribune* came to life for Lincoln, and Greeley went out on the road to lecture for his Republican nominee. In addition to this "educational work" on the stump and in editorial columns, an immense number of pamphlets and similar printed articles were produced and distributed widely. Next to the campaign lives of Lincoln and Hannibal Hamlin, of which there were many, the campaign tracts issued by the New York *Tribune* were the most widely circulated documents. There were several of these, the most popular being Carl Schurz's speech on the "Doom of Slavery," and Seward's on the "Irrepressible Conflict." Moreover, the ablest literary men in the United States wrote material for these tracts, as well as for the Republican press; for example, Horace Greeley, who claimed no knowledge of poetry, although he would like to have us remember his aesthetic qualities, called upon John Greenleaf Whittier for some appropriate verses to be included in the *Tribune.* Thus, with poems and editorials, with speeches and quotations from Lincoln's own earlier utterances, Greeley led the people toward November, hoping to usher them into Lincoln's ballot total.[20]

He lavished praise upon Lincoln as the candidate who would, if elected, foster the peaceful eradication of slavery through economic and social developments, not through coercion and law. He sought to show that the Republican policies were founded upon the best traditions of American democracy. In a manual to guide campaign speakers like himself, he reprinted the principal letters and addresses of all of the candidates, together with a copy of all four party platforms and a "History of the Struggle Respecting Slavery in the Territories, and of the Action of Congress as to the Freedom of the Public Lands." By late August, ten thousand copies of this Tribune Association manual had been sold and the work was entering its seventh printing. Greeley and his assistant editor, Charles A. Dana, spoke of local "wide-awake" clubs putting this popular handbook to practical use, exhorting such clubs, which were legion, to establish a complete organization of the community on a grass-roots level in order to get out a full vote in November. In addition, Greeley made easy the following of his paternal counsel by virtually flooding the country with printed materials; fatigue seemed never to touch him, although his letters to his friends, like Schuyler Colfax, were infrequent and were scrawled with utmost haste, and despite the fact that he continually complained of being utterly "worn out" and "exhausted" with work and anxiety.[21]

Lincoln was constantly urged during the 1860 campaign to elaborate his opinions in a public speech, but he consistently refused. From the time that he returned to Springfield after his Cooper Union address of February 27, 1860, until he read his first inaugural address on March 4, 1861, Lincoln remained silent, except for an endorsement of the Chicago platform in an acceptance letter of four hundred words. "Look over my speeches carefully," he wrote in reply to a request for a new interpretation of the opinions he had expressed in the Douglas senatorial contest, "and conclude that I meant everything that I said and did not mean anything I did not say and you will have my meaning then and now." [22]

With Lincoln silent, the national committee should have shouldered the campaign. However, in the long run, the national organization proved to be scarcely more active than the candidate. Governor Edwin D. Morgan, who headed the committee, gathered funds in the East to be spent in the West, but he never guided the party's work or program. He was governor of New York, busily seeking re-election, and subservient to Thurlow Weed. It was the Albany editor himself who took control and gave the organized campaign all of the direction that it ever possessed. Of course, Seward had suggested sadly that Weed might spend six months in Europe while Greeley directed the campaign; Weed, however, could not do that. Instead, he guided the organizational forces and machinery of the canvass, while Greeley handled the printing, distributing, and preparing of editorial, oral, and pamphlet propaganda. Although they ostensibly worked together, neither Greeley nor Weed respected the efforts of the other; and Seward predicted that Greeley would be worthless in the campaign, with Weed confirming this prediction as true at the time of the election.[23]

On the other hand, Greeley felt, as election day drew near, that his efforts had not been in vain. Out of his *Semi-Weekly* he produced the *Campaign Tribune,* but its circulation was only a fraction of what it had been when it had served an identical purpose in 1856. However, the editor believed that the *Weekly Tribune* more than compensated for this, since its mailing list remained near 200,000 during the entire year of 1860. Urging that his aggregate total of 300,000 subscribers lend their papers "as widely as possible," the editor believed that each copy passed through at least five hands before it was burned or otherwise destroyed. When Greeley sat down and considered that he had appeared on the campaign platform countless times, that he had circulated pro-Lincoln material in his *Daily,* his *Semi-Weekly,* and his *Weekly Tribune,* that he had prepared a volume for circulation on the political issues of the day, that he had turned out from his presses auxiliary publications including Republican documents and addresses, the Lincoln-Douglas debates, Lincoln's Cooper Institute speech, and other equally important printed materials—he decided that he contributed in a major way to the success of the campaign.[24]

From the moment of his nomination onward, the *Tribune* lavished praise upon Lincoln as "an able statesman who had

struggled from the impoverished surroundings of a log hut to
command the respect of a nation." He was painted as the true
political descendant of the Revolutionary fathers, as a man of
the people who would cherish and sustain the Union, as had
Andrew Jackson and Zachary Taylor before him. He alone would
draw the nation's stable, peace-loving farmers and laborers,
North and South, to the Republican banner, so that the "Sham
Democracy, which consisted of cabal and mercantile, commercial and plantation capitalists, plus a motley crowd of urban
ruffians," would be forever defeated.[25]

As the weeks and months of summer began to wear upon
politicians and journalists, as election day drew steadily nearer,
Greeley began to refer to two of Lincoln's rivals as "hypocrites."
John Bell was a "dilapidated Tennessee war horse, who had
been fighting other people's battles for years, and who was this
time backed by Democratic money for the purpose of becloud-
ing the nuclear theme of slavery restriction and frightening the
timid of the North with the ruse of disunion." Secondly, Douglas was conducting a "vague" campaign; for the Dred Scott decision had split his principle of popular sovereignty down the middle, and he was now trying in vain to stand upon the free-soil
half in the North and upon the slavery-extending remainder in
the South. In fact, Greeley so feared the little giant's popularity
in the Northwest—so doubted Lincoln's ability to carry even his
home state of Illinois—that his pen dripped venom when he
wrote of Douglas:

> It is a shame to our politics that any public man
> should in his public capacity so equivocate and deceive,
> so abandon the truth and so stick to falsehood, that,
> were it done in private life and done openly, he would
> be left without name and credit enough to buy a pint of
> rum on trust in a corner grocery.[26]

John C. Breckinridge, on the other hand, was a "manly fellow—just on the wrong side." He came out openly and admitted
that he wanted the Negro driven "across the free plains of the
West," meeting the issue of the hour squarely "so that it was a

pleasure to oppose him." Furthermore, the fundamental question before the electorate, as Breckinridge should know, was the ethics of slavery, which "should be extended if forced labor benefited the nation," but which, if it did not benefit the nation, "should be quarantined within the Slave States until it died" a normal death. The *Tribune* then placed the acceptance letter of Breckinridge and a pro-Union speech before its readers in order to prove that Douglas was engaging in the deliberate spreading of falsehoods when he warned that Breckinridge was a secessionist or a disunionist. The people must decide between Lincoln and Breckinridge. On the one hand marched honesty in government, peace with all foreigners, and an orderly development of the country's resources, with the ultimate extinction of chattel labor to be the result of his election; on the other, there slouched "corruption," "oligarchy," and costly wars to extend slavery.[27]

Hammering away in this fashion, trying to race Lincoln against Breckinridge alone—his weakest northern opponent—the editor of the *Tribune* carefully analyzed the political scene in the North, the East, and the Northwest at the end of July, 1860. In Vermont and Massachusetts, "all the factions opposed to the Republican party cannot, whether separately or combined, pull forty per cent of the whole vote." Maine, New Hampshire, Rhode Island, Connecticut, Ohio, Michigan, Wisconsin, Minnesota, and Iowa—these states were now "sure for Lincoln by a larger majority than they have ever yet given" to any candidate. Illinois, while close, "will give Lincoln from Five to Ten Thousand majority, in spite of the most desperate exertions of the Douglas men." But—Greeley warned the party faithful—"Indiana is the most evenly contested of any of the Free States." Furthermore, not sure at all of Indiana, the editor utterly despaired of California; indeed, the Breckinridgers claimed both California and Oregon. Even though he might be forced to yield these states to an opponent of Lincoln, he was much more hopeful, yet not absolutely confident, of Pennsylvania and New Jersey. This left New York still undecided; Greeley thought that the Empire

State would roll up a Lincoln majority, but he cautioned Republicans to be alert to any upsurge of Democratic strength there.[28]

In an over-all picture, Greeley felt that the choice for the people must be obvious, and he placed his faith in the future, asserting, "The signs of the times indicate that the Republican president will be inaugurated, as it were, by universal consent, amid an era of good feeling."[29]

In order to make Lincoln's election seem a thing to be universally desired, Greeley did not stress his economic program for the slaves "soon-to-be-free"; instead, he endeavored to disprove statements that the British West Indies had been swallowed up by economic starvation, writing that Jamaica had made great advancement since the slaves had been freed there. He sent a correspondent to British Guiana, whence the latter reported how freed Negroes had improved their economic status there. And a *Tribune* correspondent in Canada told how some freed slaves had recently arrived there, and how they were developing into peace-loving, law-abiding citizens. Thus, by indirection and by analogy, the Yankee farmers, merchants, and mechanics were instructed to vote for Lincoln, were assured that manumission would not "wreck the Slave States with servile insurrections." Greeley added that most southern people were honest, humble, hard-working individuals who needed the political support of their northern brothers; only a Republican victory would allow these oppressed and depressed masses to speak for themselves and to prove how close was the interrelation of their interests with those of the northern middle-class farmers and artisans. Fire-eating threats of secession? Merely belligerent language—words to be utterly disregarded and overlooked by the North. Only if one understands how many northern laborers and farmers looked to the *Tribune* for their light does one comprehend how telling an effect Greeley's words had upon the electorate.[30]

Thus, as the months passed, the forecasts of a Republican victory began to justify Greeley's prediction made immediately after Lincoln's nomination: "New England will stand like a rock;

the Northwest will be all ablaze," and Lincoln will carry the day. Yet, as the elections drew nearer, there still loomed uncertainties in California, Oregon, and New Jersey, as well as in the politically pivotal states of Indiana, Pennsylvania, and New York. Greeley had earlier listed California as one of the most doubtful states, probably hopeless, and the weeks of waiting bore out the truth of this categorical listing; few Californians were interested in antislavery, and the unifying Republican platform planks of tariff and homestead legislation appealed little to the Far West. The only reason for any Republican strength in California resulted from the feuds between the two Democratic senators over federal patronage and over the Lecompton Constitution, and from the California demands for a Pacific railroad, which Greeley had advocated and which he had written into the Chicago platform.[31]

Consequently, as the campaign progressed, Lincoln principally owed Greeley for the small measure of strength he possessed in California; and it appeared that Greeley, in his successful efforts to guide the platform committee down a road of progress, was justified. However, in his appraisal of the South, Greeley could not be justified. And it was, in part, this misinformation, which Greeley passed on to Lincoln, that caused the latter in future days to be extremely wary of Greeley's ideas. *Tribune* correspondents wrote to Greeley that the spirit of "no secession" seemed unanimous in the South, and that, were Lincoln elected, there would be no war. Furthermore, there seemed to be evidence of strong Republican elements in certain southern states; news came that the farmers of Texas had sent "three cheers for Abe" as a true conservative who would "let them keep their niggers" if they wished. Maryland would have a strong Republican vote, Greeley was told, and Republican clubs were being set up in Portsmouth, as well as in Wheeling, Virginia. A Louisville gentleman wrote to the editor that there would be no disruption of the Union; and from Memphis these reassuring words poured like balm into Greeley's ear: "Sentiments of disunion are uttered only by violent political aspirants, and are seriously entertained by no one possessed of an ordinary amount of common sense. Let not threats or predictions of disunion intimidate the friends of honest dealing and righteous government. . . ." [32]

In printing these statements to reassure the North, Greeley also included what he termed a "genuine" letter from Alabama, supposedly written by an overseer, which declared that the South was divided into two classes—the rich and the poor—with the non-slaveholders ready to overthrow the "hated slaveocracy" as soon as the Republicans were in power. Perhaps such statements reassured Northerners; perhaps Lincoln's small total of popular votes was swelled by people who voted Republican because Greeley printed these "authentic" letters. However, when news of them reached the South, that section searched in vain for the proper invective to employ against Greeley's columns of campaign propaganda. And when Lincoln at last realized how Greeley had misinterpreted southern public opinion, he was inclined to deprecate the assistance in the campaign and to doubt the editor's sanity or his sincerity. [33]

According to one who lived through this memorable campaign, who read Greeley's visions of Republican victory as they appeared from day to day in the *Tribune,* "the campaign was exceedingly animated, on the part of the Republicans, from the moment of Mr. Lincoln's nomination." Continuing in this contemporaneous view:

> As with General Harrison, there appeared to be something in his homely life and character to bring out the affections and enthusiasm of the people. The nominations at Baltimore but increased the excitement. . . . It was certainly the liveliest Presidential campaign in the history of our country, excepting only that of 1840. Companies of "Wide-Awakes" were formed by Republicans in every neighborhood, followed by "Hickory-shirt Boys" on the part of the Douglasites in many portions of the North. It was astonishing, too, how much

noise the "Bell-Everettites" made even in communities
where they were outvoted ten, twenty, fifty, or even a
hundred to one. All the orators and all the journals of
each party undoubtedly did their best. . . .[34]

Greeley did his best. Sometimes, however, he was misin-
formed; other times, he misunderstood political trends. A Savan-
nah correspondent wrote to the editor warning that, if Lincoln
should be elected, for the sake of the South, "he had better receive an overwhelming popular majority"; to be a "Constitutional President was not enough—he needed to be the people's
President." If he were not so elected, he quite possibly might
be unable to hold the Union intact. In some quarters—at least
in certain private statements—Greeley's anxiety was evident; and
although he expected Lincoln to win a majority of the electoral
votes, he feared that he would never receive a popular majority,
which fact would furnish the fiery disunionists with potent propaganda. Sectional charges continued to be heaped against the Republican Party; and, in the *Daily Tribune*—but only there—Greeley permitted himself to utter a public regret that Edward Bates
had not been nominated.

With Greeley thus nursing his regrets, the time approached
for the October elections. Once they were over, Lincoln was assured of success in the pivotal states of Indiana and Pennsylvania. He "will certainly be the next President," Greeley wrote,
as he turned again wistfully toward the South, pleading for
peace and for harmonious acceptance of the people's verdict. "It
is most desirable that the sensible, patriotic citizens—who are far
more numerous in the Slave States than they would seem to be—
if we judged the South by what appears in her newspapers—
should interpose at once to stop the ridiculous gasconade" of
disunion which "some who know better, with many who know
scarcely anything, mischievously persist in. . . ." [35]

Then, in a tone hovering between wrath and solicitation,
Greeley cried out to the South, where his words were muffled
beyond recognition:

To undertake to browbeat the North out of her convictions by threats of rebellion and revolution, is to renounce the whole machinery of popular elections, and to convert our country into another Mexico or New-Granada, where each election is expected to be followed by a civil war between those who carried it and those who were defeated.[36]

Greeley was writing in this half-belligerent mood when November 7 came and passed. On November 8, it was announced that Lincoln had been elected.[37] He and his running mate, Hannibal Hamlin, had received a popular vote of 1,866,352, while Stephen A. Douglas had received 1,375,157, with John Bell receiving 587,830, and John C. Breckinridge receiving 847,514 popular votes.[38] However, the arrangement of votes in the electoral college appeared in a far more astounding light, revealing the true source of Lincoln's strength and victory, proving, beyond all fabrications, even by Greeley, that the triumph of Lincoln was a sectional victory. For in this election, aided by Greeley, Lincoln had carried every free state except New Jersey, with even a portion of the electoral vote of that state accruing to him. Next in popular strength to Lincoln stood Douglas, followed by Breckinridge, with Bell trailing; in electoral votes, however, Douglas received only 12, Bell 39, and Breckinridge 72, while Lincoln captured 180.[39]

Thus, Lincoln's victory was a sectional one, but it was a victory, and a victory Greeley had craved. A victory he had helped to bring about, moreover. For, as his contemporary biographer indicates, the attacks upon him by Weed and Seward and Raymond, at the very inception of the campaign, "aroused his ambitions and energies to their best endeavor." Consequently, it is certain that the *Tribune,* in all of its editions, "was one of the most potent means in bringing about the desired result"—the election of Lincoln.[40]

Therefore, with Lincoln's November 7 election a fact, many remembered Greeley's prophecy of January 5, 1854, in regard to a new antislavery party which must of necessity take shape and form, then conquer the widely divided Democratic ranks: "[It will be] the most gigantic, determined and overwhelming party the world has ever known. . . . Overcome it may be, but beaten it cannot be." [41]

Less than seven years later, here was the prophesied victory for that new party, and the *Tribune* jubilantly assured its readers that "the result may be to the highest good of the country will be the prayer of every patriot, every philanthropist and every Christian." By supporting Lincoln, eighteen northern states, Greeley implied, had acquiesced in his arguments; and the Lincoln victory could be partially attributable to the *Tribune*'s persistent adherence to Republican principles and to the Republican candidate.[42]

Nevertheless, this victory, which Greeley had seen in his political vision, which he had helped to bring about, proved to be but a brief interlude of joy amid the bitter concern Greeley felt for the Union. On the day after the victory was signally announced, he wrote strangely, "We hope never to live in a Republic whereof one section is pinned to the residue by bayonets." In other words, Greeley was launching his policy of peaceable secession almost before Lincoln had accepted the verdict of the people; if the South wished to secede, it must do so as a whole section, with the majority of the people concurring in the step. It should not be brought about by the hasty actions of "political fire-eaters," but it could be accomplished by the masses, and, in such a case, the North should accept the decision, without a war, without coercion, without complaint.[43]

Lincoln, who had accepted Greeley's support during the campaign with open eagerness but with inward reservations, read of Greeley's position with horror but not with surprise. This editor, whose opinions were so widely read and so readily believed by so many people throughout the North, had twice visited Lincoln, in Springfield, during the campaign. His ambivalence, together with a tendency to think in "running circles," made him one "not overly gifted in his estimate of the South, as well as of the national crisis"; and Lincoln saw this on both occasions. Greeley had visited Lincoln for two reasons—to secure aid from the candidate in his campaign to become United States senator from New York, and to give Lincoln some "valuable advice." "Speak freely," the editor had urged; "show a strong hand, pull hard, and make this leviathan of the South aware of what the President can do if it will not come to terms." But Lincoln had disregarded Greeley's advice and had made him no political promises of support or aid. Both men came away from these meetings discouraged; the fact that Greeley had not really touched Lincoln may be seen from reports that "Lincoln offered him no apt bits of humor." Consequently, Greeley remained outside the inner circle, becoming, so he imagined, a free agent.

Hence, he gave advice frequently, quixotically, always proving himself, during the campaign and afterward, an erratic editor with an ample amount of eccentricity—eccentricity which made him deal in ideologies, not in facts, in idealisms, not in realisms. Therefore, he misunderstood the position of the South during the campaign, and the advice he gave to Lincoln proved fallacious. The President-elect rapidly realized this; yet he remained silent in the months prior to his inauguration, not exposing the errors of the editor whose support he needed, but waiting patiently for events, not editorials, to shape his future policy.[44]

CHAPTER FIVE

Two Pressing Problems

From the day of his election in November, 1860, to the day of his first inauguration in March, 1861, and even from that day until the attack had come upon Fort Sumter, two primary problems of paramount significance faced Abraham Lincoln—two problems in which Greeley's interest was tantamount to that of Lincoln, and in which Greeley sought to establish a definite and a lasting influence upon America's first Republican administration. These problems, in brief, were, first, the attitude which Lincoln must pursue toward the seceding states of the South, and, secondly, the construction of a capable, durable, geographically and politically satisfactory presidential Cabinet.

Shortly after Lincoln's election, with the President-elect living quietly in Springfield, Horace Greeley came to the city to impart his storehouse of wisdom to fill the needs of the candidate, who, the editor felt, owed to him in great part the successes at the polls a few days before. However, Greeley did not immediately seek out Lincoln; therefore, this time, the President-elect called upon the editor at his hotel, uninvited. The two men conversed for more than an hour without coming to a real understanding, and Lincoln took his leave, discouraged, not having told the influential editor a single anecdote, not having found in him either a friend or a communicable consort.[1]

As the days passed between this unfruitful meeting and the December 20 secession of South Carolina—which act added measurably to the crisis—Lincoln began to be burdened by callers, overwhelmed by mail, perplexed by questions of Cabinet appointments and of policy toward the South, and he grew daily more careworn. Yet, apart from Greeley, he continued to impress newspapermen with the quaint sagacity of his words and the amazing originality of his language. "Historic phrases are not ceremoniously set," wrote Henry Villard, "but pervaded with a humorousness and, at times, with a grotesque joviality, that will always please. . . . I think it would be hard to find one who tells better jokes, enjoys them better, or laughs oftener than Abraham Lincoln." [2]

Never in any public crisis, declared Greeley, as he departed from Springfield, had he seen such calmness, steadiness, and firmness as the masses now displayed. Was this statement true? Unfortunately for Lincoln and for Greeley, quite the contrary state of affairs prevailed, for almost every newspaper, diary, and bundle of letters of the time exhales bewilderment and anxiety. From the three million square miles of the country, from thirty million people, came an audible cry for rescue. Perhaps Greeley did not hear this cry, but Lincoln did, and he winced.[3]

Meanwhile, all through the stormy winter before Lincoln's inauguration, while he anticipated the future with dread, while Greeley traveled blandly forward without seeing the impending crisis, evidences of actual demoralization within Republican ranks grew rampant, becoming increasingly apparent to Republicans and Democrats, North and South, with equal results of fear and confusion. It seemed as if the party had become frightened at its own victory and at the consequences entailed by it. The municipal elections following the state and national elections exposed a great defection from Republican Party allegiance. Moreover, the leading party journalists appeared to be utterly at sea, with neither compass nor rudder. To those who read Greeley's editorials, it seemed that never, until the moment of victory, had he considered what must be the principle of his party—apart from his own personal opinion—in regard to the question of sovereignty. As this is the deepest question of any and every political system, and as the new party in power must take some position even prior to election, it seems strange that Greeley associated his own personal beliefs with the tenets of Lincoln and the party.

Many of the readers of the *Tribune*, scarcely aware of Greeley's ideas of political economy and social doctrine, glanced with horrified gaze at the first in a long series of editorials appearing in Greeley's paper on the subject of southern secession. On November 9, 1860, Greeley first put his doctrine into newspaper print, writing sincerely:

> We hold, with Jefferson, to the inalienable right of communities to alter or abolish forms of government that have become oppressive or injurious; and, if the cotton States shall decide that they can do better out of the Union than in it, we insist on letting them go in peace. The right to secede may be a revolutionary right, but it exists nevertheless; and we do not see how one party can have a right to do what another party has the right to prevent. We must ever resist the right of any State to remain in the Union and nullify or defy the laws thereof; to withdraw from the Union is quite another matter. And whenever a considerable section of our Union shall deliberately resolve to go out, we shall resist all coercive measures designed to keep her in. We hope never to live in a Republic whereof one section is pinned to the residue by bayonets.[4]

In expressing this view, Greeley did not voice the thoughts of Lincoln; instead, he set forth the doctrines of Jefferson Davis and Alexander H. Stephens.[5] In publishing this editorial and those which followed, Greeley, as the nation's leading Republican journalist, endorsed the position held by the fire-eaters of the South, and these southern leaders made the best possible use of Greeley's thoughtless statements.[6]

Although Greeley had the audacity to talk of "peaceable secession," although he wished Lincoln to follow his own policy toward the South, certain other Republican leaders felt that Lincoln should not acquiesce in the southern revolt, and that he should make no statement before his inauguration, leaving all of the administrative decisions in the hands of James Buchanan. Thinking in this vein, Preston King wrote to John Bigelow only five days after Lincoln's election:

> I think there is no danger of Lincoln making any declaration to anticipate the day of his inauguration, but I am glad that Mr. Bryant [William Cullen Bryant, of the New York *Evening Post,* a Republican newspaper] wrote [to Lincoln on this matter]—for we cannot be too secure on such a point.[7]

Because Greeley had already begun indulging in what Lincoln's biographers have termed "damaging vagaries" in regard to a policy of "peaceable secession," Bryant wrote to Lincoln, as the representative of a number of anti-Greeley eastern Republicans, urging that the President-elect make no public statement prior to his inauguration, urging that he refuse to endorse the "unusual" policy being advocated by the editor of the New York *Tribune.*[8]

However unusual Greeley's policy may have been, and no matter how horrified Lincoln may have appeared when he learned of it, the editor's pronouncement of November 9, 1860, was no editorial flash of false genius; it was the expression of a premeditated, if not a public, policy. For as early as nine years prior to 1860, in discussing South Carolina's perennial threats of withdrawal from the Union, Greeley had remarked, "If a State, by a decided, unquestionable majority of her People, should resolve to quit the Union, we should prefer to let her go rather than retain her by military force." The editor added that, "If any [state] did [go], she would be glad to walk in again before she has been out two years." [9]

Hence, Greeley's controversial position as it unfolded before his readers in the autumn, winter, and spring of 1860 and 1861 was changed in only one particular point. He felt it impracticable for a single state, by itself, to leave the Union, viewing such a step as unconstitutional. Although the position of such a state would be untenable, the action of any one state in seceding from the other states should in no wise be prevented by military force. At the same time, Greeley found the Union to be "irrevocable"; only the earthquake of sectional revolution could "shiver it." [10]

Thus, the *Tribune* of November 9, after weakly advocating the principle of peaceable secession, added laconically:

> But while we thus uphold the practical liberty, if not the abstract right, of Secession, we must insist that the step be taken, if it ever shall be, with the deliberation and gravity befitting so momentous an issue. Let ample time be given for reflection; *let the subject be fully canvassed before the People;* and let a popular vote be taken in every case, before Secession is decreed.[11]

Thus, if the people should vote to secede, Greeley would grant this "revolutionary right" to the "eight Cotton States" and, if they concurred, to their contiguous neighbors, in view of "Jefferson's Great Principle" that "governments 'derive their just powers from the consent of the governed: and that, whenever any form of government becomes destructive of these ends, it is the right of the People to alter or abolish it.' " [12]

Greeley sincerely believed—and he told Lincoln so—that "this Principle would either allow the Unionist masses in the South to overthrow their leaders or the Cotton States to depart in peace." The first alternative seemed much more likely to the editor, in view of the reports he had received from his faithful southern correspondents, who informed him daily "that the Unionists are in a vast majority" throughout the entire "Southern region." Therefore, Greeley would permit no compromise, would bow to no "Southern stand of firmness," would insist that war was impossible, that the South must depart in peace or the loyal masses must remove their aristocratic overlords. Lincoln disagreed, but said nothing.[13]

Thurlow Weed, however, could not keep silent; he disapproved of Greeley's position, writing to a friend some years later that, because of the *Tribune* editor's philosophy, secession became an accomplished fact, and, for this reason, he could never support nor even tolerate Greeley and his whims:

> For several months before the Rebellion, while that question was rife in the Southern States, Mr. Greeley was an avowed, earnest, and persistent Secessionist. As the editor of a leading and widely circulating Republican journal, he exerted an influence at once powerful and malign. Indeed, but for that influence it would have been difficult, if not impossible, to have withdrawn North Carolina, Tennessee, and Georgia from the Union. [In order to prove these statements, Weed quoted from the *Tribune* editorial of November 26, 1860:]
>
> ". . . If the Cotton States unitedly and earnestly wish to withdraw peacefully from the Union, we think they should and would be allowed to go. Any attempt to compel them by force to remain would be contrary to the principles enunciated in the immortal Declaration of Independence, contrary to the fundamental ideas on which human liberty is based. . . ." [14]

In addition to condemning Greeley himself, Weed did all that he could to discredit the editor in the eyes of the President-elect. He found his task not too difficult, for Lincoln already possessed grave doubts concerning Greeley's intellectual sense of proportions.

If there had been in all of the states of the North any newspaper which was thoroughly but not altogether radically committed to the antislavery cause prior to 1860, it was the New York *Tribune*. Republicans throughout the North had, in great measure, been socially and politically educated by the teachings of Horace Greeley, and had accustomed themselves to take a major portion of their knowledge and their opinions, in matters political, from the editor's pen. Hence, it was a misfortune for Lincoln—one which cannot be overrated—that from the moment of his election to the day of his death, the *Tribune* was principally engaged in criticizing his measures and in condemning his policy or lack of policy. No sooner did all that for which Greeley had been striving during more than a decade seem to be on the point of consummation than the virtually demoralized and totally panic-stricken reformer begin to fear for the safety of the Union. But not knowing how to save it, he became desirous of undoing his own achievements and using all of the influence which he had gained by virtue of his hitherto bold leadership for the purpose of effecting a sudden retrogression. From November 9, 1860, onward, Greeley began preaching peaceable secession; not nullification, but secession. Unwittingly, he was striving to shipwreck Lincoln's administration before it had been launched.[15]

However, Lincoln did not intend that anyone should shipwreck his administration before it sailed from port; therefore, until his inauguration, he left James Buchanan exclusively at the helm of the ship of state, waiting until his hour at the wheel had been officially announced. Consequently, Buchanan steered through the troubled straits with what skill he possessed, bearing Greeley's criticism and forecasting to Lincoln the type of opposition the *Tribune* might afford him.

Yet, despite Greeley, one must admit that, however blameworthy President Buchanan may have been, he was still the "victim of his period," as was Lincoln. While the Buchanan administration seemed to possess no settled belief or opinion, the *Tribune* harassed the incoming and the outgoing executives with its demure banner—"Let the erring sisters depart in peace." Furthermore, Greeley's position rapidly began to attract a host of followers, for many northern abolitionists were willing to send the South on its way in order to free the Union of slavery. Such men abandoned the silent Lincoln and flocked to the support of the noisy Greeley.[16]

Rejoicing at this new-found aid, Greeley continued his "peaceable" policy, disregarding the fact that Lincoln disapproved of it. And as the weeks passed, the South began to act. December

17, 1860, dawned across the united nation, and Monday passed placidly into history as a leading diarist of the time wrote pensively:

> The South Carolina convention has met and is to adjourn from Columbia to Charleston, being driven away by an epidemic . . . of small pox. [Francis Wilkinson] Pickens is elected governor of that insolent commonwealth. He seems committed to secession and treason now, but when he crossed the Atlantic a few months ago with Mr. and Mrs. Philip Allen, he said his object in coming home was to tell his fellow citizens that they were making themselves the laughingstock of Europe. This foul disunion disease is frightfully contagious, however (like other cachetic, asthenic distempers, jail fevers, and the like), and Pickens may have caught it. . . . Seward in town yesterday. Report of schism in Republican party of this state [New York]. A lot of extreme Free-soilers headed by Horace Greeley and including D. D. Field and Austin Stevens, Jr., pronounce against Seward and Thurlow Weed [on every issue], and mean to establish an Albany newspaper organ in opposition to Weed's.[17]

Despite the fact that this venture in founding a new anti-Weed newspaper proved unsuccessful, Greeley and his associates managed to create a maximum amount of difficulty for New York's Weed Republicans and for Lincoln with the new doctrine of peaceful secession for the South. Greeley continued his philosophy of permitting the South to withdraw in peace, even as the crisis grew more appalling to other leaders. And, on December 17, the very day that the South Carolina secession convention adjourned from Columbia to Charleston, the *Tribune* carried an editorial which declared that the South had as good a right to secede from the Union as the colonies had to secede from Great Britain. Furthermore, Greeley concluded that he "would not stand up for coercion, for subjugation," because he did not think it would be just.[18]

Greeley, moreover, had not changed his opinion two months later, for, on February 23, he wrote in an editorial, "If the Cotton States or the Gulf States choose to form an independent nation, they have a clear moral right to do so," and "if the great body of the Southern people" become alienated from the Union and wish "to escape from it, we will do our best to forward their views." [19] In truth, a volume could be filled with like writing of Greeley's during this period, and "every sentence of such purport was the casting of a new stone to create an almost impassable obstruction in the path along which the new President must soon endeavor to move." [20]

On December 20, 1860, South Carolina actually seceded. As the fateful step was taken, Greeley suppressed his surprise and continued his peaceful policy, hoping to see the state hurry back into the fold before Lincoln was inaugurated. Generally, among those who had voted the Republican ticket in November, the secession of South Carolina was received with feelings of dismay. Many recent adherents of the party came to a sharp realization that the antislavery movement had gone too far. They would have been willing to grant concessions, and would probably have done so if they had had leaders and the means of making their influence felt. The great body of Republicans, having just gone through a difficult campaign, were not disposed, however, to think kindly of proposals of compromise which were likely to deprive them of the fruits of victory. The most extreme group—the so-called radicals—welcomed the dissolution of the "unnatural Union" between themselves and the slaveholders, because they would no longer have to bear the reproach of being accessories to slavery. And Greeley's famous expression—"Let the erring sisters depart in peace"—exactly suiting their sentiments, became the watchword of the abolitionist radicals. Consequently, Greeley, who claimed to be a moderate, who had desired a conservative Republican candidate, found himself in the radical-abolitionist fold at last, among those who could use his propaganda.[21]

With the secession of South Carolina, Greeley became desperate. He wished to influence Lincoln to speak on behalf of peaceable secession, feeling confident that a reassuring statement from the President-elect would bring the "rebellious" states scurrying back to their proper legal relationship with the Union. He believed that if Lincoln announced that he had no intention of manumitting all of the slaves immediately the southern mind would be eased. In addition, striving to win Lincoln over to his point of view, the editor of the *Tribune* endeavored to clarify his own position both to Lincoln and for himself. Thus, he wrote a private letter to the President-elect, headed "Office of the *Tribune,* New York, December 22, 1860":

. . . Let me try to make my views a little more clear:

1. I do not believe that a State can secede at pleasure from the Union, any more than a stave may secede from a cask of which it is a component part.

2. I do believe that a people—a political community large and strong enough to maintain a National existence—have a right to form and modify their institutions in accordance with their own convictions of justice and policy. Hence if seven or eight contiguous States [not one small one] were to come to Washington saying, "We are tired of the Union—let us out!"—I should say, "There's the door—go!" And I think they would have a *right* to go, even though no one recognized it. If they should set to fighting and whip us, every one would say they had a right to govern themselves; and I do not see how their having a few more or less men, or a better or worse general plan than we, can make or mar their right of self-government.

3. If the seceding State or States go to fighting and defying the laws,—the Union being yet undissolved, save by their own say-so—I guess they will have to be made to behave themselves. I am sorry for this, for I would much sooner have them behave of their own accord; but if they won't, it must be fixed the other way.[22]

4. We shall never have peace nor equality in the

Union till the Free States shall say to the Slave, "If you want to go, go; we are willing." So long as they threaten secession and we deprecate it, they will always have us at a disadvantage.

5. The Cotton States *are going*. Nothing that we can offer will stop them. The Union-loving men are cowed and speechless; a Reign of Terror prevails from Cape Fear to the Rio Grande. Every suggestion of reason is drowned in a mad whirl of passion and faction. You will be President over no foot of the Cotton States not commanded by Federal arms. Even your life is not safe, and it is your simple duty to be very careful of exposing it. I doubt whether you ought to go to Washington via Wheeling and the B. and O. Railroad unless you go with a very strong force. And it is not yet certain that the Federal District will not be in the hands of a Pro-Slavery rebel array before the 4th of March.

6. I fear nothing, care for nothing, but another disgraceful backdown of the Free States. That is the only real danger. Let the Union slide—it may be reconstructed; let Presidents be assassinated—we can elect more; let the Republicans be defeated and crushed—we shall rise again; but another nasty compromise whereby everything is conceded and nothing secured will so thoroughly disgrace and humiliate us that we can never again raise our heads, and this country becomes a second edition of the Barbary States as they were sixty years ago. Take any form but that!

(So many people entertain a violent prejudice against my handwriting that I have had the above copied to save you trouble in deciffering [sic] it.)[23]

On the same day that Greeley penned this hysterical epistle to the speechless President-elect, without waiting for a reply or even for Lincoln to have an opportunity to read the missive addressed to him, the *Tribune* editor editorialized in the columns of his paper:

We are enabled to state in the most positive terms that
Mr. Lincoln is utterly opposed to any concession or compromise that shall yield one iota of the position occu-
pied by the Republican party on the subject of slavery
in the territories, and that he stands now, as he stood
in May last, when he accepted the nomination for the
Presidency, square upon the Chicago platform.[24]

In printing this unauthorized avowal of Lincoln's stand,
Greeley hoped that somehow he might appease both the South
and the North, alleviating fears and easing tensions. While he
was urging Lincoln to be firm and forceful, he himself refused
to follow a consistent policy toward any section. Thus, as the
weeks passed, the Senate Committee of Thirteen failed to agree,
and John J. Crittenden's insistent and pathetic efforts to bring
forward any form of North-South compromise failed, because
Lincoln was silent, pondering which position to take, and because
Greeley was eagerly beating his drums for the South. Although
Greeley later declared that Crittenden's proposals should have
been followed in order to avert a war, he now demanded that
Lincoln refuse any suggestions of compromise, telling himself
daily that there was no real danger of war, that the South Carolina action would soon prove to be a fiasco, and that Lincoln
would become President in an atmosphere of hopeful harmony
in which the dreadful days of December would be forgotten and
pushed aside in the sunshine of the hope of spring.[25]

In spite of Greeley's later lamentations that no compromise
had been effected, he eschewed the thought of weakness on Lincoln's part from the beginning, not attempting in any way to
co-ordinate his policy of peaceable secession with his unheeded
instructions to Lincoln. On December 26, not having received
a reply from the President-elect in regard to the missive of December 22, the *Tribune* director wrote to his old correspondent,
William H. Herndon, in frightened phrases:

The danger of compromise is nearly over; the peril of
disunion is just rising into view. The Secessionists are
now doing their utmost to coerce Governor Hicks of

Maryland into calling the Legislature [Democratic] which is to call a state convention. If they fail, I think the Legislature will be called irregularly—that is, will get together in something which will be made to pass for authority. If they can get Maryland into their clutches, *every Slave State but Delaware and perhaps Missouri will have seceded before the 4th of March, and Mr. Lincoln must fight for the possession of Washington City.* Of course, the plot may miscarry; but Yancey, Wise and Co. are pushing it with all their might, and the virtual dissolution of the Government gives them every facility. I tell you I think it today an even chance that Mr. Lincoln will not be inaugurated at Washington on the 4th of March . . .[26]

When Herndon disclosed the contents of this second hysterical letter to the President-elect, as he doubtless did, Lincoln, still reading Greeley's peaceable-secession editorials in the *Tribune,* evidently decided that the editor was either a deliberate prevaricator or an insane idiot, definitely not a political mind. That Greeley instructed Lincoln privately "to be firm," and then publicly urged the South to "quit the Union," seemed no more logical to the President-elect than it has appeared to posterity. Of course, certain Northerners of the "hopelessly abolitionized type" rejoiced that Greeley had concurred in their tenet—"Let the erring sisters depart in peace." If some of these men—Republicans—talked of the rights of the South to self-government and self-determination, it is candidly clear that their deeper motive was to rid the nation of responsibility for an "undesirable institution." Wendell Phillips was presented with the opportunity of renewing his old abolitionist slogan—"No Union with slaveholders." [27] In thus furnishing Phillips and his abolitionist associates with new ammunition for their fanatical cannons, Greeley actually aided the South and "pulled the rug from under" Lincoln. Greeley did not understand the true motives of that section which stretched from Virginia to Texas; therefore, he unwittingly gave encouragement to those whom he should have opposed. At the same time, he thwarted Lincoln's silent efforts, for the President-elect, like William H. Seward, was gradually retreating from a "house-divided," "irrepressible-conflict" policy to one of moderate conciliation so that, with or without slavery, the Union might be held intact.

Greeley did not understand the motives, did not fathom the position, of the South, because he adhered to a political theory, popular at the time of the American Civil War, that the whole secession movement at the outset was nothing more nor less than a "conspiracy." Greeley, in the North, in intonations equivalent to those of Edward A. Pollard in the South, declared that the secession movement represented absolutely no popular sentiment, that it was engineered by greedy politicians in the interest of a minority of rich planters determined to protect their wealth and to increase it. To prove this, Greeley publicly "exposed" the folly of the southern attitude, and published "authentic" letters from southern correspondents in the columns of his *Tribune*. Hence, Greeley told his readers, if there was to be a "Great Rebellion," it would merely be a plotting of vested interests to overthrow certain shackles placed upon them by the North and by the Union. Upholders of this economic interpretation, led by Greeley, even fixed the date and place of its beginning; then, further embarrassing Lincoln before he took office, Greeley and his adherents accused the South of guilt in conspiring to attack the North, thus initiating a civil war, when that "backward" section could have, and should have, withdrawn from the Union peaceably.[28]

Nevertheless, although Greeley called the southern action a "conspiracy," yet publicly approved it, he found certain antagonists in the North—men who sought to discredit his influence in the eyes of Lincoln—men who called the southern action outright "rebellion" and "treason." In reply to these accusations, the leaders of the South declared that such epithets did not deter them from the assertion of their independence. In vindication of the right of secession, the South appealed to the essential doctrine that "the right to govern rests on the consent of the governed." In addition, appealing to the acts and opinions of the

Founding Fathers, to the rights of independent action reserved
to the states and "reserved by the states," and to the report of
the Hartford Convention, which asserted the power of each state
to decide as to the remedy for the infraction of its rights, the
South repeated with elation and with alacrity the declarations of
Horace Greeley, the man who stood forth as the mouthpiece of
the Republican Party. Lincoln was quoted as saying that there
arose difficulty in regard to the question of force, "since ours
ought to be a fraternal Government," and the South implied
freely that Greeley and his *Tribune* spoke for Lincoln and for
the Republican Party. Thus, daily, Greeley placed the President-
elect in an increasingly untenable position, despite the fact that
Lincoln was hesitant to heed Greeley's advice.[29]

During the dull weeks of December and the jittery ones of
January, there developed among the people of the North a wide-
spread feeling that rampant abolitionism, supported by Greeley's
peaceful-secession slogans, must be on the verge of pushing the
nation over the brink of a precipice. In numerous localities citizens proceeded to make life uncomfortable for the antislavery
agitators; instances were frequently reported of violence, ranging from the harassing of individuals to the breaking up of meetings and even to more devastating actions.

Decidedly disappointing to the radical element was the conciliatory position taken by such newspapers as the Albany *Evening Journal* (Thurlow Weed's sheet), the New York *World,* the
New York *Times* (Henry J. Raymond's paper), and the New York
Herald (whose editor was Greeley's enemy and rival, James Gordon Bennett). The attitude of "outstanding patriots" indicates
the favor with which the North looked upon sincere efforts to
avert war. Edward Everett, Thurlow Weed, William H. Seward,
James S. Thayer, and President Buchanan—all evinced a desire
to co-operate in the interest of conciliation. Stephen A. Douglas
and John J. Crittenden went so far as to telegraph Union stal-
warts in the South of their belief and hope that the rights of
that section would be protected within the Union. Moreover, a
large element of the John C. Breckinridge and John Bell factions
seems to have been fearful of the prospect of armed strife and

desirous to avert war at all cost. Northern Democrats wished to
hold the states of the South in the Union and to avoid a bloody
conflict; and Greeley, who later deliberately declared that, had
the Crittenden proposal been submitted to a vote of the people,
it would have been adopted "by an overwhelming majority,"
now sought to avert war merely by dividing the Union, hoping
that, in a brief space of time, the "erring sisters," lacking oil for
their lamps, would return to the safety and sovereignty of the
Union.[30]

Meanwhile, Greeley found himself assailed violently in certain border-state quarters for his prophecies that Lincoln's election would quiet the nation's pulse and for his unimaginably
ignorant policy in regard to secession. An editorial in a Kentucky
newspaper summed up succinctly the feelings of many border-
state editors who regarded Greeley, with his foster-child, Lincoln,
as the primary reason for the disunionary actions of the southern states:

> "Touch it off," gently said Pat standing before the
> mouth of a cannon and supposing it was only primed.
> "Touch it off gently, and I'll catch the ball in this
> basket." It was touched off as gently as possible, but
> Pat and the basket were never seen again. Thus do
> many of the Republican leaders of the present day
> blunder along as they approach the terrible crisis of our
> country's destiny. They seem to think that they can
> manage the explosive forces of human passion and civil
> war, and pocket a neat profit upon the whole opera-
> tion. Notwithstanding the repeated declarations of Con-
> gressmen from Southern States, notwithstanding the
> emphatic declarations of a dozen Gubernatorial messages
> and the solemn acts and resolutions of a majority of
> Southern Legislatures, notwithstanding a thousand un-
> mistakable indications of deep, strong, and unchange-
> able feeling in the Southern States, a portion of the
> leaders of the Republican party have gone on steadily
> ignoring all these portentous signs of the times in a pol-

icy which they must have known, if they had capacity
to understand the plainest indications, would imperil
the Union. . . .

Just before the Presidential election we were gravely
assured by Mr. Greeley of the *Tribune* that the election
of Lincoln would have a wonderfully quieting effect
upon the country, that it would be *like oil poured upon
the waters,* and would promptly remove all sectional ex-
citement. Not believing Greeley altogether a fool, we
were compelled to suppose that he had reconciled his
conscience to the necessity of winning an election by
transparently false pretences. If he would now claim
credit for sincerity in that prediction, he would prove a
degree of ignorance or imbecility which would excuse
his present transcendent follies [his editorials on peaceable secession]. At the same time [the *Tribune*] . . .
and other leading Republican papers are gravely urging the coercion of all the seceded States by an embargo
or blockade, which, they maintain, would gently switch
them back into the Union without involving the calamities of war or inflicting any injury upon the North. Nay,
they are even calculating that all the commerce of the
country would be driven to Northern ports; that Southern cotton would be sent North by land, and that the
Northern cities would make a handsome speculation
by thus playing gracefully and daintily at the great
game of war. To such stuff as this we would reply emphatically—gentlemen, unless you are resolutely bent on
realizing all the horrors of war, you need not deceive
your readers any longer by such delusive assurances. If
you know no better yourselves, if you really believe that
your nice and comfortable calculations will be verified,
and, that the Southern States will succumb like mis-
chievous little children to a little flagellation, we are
amazed at your folly and can scarcely conceive how men
of . . . intelligence on other subjects could be so ut-

terly deluded in reference to this great question. . . .

We have done nothing to bring on this crisis, nor have we expected to make any political capital out of our country's misfortunes. We address you, Republican leaders, not as politicians, but in the name of humanity, in the name of patriotism, when we ask you to forget, as others have done, the paltry interests of party and give our country once more peace and prosperity. We need not repeat for the thousandth time our expression of the conviction that the Southern Secessionists have acted unadvisedly, rashly, flagrantly, acted in strange and manifest disregard of the great interests of their own section and in violation of all loyalty to the Constitution and the laws, but a little calm and dispassionate reflection would convince you that the sectional and aggressive language . . . of yourselves . . . could have no other tendency than to inflame and provoke the fiery spirits of the South to such a course as they have taken. . . .[31]

Greeley could have read such an editorial, sifted the truth from the exaggeration, and perhaps profited by it. However, it is doubtful that he did read such an editorial; furthermore, it is doubtful that, had he done so, he would have awakened to the incongruity of his own position. In 1860 and early 1861, his *Tribune* was the most influential force in the nation's Republican elements which favored the philosophy of peaceable secession for the South. Greeley's solution was a fraud from the start. He was prepared to let the "South depart in peace" only so long as there was danger of the Republicans abandoning their principles; moreover, from the very beginning, he placed so many unusual qualifications on the process as to render it absolutely meaningless. Furthermore, almost every other advocate of this peculiar course, most of them Greeley's disciples, soon became guilty of the same deception. The peaceful secession envisioned by Greeley, spokesman of the northern nationalists, hardly fitted the pattern of the states'-rights concept; it was not a matter to be initiated and consummated by a single state upon its own terms.[32]

According to Greeley's elaborate but illogical plan, the South, as a section, not state by state, would first have to satisfy the North that the southern desire for secession was unanimous. Secondly, the southern states would have to apply formally for permission to secede; the request could be submitted to Congress, which in turn could refer it directly to the people, or to a national convention, for approval. Until such consent had been granted, "the Government must maintain its authority even in South Carolina, and punish [those defying the government] if assailed." [33]

Finally, should separation ultimately be approved, a constitutional amendment should still be required to make it legal. Meanwhile, the southern states must wait quietly until the federal government and the people of the northern states had sufficient time for deliberation. Secession, therefore, would be slow and painless, respecting the federal government, protecting the interests of the nonseceding states. However, if one follows this plan to the letter, it must be admitted in the succeeding step that secession or separation as South Carolina and the other states attempted it was impossible, because it was attempted illegally through violence against the federal government and national laws.

At length, after much hesitation and many masterfully erratic maneuvers, the *Tribune* finally escaped through this wide opening—the escape for all peaceful secessionists of the northern states—that, because of the method pursued by the seceding commonwealths, their attempts were illegal, and the process was rendered an impossibility. Greeley at last soliloquized sorrowfully:

> That we no longer advocate acquiescence in the demands of the seceding States is because the nature and tone of these demands have altogether changed. Instead

of asking for a peaceable and legal separation, the seceding States . . . have resorted to violence . . . and now stand defiantly in the attitude of traitors and rebels.[34]

Peaceful secession was desirable, according to Greeley; but it must be on northern terms and in accordance with a strict and rigid formula. Since the southern states rejected both the terms and the formula, there could be no peaceable secession. Greeley's deception seems to have been chiefly motivated by his implacable hostility to any form of compromise. A few Republicans adopted his position in good faith, however, but added the nullifying qualifications as they slowly appreciated the serious complications which would result from disunion. And Greeley's *Tribune* ultimately confessed, "The right of secession has been almost universally denied at the North . . . and but a very small proportion of the Northern people have been willing to acknowledge that the bonds of our Union were utterly broken. . . ." [35] Thus secession occurred, in spite of denials in the North that it could occur.

In December of 1860, at the time Greeley wrote to Lincoln privately expounding his doctrine on the matter, but a few Garrisonian abolitionists and extreme pro-southern Democrats still adhered to the scheme of peaceful separation or secession. Furthermore, Greeley's powerful *Tribune* had had absolutely no influence upon Lincoln's policy. The editor's private letter to Lincoln, in which he admitted that "the Southerners would have to be made to behave themselves," was studied by the President-elect with interest, but he was by no means influenced by it. Thereafter, the *Tribune*'s columns contained a confused mixture of empty talk about qualified peaceful disunion and increasingly violent demands for the enforcement of the laws and the suppression of rebellion. By a devious route, like so many others, Greeley finally arrived in the camp of the proponents of force; then the President—his President—could not act swiftly enough to satisfy the bustling, hurrying, squeaking Greeley.[36]

Lincoln's patient policy in regard to the problem of south-

ern secession was not implemented by the inconsistent demands
of Horace Greeley, was not influenced either by the private correspondence or the public utterances of the *Tribune* editor. However, Lincoln was faced with another equally difficult problem—
that of constructing a durable, advisable, geographically and
politically satisfactory Cabinet—in which Greeley also possessed
a paramount interest, and in which he endeavored to mingle his
influence with the President-elect's objective judgments. After
Lincoln's election, a great many men were summoned to Springfield in order that he might learn their views more perfectly.
Among those who came, either by direct or by indirect invitation, were Edward Bates, Thurlow Weed, David Wilmot, A. K.
McClure, George W. Julian, E. D. Baker, William Sweeney, Carl
Schurz, and Horace Greeley. With many of them, Lincoln did
not hesitate to talk over his problems of forming a Cabinet;
Thurlow Weed declared that, when he visited the President-elect
in December, the latter introduced the subject of the Cabinet,
remarking that "he supposed I had had some experience in
Cabinet-making, and that he had a job on hand, and as he had
never learned that trade, he was disposed to avail himself of
the suggestions of friends. . . . The making of a Cabinet, now
that he had it to do, was by no means as easy as he had supposed; that he had, even before the result of the election was
known, assuming the probability of success, fixed upon two
leading members." However, he added that, "in looking about
for suitable men to fill the other departments, he had been much
embarrassed, partly from his want of acquaintance with prominent men of the day, and partly . . . because that, while the
population had greatly increased, really great men were scarcer
than they used to be." [37]

If Lincoln disclosed to Weed the names of the two men whom
he had already decided upon as members of his Cabinet, there
is no record of it. However, it is certain that one of them was
the leading Republican figure of the day, the man whom he
had defeated for the nomination against overwhelming odds,
Greeley's favorite enemy—William H. Seward. By the first of
January, it appeared that the problem of Seward had been set-

tled, at least temporarily—that Seward had accepted his appointment with eagerness and alacrity, feeling himself to be the best possible choice for Secretary of State, since he knew more about national, world, and Republican affairs than Lincoln or any other man in the party. Nevertheless, the problems of Simon Cameron and Salmon Portland Chase still remained unsettled.

Greeley, chagrined at not being informed of Seward's selection, angry because Seward was chosen at all, hoped that he might either find a place in the Cabinet himself or at least suggest some of the members to Lincoln. Early in January, a deputation started for Springfield, representing the influential wing of New York politicians who for years had been "daggers'-drawn" enemies of the powerful Weed-Seward machine. These men— George Opdyke, Hiram Barney, and others—came primarily to protest against Seward being placed in the Cabinet, but they were equally emphatic in denouncing Cameron and in advocating Chase. Greeley did not come with them; despite the fact that he wished to influence Lincoln's selections, he was reconciling himself to Seward's Cabinet appointment and beginning to entertain the hope that he might gain Seward's Senate seat if he did not openly antagonize Weed and his Auburn puppet. However, he secretly encouraged the Opdyke-Barney forces, and urged them to speak favorably for Chase and for Gideon Welles. Moreover, in an unofficial capacity, the two most powerful and influential New York City dailies, Greeley's *Tribune* and William Cullen Bryant's *Evening Post,* had joined hands in this sly campaign to keep Seward and Cameron out of the Cabinet, while pushing Chase and Welles into the administration. "Now I am even with Seward," Greeley had exclaimed after the defeat of his enemy at the Chicago convention, but his appetite for revenge had not been satiated.[38]

Therefore, the editor proffered his secret support to the Opdyke committee (known as "the Committee of Ten"), which traveled from New York to Springfield, by way of Columbus, Ohio. On January 10, 1861, the committee stopped at Columbus in order to discuss matters fully and freely with Governor Chase, and to hear, no doubt, all that had been said during Chase's

conference with Lincoln a few days before. Arrived in Springfield, the committee was cordially received by the President-elect,
but politely informed that no further appointments would be
made until he reached Washington. Lincoln indicated, however,
that, if the Pennsylvanians could be placated, he expected to
name Chase Secretary of the Treasury. Of course, the President-
elect was cold toward any efforts that were made against Seward or Cameron, for he envisioned the political expediency of
appointing these two men, one of whom had been bargained
out of the nomination, the other of whom had been defeated
in open warfare and in secret deals. Consequently, when Greeley
and Bryant heard the report of the committee, they joined Opdyke in writing letters to Lincoln, urging him to appoint Chase
at once. For they feared that, unless Chase was received into the
Cabinet soon, Weed, acting through Seward, would gain complete control of the administration.[39]

Lincoln refused, however, to be stampeded, standing by his
original statement that no further appointments would be made
until he arrived in Washington. Quite frustrated, Greeley began
a definite campaign to secure Seward's Senate seat; he even sent
an emissary to Lincoln to see whether the President-elect would
support him in his effort. When the informal ambassador returned from a visit with Lincoln, he took extraterritorial powers
with the words of the President-elect, much to the anger and
fear of Weed, who wrote hurriedly to Lincoln, on January 28:

> A member of our Legislature [Mr. Camp] who recently
> went to Springfield, comes back misusing your name
> abominably. He says that you desire the election of
> Greeley to the Senate, and that if chosen he will have
> the disposal of Offices. This is an absurd falsehood, we
> know, but it fools some who are sharp for Office and
> credulous. . . .[40]

Weed, fearful that this letter, urgent as it seemed to him,
might not receive Lincoln's personal attention in the immediate future, also wrote to Judge David Davis, whom he had met
and in whom he had confidence, since both men appreciated the

political prowess which each now knew the other to possess. The time before the senatorial election took place in the Albany legislative chambers was short. But Lincoln responded immediately to Weed:

DEAR SIR:

I have both your letter to myself and that to Judge Davis, in relation to a certain gentleman in your State claiming to dispense patronage in my name, and also to be authorized to use my name to advance the chances of Mr. Greeley for an election to the United States Senate.

It is very strange that such things should be said by anyone. The gentleman you mention did speak to me of Mr. Greeley in connection with the Senatorial election, and I replied in terms of kindness toward Mr. Greeley, which I really feel, but always with an expressed protest that my name must not be used in the Senatorial election, in favor of, or against, anyone. . . .[41]

Although no records indicate that Greeley authorized his emissary to use Lincoln's name in an official manner, without the consent of the President-elect, the entire affair caused Lincoln to be even more suspicious of Greeley's integrity than he had been during and before the campaign and the disagreement over a secession policy.

At this point, in connection with the Weed-Greeley senatorial controversy, which, unfortunately for Greeley, was brought out into the open, it is significant to emphasize that, in the beginning of 1861, the Republican Party found itself deeply divided into two factions. These factions searched for prominent personal leaders, finding them in William H. Seward and in Salmon P. Chase. In regard to the secession problem, Seward, in an attitude of retrenchment, now favored compromise, while Chase, ever a radical, favored coercive action; the moderates lined up behind Seward, while the abolitionist radicals began to seek guidance from Chase. And as Congress labored throughout February in efforts to avert civil war, Seward and Charles Francis

Adams still cherished the idea—the dream—of conciliation, while
Chase and his active cohort Charles Sumner steadily opposed all
forms of compromise. In this atmosphere, one of Chase's phrases
gained wide currency—"inauguration first, adjustment afterward"—by which he meant that unconditional submission by the
southern states must precede any concessions. On the other hand,
Seward, who believed it imperative to hold Virginia and the
border states in the Union and to build a groundwork of fraternal
feeling for ultimate reconstruction, regarded such an attitude as
calamitous. He had been intensely worried lest a a secessionist
victory in Virginia, which held elections for her convention on
February 4, might precipitate an attack by Governor Henry A.
Wise upon Washington, which attack would be but the first
step in what might prove to be a long and bloody war. Thus,
the victory of the Union men heartened him enormously, seem-
ing to indicate to him and to his followers that his policy might
well succeed. When mid-February came and then passed without disturbance, he was still more relieved. However, with every
passing week the antagonism between the Seward and the Chase
factions became more acidulous and more threatening to the
harmony of the new administration.[42]

Early in February, Greeley added to Lincoln's discomfiture
by opening all of the *Tribune* batteries upon Seward. He had reserved his fire for a time merely because a severe struggle was
raging at Albany for the Senate seat soon to be vacated by Seward. The Weed-Seward forces had united behind the brilliant
young lawyer William Maxwell Evarts, who had placed Seward's
name in nomination at Chicago; the opposition, rallying against
Weed with the cry, "Down with the dictator!" had unwisely divided its votes between Ira Harris and Horace Greeley. As has
been seen, Greeley did all in his power, even attempting to use
Lincoln's name, in order to secure the Senate seat. The outcome
left Greeley half-elated, half-frustrated. When Weed, sitting in the
executive chamber nervously smoking, learned that Greeley was
leading and that Evarts was about to be overwhelmed, he suddenly transferred his votes to Harris, thus robbing the editor of
the prize. Nothing was now too harsh for Greeley to say about

the humiliating surrender of Seward to the compromise spirit. "Mr. Seward Renounces the Republican Party," ran one of the *Tribune* headlines, as Greeley vented his wrath upon the back of the new Secretary of State, the product of Weed's New York politics, and from there upon the back of Lincoln, whom Greeley thenceforward associated with Seward and Weed.[43]

What Lincoln had remarked to a friend, as well as to the anti-Seward delegations who visited him at Springfield, about deferring Cabinet appointments as long as possible to avoid being teased into insanity to make changes was one of the early illustrations of his growing foresight. When he arrived in Washington, but one other department chief besides Seward had been positively chosen. This was Edward Bates, the future Attorney-General, Greeley's candidate for the presidency. Lincoln had almost decided to nominate Chase, the radical governor of Ohio, as Secretary of the Treasury, Caleb B. Smith of Indiana as Secretary of the Interior, Gideon Welles of Connecticut as Secretary of the Navy, Simon Cameron of Pennsylvania as Secretary of War, and Montgomery Blair of Maryland as Postmaster-General. However, the firm friends of these prospective appointees did not, in all cases, know of Lincoln's decisions and of his doubts. Nevertheless, the friends of all of the Cabinet aspirants sought Lincoln's ear both in Springfield and in Washington; and eventually, in every case, they became associated either with the moderate Seward faction or with the radical Chase faction. Consequently, the Seward men expected the new administration to be conducted along the lines of policy advocated by their idol. Chase's associates counted among their number most of Seward's enemies of 1860, as well as the radical Republicans, some of whom believed in recognizing secession as a fact, others of whom favored coercion. Furthermore, there was considerable personal antipathy between the two branches of the party, but the antagonism was essentially legitimate, because it grew out of two distinct theories as to future administrative and congressional action.[44]

Shortly after the election, William Cullen Bryant had urged Lincoln to make Chase Secretary of State. When Seward's selec-

tion had become known, Bryant again praised Chase's qualities
to the President-elect, speaking of the "need of his presence there
[in the Cabinet] as a counterpoise to the one who joins to com-
manding talents a flexible and indulgent temper of mind and
unsafe associations." [45]

In the same vein, the old hostility to Seward in New York
State had recently been made sharper, because, as has been seen,
Weed and Seward had defeated Greeley in his attempt to succeed Seward in the United States Senate. During the entire
month of February, leading up to the day of Lincoln's inauguration, the *Tribune* assailed the prospective Secretary of State
with unwonted virulence; the criticisms became so exasperating
to Weed that he declared Greeley to be willing "to dissolve the
Union, destroy the Government, and bankrupt and ruin the
people to keep Seward out of the Cabinet and secure [for him-
self] . . . the 'spoils of office.' " [46] In Springfield, before he left
for the East, and in Washington, before the day of his inauguration, Lincoln found Greeley daily attacking him, demanding
that Seward be forced out of the prospective Cabinet.

Thus, about the incoming President, whose primary task was
now completion of his Cabinet, swirled deep and murky currents of intrigue. To Seward, a perfect Cabinet would be one
which included Charles Francis Adams for New England, Simon
Cameron for Pennsylvania, and Henry Winter Davis for Maryland—and did *not* include Salmon P. Chase. Weed was in Washington, in New York, in Springfield, ably abetting the Secretary
of State, endeavoring to bring about the formation of Seward's
"perfect Cabinet." On the other hand, to leaders of the party's
radical wing, who avoided all contact with Weed and Seward,
an ideal Cabinet would be one which included Gideon Welles
for New England, someone like David Wilmot for Pennsylvania,
and Montgomery Blair for Maryland.[47] Furthermore, a Cabinet
would not be "ideal" with Seward in it, and there seemed no
indication that Lincoln would part with his first choice. Hence,
every motion which Lincoln made was watched by these rival
forces with hope, dread, and suspicion. Greeley, who was almost

frantic with animated anxiety over the whole situation, wailed
pathetically that Seward kept Lincoln perpetually surrounded,
that the compromisers would have full swing with Lincoln and
in the Cabinet. Finally, Greeley cried out in despair:

> Old Abe is honest as the sun, and means to be true and
> faithful; but he is in the web of very cunning spiders
> and cannot work out if he would. Mrs. Abe is a Ken-
> tuckian and enjoys flattery—I mean deference. And God
> is above us, and all things will be well in the end. Life
> is not very long, and we shall rest by and by.[48]

Thus Greeley, disappointed in his failure to acquire public office, lamented his prostrate state, and William Cullen Bryant,
Hiram Barney, George Opdyke, and the other New York anti-
Weed Republicans gained a new supporter in pressing Chase
for the Cabinet. Greeley was only too happy to hurl a political
bomb or two at Seward, whose presidential candidacy he had so
violently opposed at the Chicago convention; and, if Lincoln
happened to be jarred by the explosion as well, so much the
better. Moreover, Greeley was the mentor and staunch friend of
Schuyler Colfax, and Colfax's rival for a Cabinet seat, Caleb B.
Smith, was in communication with Judge David Davis, seeking
aid against Colfax.[49] The latter, meanwhile, had become the
anti-Weed Republicans' choice for the Indiana member of the
proposed Cabinet. Greeley now placed the immense power of
his *Tribune* behind the candidacy of Chase and Colfax. In the
meantime, Greeley's assistant editor, Charles A. Dana, used his
persuasive powers upon Chase, easily forcing the Ohio politician
into agreeing to accept a Cabinet post should it be tendered
him.[50]

Furthermore, while Greeley was eagerly striving to dictate to
Lincoln the names of his Cabinet members, the editor himself
was proposed for a Cabinet post by at least one person. On December 15, 1860, Mrs. Rhoda E. White wrote privately to Lincoln, suggesting that Greeley be given the office of Postmaster-
General, in this roundabout manner:

Permit me to command a few moments of your valuable time, in order to express the sentiments and wishes of a *large Class* here and elsewhere.

Before going further allow me to introduce myself—I am twenty-six years a resident of New York and during that time have formed a large acquaintance with our good citizens of my own sphere in society, and am well known to the Irish and German Catholic portion of the Lower or rather middleclass, and with these latter I have almost unbounded influence in consequence of having been at the head and the Directress of almost every public undertaking gotten up by them, which, through the blessings of God, has on all occasions been successful—It would seem egotistical to mention this but for the necessity in order to show you dear Sir, the means I have of understanding the feeling of *the people* here on public matters—Therefore you will pardon me for speaking of myself—I must not allow you to imagine me a *Large Virago-looking* woman politician, who belongs to a class (*I detest*) "woman's rights" . . . I was forced to mention these facts to remove an impression from your mind that you might be in communication with a *"strong minded* woman"! . . . My husband, James W. White (one of the Judges of the Superior Court of our City) and myself are warm personal friends of Horace Greely [*sic*], and to us, as well as yourself, dear Sir, his unwearied and faithful labors during this last campaigne is a subject of greatful appreciation. His friends here and elsewhere are looking for a place for him in the Cabinet, and it will cause *great disappointment* should he not receive a favor worthy of his acceptance. He is a man who will *never* approach or present the slightest claim himself, his sensitive, high minded pride will prevent him from doing so, but I do not know a man who better understands what should be recognised by the Higher powers as due to him.

You must pardon the suggestion of a doubt, that you

will forget one from whom you have received such aid, but having heard it on all Sides rumored "that Horace Greely would of course be offered the office of Post Master General" I concluded to write privately on the subject to you. Mr. Greely has not the remotest idea that I would do so, but I am sure he would object to it, feeling that no suggestion should be necessary.

. . . This City is largely Democratic in consequence of the prevailing prejudice among the ignorant class of Irish and German, that the Republican party are opposed to giving patronage to foreigners—Now if this could be removed by judicious appointments in our City thousands can be won over to the Republican party. No one in New York understands this better than Mr. Greely and no one would be better calculated to direct or counsel with on the subject than he. . . .[51]

Mrs. White's appeal to Lincoln was not the only such plea which the President-elect heard in the months prior to his inauguration. Among others, John W. Forney asked Lincoln to make Greeley Postmaster-General, describing his request and the polite refusal it received in these words:

When I was defeated for Clerk of the House in March, 1861, Mr. Lincoln called upon a number of Senators and asked them to vote for me for Secretary of that body. . . .

[During this period] I recommended Horace Greeley for Postmaster-General, because dear old Horace four years before, without knowing that I had fallen from grace under Mr. Buchanan, recommended me for that office. But as Lincoln had selected Seward for Secretary of State from New York, he could not, of course, appoint Greeley from the same State, and so he replied, and that proposition fell.[52]

However, Lincoln ignored or politely refused to acquiesce in these requests, for he doubted Greeley's ability, if he did not already doubt his sincerity and his truthfulness. Nor did Greeley receive any other political plum from Lincoln's ample Republican pudding. Politically and financially, the collectors of the customs posts were among the most important at the disposal of the administration. Particularly was this true of the collectorships of the more significant American seaports. And that at the metropolis of the Empire State was the most lucrative. "There is no situation in the United States which enables the incumbent to exert such influence (and at the same time do his duty) as the Collectorship of New York," one political observer correctly wrote. To another, this position was second only "in influence to that of Postmaster-General." Furthermore, under the caption "Fat Offices of New York," Greeley's *Tribune* informed its readers, in 1860, that ranking first in importance and in revenue was this collectorship, with its fixed salary of $6,340, and some $20,000 in the form of "pickings and fees." Before Lincoln's first administration had run its course of four years, the Surveyor of the Port estimated the number of employees in the New York customs house at 1,200, and the assessment on their salaries for political party purposes at 2 per cent. Over the award of this rich New York collectorship, a bitter fight was waged between the Seward-Weed wing and the Bryant-Barney-Greeley forces in the New York Republican organization. The wrangling grew even bitterer as the month of February progressed, with Chase supporting the Bryant-Barney forces, and with Greeley's *Tribune* openly aiding and abetting the anti-Weed faction.[53]

Actually, the two New York factions had crossed swords in early January, when in party caucus DeWitt C. Littlejohn, candidate of the Seward-Weed interests, had defeated Lucius Robinson for the party's nomination for the speakership of the State Assembly. "His [Weed's] friends," declared an Albany observer, "have made the rural members [of the Assembly] believe that Thurlow is to be the person that will deal out the soup for New York, and every person who is expecting to share in the good things of Lincoln's administration from the Empire State must apply through him and at his favor." "Upon this point and this alone, was Mr. Littlejohn nominated and Mr. Robinson defeated." [54]

Soon after this incident, the anti-Seward-Weed faction complained to Lincoln that Weed was giving the impression that he was to be the chief distributor of federal jobs for New York. This brought forth a mild rebuke from the President-elect:

> . . . As to the matter of dispensing patronage, it perhaps will surprise you to learn that I have information that you claim to have my authority to arrange that matter in New York. I do not believe that you have so claimed; but still so some men say. On that subject you know all I have said to you is "Justice to all," and I have said nothing more particular to anyone. [55]

It was at this time that Horace Greeley returned to Springfield, hoping that he might talk with Lincoln again about the problems of the secession movement and about the Cabinet appointments and the distribution of patronage. On February 5, 1861, Greeley arrived in Springfield, to deliver a lecture there that evening. He registered at a hotel, and Lincoln called on him in the afternoon. The two men talked this time for hours, and, according to a story published the following day in Greeley's *Tribune*, he did most of the talking. This dispatch appeared in the *Tribune* on the morning of February 6:

> Horace Greeley returned from the West this morning. This afternoon he was called upon at his hotel by Mr. Lincoln. The interview lasted several hours. Greeley urged a strict adherence to an anti-compromise policy, and is said to have received gratifying assurances. His opinion as to the Cabinet and other appointments was freely solicited and given. He is known to be strongly opposed to Cameron, and very much interested in the appointment of Chase and Colfax. Colonel Fremont, he thinks, should have the mission to France. Although just defeated in Albany, he did not ask anything either for himself or friends. [56]

This rambling dispatch was, in all probability, written by Greeley himself; it sounds exactly like him. The denial that he was seeking any political favor was Greeley's theme song. It is unfortunate that no more elaborate record of this meeting exists; however, it is clear that Lincoln refused to yield in any measurable fashion to Greeley's influence.[57]

Declaring that, at this time and in future days, during the Civil War, he spent many hours with Lincoln, Greeley has remarked sadly that he never heard the President tell an anecdote except on one occasion. This was the occasion. On his way to Washington to be inaugurated, Lincoln stopped in New York, where the people asked him, "Are we really to have civil war?" Lincoln, looking at Greeley in the audience, responded by telling a tale of his circuit-riding days. He and his companions had crossed numerous swollen rivers, but the Fox River still lay ahead of them.

And they said one to another, "If these streams give us so much trouble, how shall we get over Fox River?"

When darkness fell, they stopped for the night at a log tavern where they fell in with the Methodist presiding elder of the district who rode through the country through all weather and knew all about Fox River. They gathered about him and asked him about the present state of the river.

"Oh, yes," replied the circuit rider, "I know all about the Fox River. I have crossed it often, and understand it well; but I have one fixed rule with regard to Fox River: I have never crossed it till I reach it." [58]

Despite the fact that Greeley was disappointed that this was the one anecdote he ever heard Lincoln tell, and in spite of the fact that this one was not addressed exclusively to him, the editor could have profited from the sagacity of the President-elect. Always bemoaning the fact, during these pre-inauguration months, that his influence did not reach into Lincoln's mind and heart, Greeley might have learned the reasons for his failures had he paid careful attention to Lincoln's narrative. For the editor invariably endeavored to cross the Fox before he or any other man had reached it. Lincoln, disapproving any policy of anticipation, learning by experiences of past and present, not by forecasts of a probable future, disregarded Greeley's advice as words without weight.

Thus disheartened, as February ended, Greeley watched Lincoln depart from Springfield, speaking at every stop on the route to Washington. From the moment the coercion remarks of the President-elect, made at Indianapolis, reached the country, he had received telegraphic congratulations and remonstrances at almost every stop of the train. When his remarks at Columbus produced a similar result, Lincoln thenceforward made his speeches even more general, with almost less substance than Greeley could bear. At Cleveland, Buffalo, Albany, and New York City, there was nothing in what he said that his enemies could condemn—nothing that his admirers could praise. Furthermore, his journey from Pittsburgh eastward was no different from the western leg of his trip. The same crowds at every station, the same booming of cannon, gifts of flowers, hotel receptions, breakfasts, dinners, luncheons with local magnates—these were his greeting. All during the journey, the people mobbed the train at every halting point; flags, banners, mottoes, decorated every available space. As the locomotive proceeded eastward, the party inside the train continued to change in complexion as it had done throughout the western states, committees and "leading citizens" replacing each other in rapid succession. None of these accessions aroused more interest among the other members of the party than did Horace Greeley, who, still hoping to impress Lincoln before the latter fell into the clutches of Seward at Washington, arrived unexpectedly at Girard, Ohio, bag and blankets in hand. After riding with Lincoln for twenty miles, Greeley departed as auspiciously as he had arrived; and, although everyone wondered what he had discussed with the incoming executive, nobody knew and nobody was told.[59]

Certain it is that Greeley discussed the problem of the New York Republicans. Lincoln doubtless informed him that he wished the two factions to pursue a policy of "give and take," that he wished to show favors to neither side. Greeley replied, angrily, "But the thieves [the Weed men] hunt in gangs, and each helps all the rest. Three quarters of the post-offices will go into the hands of the corruptionists." [60]

Others, more fair-minded than Greeley, less anxious to dictate the plans and policies of the new administration, told the editor that Lincoln was being equally generous to both sides. Charles A. Dana believed this to be true, but Greeley doubted it; hence, he spent some of his valuable time on Lincoln's train struggling to convince the latter that Greeley's faction should be granted a larger share of the patronage.

One important reason for Greeley's en-route visit with Lincoln was the fact that the Greeley-Bryant-Barney-Chase New York faction was pressing George Opdyke, defeated Republican candidate for mayor of New York, for the important post of Collector for the Port of that city. On the other hand, the Weed-Seward group backed the important merchant, Simeon Draper, hoping that, by securing the position for him, they might ease some of the mercantile demands that the city secede with the South. Knowing, therefore, that Draper might be unacceptable to Lincoln and some of his advisers, Weed indirectly informed the President-elect that he would accept Richard M. Blatchford, a powerful New York banker, but would not acquiesce in the nomination of "that upstart" Opdyke. Lincoln refused all three suggested nominees. And, much to the chagrin and embarrassment of Weed and Seward, the incoming chief executive bestowed the New York collectorship upon Hiram Barney, one of the principal anti-Weed leaders and bosom friend of Salmon P. Chase. In fact, the hand of the soon-to-be Secretary of the Treasury was clearly seen by Weed in this selection, while Greeley considered the appointment a signal victory for his forces.[61]

Lincoln's Cabinet appointments and prospective appointments, his cautious speeches on his journey to Washington, his refusal to lay down a policy in these or in any other speech or public statements, his surreptitious entrance into the capital on February 23, 1861, in order to escape a rumored assassination plot (an idea of which Lincoln himself did not approve), these steps convinced the radicals, the followers of Chase, that the President lacked the resolution and courage to crush the secession movement. By this time, they believed that he had placed himself completely under the influence of Seward and the compromisers. Even such a moderate as Samuel Bowles of the Springfield *Republican* thought Lincoln to be a "simple Susan," speaking scornfully of Seward's "Illinois attachment." In an attempt to frustrate this Seward power in the Cabinet, the American Jacobins concentrated their forces even more firmly behind Chase's candidacy for the Treasury post, seeing in Barney's appointment to the New York collectorship a forecast of success.[62]

However, Greeley, who had returned to New York after discussing this problem with Lincoln as the latter traveled through Ohio, after hearing the famous Fox River anecdote, now heard rumors that the Weed-Seward forces were causing Lincoln to waver from what Greeley considered to be the former's promise to appoint Chase to the Treasury post. Consequently, the editor temporarily abandoned his *Tribune* and hastened to the national capital to direct the pro-Chase campaign. After days of intrigue and backstairs politics, Greeley wrote gloomily, exhaustedly, "I think we have fought through the nomination of Chase for the Treasury, but I am not sure he will go in with much company." [63]

Chase received the post, but he had little radical company. Greeley found scant reasons for rejoicing. Everywhere it seemed apparent that Lincoln stood close to Seward, listening only to his advice. A leading New Yorker of the day wrote in his diary: "It appears that Abraham Lincoln sympathizes with Seward and the Republican Right, and not with Greeley and Sumner and the Extreme Left. Glad of it." [64]

On the day after the diarist George Templeton Strong wrote this opinion, Chase, realizing that he would receive the Treasury post but that Seward would hold the upper hand, concurred in the statement that Lincoln was following the moderately conservative rather than the radically Jacobin view.

Fully appreciating that, in the matter of New York patronage, the Weed-Seward faction and not the Greeley-Chase forces controlled the dispensation of awards, the Secretary of the Treasury, under date of March 27, 1861, wrote to Seward reluctantly, even with dread, informing him that the appraisership at New York was vacant, and inquiring, "Which of the applicants do you prefer?" [65] Two weeks earlier, Chase had indicated to John Bigelow that New York appointments were only "very partially" under his control, and even less under the control of Greeley. Chase wrote sadly that "the President desires that all the Republican interests be consulted and in doing so it is necessary to make . . . concessions." [66]

This rivalry between the two New York factions—a rivalry which characterized even the minor appointments—once provided Lincoln with an opportunity to indulge in a bit of humor at Greeley's expense. On one occasion, he wrote to Chase:

> Ought Mr. Young to be removed, and if yes, ought Mr. Adams to be appointed? Mr. Adams is magnificently recommended; but the great point in his favor is that Thurlow Weed and Horace Greeley join in recommending him. I suppose the like never happened before, and never will again; so it is now or never. What say you? [67]

Lincoln intended, come what would, to be master in his own house. He meant to rule by a balance of factions and forces, in which he would hold the pivotal authority. From the outset, he had been determined, if possible, to have both Seward and Chase in his Cabinet, although he knew that he would be forced to maneuver factors in a certain way in order to accomplish it. For while he wished to keep both men in important positions, he wanted to surrender direction to neither individual. He had no intention of yielding on the one side to Seward's objections against a "compound Cabinet," nor on the other side to the last-minute battle of Chase, Greeley, and other radicals to close the door against Seward's ally in a policy of moderation, Simon Cameron. Lincoln listened for a week after he arrived in Washington to the voices of the contending factions, and then found his original judgment as to the need for a balanced combination of talents unshaken. He refused Seward permission to carry out the alleged agreements of a conference held the previous summer with David Davis; he did not permit the Chase-Sumner-Greeley group to be equally proscriptive on the other side. In the end, he decided to appoint Cameron to the War Secretaryship—a position which gave deep offense to the "iron-back" radicals. But he also appointed Gideon Welles to the Navy Department and Montgomery Blair to the Post Office Department —which brought protests of anger from Seward and his backers. By March 2, the heat generated by the two factions had almost reached the point of explosion; Seward refused to remain in the Cabinet were Chase to serve with him, and Chase refused to join the Cabinet unless Lincoln removed Seward. The President-elect remained adamant. If he must part with one man, he would part with both men. And at last both men agreed to remain. Greeley sighed. His efforts to thwart Seward's power had failed.[68]

March 4 came. On the morning of Lincoln's inauguration, the *Tribune* asked "for our new ruler the generous confidence and support of the American people. With a hearty good-will we bid Lincoln God speed." Nor did Greeley extend his greetings only in print. At noon that day, among the thousands gathered to hear Lincoln's first inaugural address, there was not a more hopeful or a more fearful listener than Horace Greeley. The editor sat near Stephen A. Douglas, very close to the President, and as Lincoln faced the crowd, beginning his address in the customary manner that the people had come to know, everyone seemed to have but one thought anxiously in mind, according to Greeley. Would he "get through unharmed"? Was an assailant lurking in that immense throng, "awaiting only an opportunity to make a target of that tall form, towering above all those around him"? "I shared that feeling," declared the editor. "As he delivered his address I expected it would be arrested at any moment by the crack of a rifleshot aimed at his heart. . . . But it pleased God to postpone the deed."[69]

Therefore, the speech was finished. Of it, the *Tribune* urged that "it should command the support of all good citizens. . . .

To twenty million people it will carry the tidings, glad or not as the case may be, that the Federal Government is still in existence, with a Man at the head of it." [70]

Because Lincoln's first inaugural address contained no direct reference to compromise proposals, the *Tribune* praised it as guaranteeing "the Constitution, the Union, and state sovereignty." Greeley believed that perhaps the firm, courageous, conciliatory inaugural would elicit from the southern seceded states a Unionist response. When it did not, he warned the fire-eaters and the President, his faith in peaceable secession still scarcely shaken.[71]

Yet, deep in his mind and heart, Greeley was secretly disappointed in Lincoln's mildness, for the editor was gradually, almost unconsciously, aligning himself with the Jacobin radicals. Consequently, before leaving Washington, Greeley sought out Lincoln at the White House, and there made the first of many vain efforts to influence the man who was now actually President. Unhappily, the "drumbeat of the nation" in 1854, the triumphant strategist of the 1860 convention, failed to realize that the people had since chosen a man to lead them in the effort to save the Union, and that that man had his own ideas. During this conference with the President, an astonished Greeley found him to be possessed with "an obstinate calmness of manner" which was unalterable. "Do you realize," the editor asked him, "that you may have to fight for the place you now hold?" The President seemed undisturbed by this question, and Greeley thought him deluded, thinking that forbearance, patience, and soft words would yet obviate "all necessity for deadly strife." He did not reproach Greeley for his doctrine of peaceable secession nor did he acquiesce in any of Greeley's demands for Cabinet appointments or for actions to warn the southern states against violence. Instead, he listened calmly, and was unmoved.[72]

CHAPTER SIX

The Road to Richmond

As the months of spring, 1861, advanced toward summer, almost
imperceptibly a new sentiment began to take shape which in-
validated the predictions of the South that the Democrats of the
North and the West would checkmate any Republican policy
of coercion. An undefined impatience with unproductive discussions and chimerical panaceas suddenly appeared. While politicians had been occupying the center of the now-divided national stage, while federal administrations had been changing,
a development in the popular psychology—one of deep significance—had been taking place. The mass of people, at first
fearful at the thought of war, had been growing constantly more
exasperated at the failure of their leaders to enter upon a course
of action. Humiliation at the apparent impotence of the North,
as one after another of the southern states withdrew from the
Union, begot a rising anger and demands for some solution that
would speedily bring to an end the harrowing uncertainty—
some policy that would bridge the impassable gulf between peace
and war. In such a frying pan, the idea of leaping into the fire
began to have its appeal. A young man who would soon don
the uniform of a soldier expressed a sentiment which thousands

had come to share: ". . . I have grown impatient to see the power of the Government and the loyalty of the people put to the test. . . ." [1]

One factor behind this growing impatience for action—an impatience the ever-dynamic Horace Greeley was himself beginning to feel—was the nineteenth-century factor of nationalism. Nationality stood forth in print and on the tongue as a common word in 1861. Hence, Greeley could write with exalted fervor of "the majestic development of nationality" occasioned by the firing on Fort Sumter. Nevertheless, the shoutings and enthusiasm which he translated into nationalism may also be understood as the expressions of sectional or state pride and patriotism, overt manifestations of class interest.[2]

Greeley was a patriot. He loved the nation that had begotten him as he loved its problems and its politics. From March 4 to April 17, he secretly hoped that Lincoln would do something drastic and decided to bring the South "to its senses"; he told Lincoln so when he called on him in the presidential mansion after the latter had delivered his inaugural address.

Although confused in his own mind and heart about what should be done in the South, Greeley preached to Lincoln that secession could be met "in one of four ways": (1) by substantial acquiescence in the movement and in its proposed results; (2) by proffering such new concessions and guarantees to slavery as should induce the "conspirators" to desist from their purpose and return "to loyalty and the Union"; (3) by treating the act of secession as "Rebellion and Treason," and putting it down, if necessary, "by the strong arm"; and (4), finally, by "so acting and speaking as to induce a cause and movement and permit an appeal to Philip sober," trusting that the seceded section might be transformed "from a South inflamed by passionate appeals and frenzied accusations" to a "South which would be enlightened, calmed, and undeceived, by a few months of friendly, familiar discussion and earnest expostulation." [3]

As time passed, Greeley advocated each of these four measures. And he tried, without success, to bring Lincoln into agreement with his point of view—on peaceable secession, on conciliation, on lengthy bilateral discussions, and then on war to "end the Rebellion." As March waned, Greeley declared that President Lincoln should have invited the people "to assemble at any early date in their designated wards and townships, because the South was assailing the nation." At these meetings, "the people should swear to support the Government and the Union, and to enroll themselves for volunteers" for the army, if war came.[4]

As early as four days after the inauguration, the *Tribune* editor had been forced to admit belatedly that the only two serviceable choices which the nation possessed were compromise and preparation for war. And, when one must choose between compromise and some other alternative, it appeared to Greeley that the other alternative was always preferable. Therefore, he at last publicly began to advocate that which he had secretly and almost unconsciously advised since the day of Lincoln's election. From late March onward, Lincoln could not and, according to the editor, would not move fast enough to "end the Rebellion" honorably. Delay "would only give credence to that absurdity" held by the South—that the "free states were ready to submit" peacefully to the withdrawal of their neighbors from the Union.[5]

By the first of April, Greeley's policy of peaceable secession had been merged with Charles A. Dana's policy of belligerent action.[6] Nevertheless, Greeley endeavored to maintain faith in his convictions, forcing his convictions to modify themselves when expediency demanded it, but never admitting to compromise. Hence, when Greeley began to see that peaceful efforts to mend the national schism were proving ineffective, he wrote that everything possible had been done to avert a war; and if the secessionist fire-eaters precipitated armed conflict, he would battle in self-defense: "Within a few days at farthest the cannon of the insurgents will be battering down the defenses and slaughtering the defenders of the American Union." "Slavery makes open war upon that Union," he cried in early April, "upon that Union which has so long been its protection and its security." [7]

A spell seemed to have been cast over the federal government,

especially over Lincoln, Greeley now complained. Paralysis had
deadened the faculties of the President and of his government.
"Let the spell be broken," the *Tribune* thundered. Make "some
kind of decision"! Take some action! Human nerves could no
longer bear such a situation in which no policy was determined
and nothing was done. "Let this intolerable suspense and uncertainty cease!" continued the former pacifist, Greeley. "If we
are to fight, so be it." [8]

However, Greeley still doubted that war would come. His "so
be it" seemed very unlikely in early April. But with the coming
of the middle of the month, with the firing upon Fort Sumter,
many of the editor's dreams were shattered. Many of his pacific
hopes crumbled to the ground, bombarded by shells of war. In
his erratic manner, the editor of the *Tribune* made this unexpectedly colorless comment on the earth-shaking incident:

> The fleet from New York, laden with provisions for the
> garrison, had appeared off the bar by noon of the day
> on which fire was opened but made no effort to fulfill
> its errand. To have attempted to supply the fort would
> have, at best, involved a heavy cost of life, probably to
> no purpose. Its commander communicated by signals
> with Major [Robert] Anderson, but remained out of
> range of the enemy's fire till after the surrender, when
> he returned as he had come.[9]

In spite of the colorlessness of Greeley's official statement in
regard to the Sumter crisis, his heart leaped for fear as he hoped
that sudden, quick action would end the problem of secession
and bring the "wayward sisters" home. Many public minds
blamed Greeley for the crisis; others saw in it the hand of Lincoln or the work of Seward. On April 15, a leading citizen of
New York with hopeful heart wrote in his diary:

> Events multiply. The President is out with a proclama-
> tion calling for 75,000 volunteers and an extra session
> of Congress July 4. It is said 200,000 more will be called
> within a few days. Every man of them will be wanted

before this game is lost and won. Change in public feeling marked, and a thing to thank God for. We begin to look like a United North. Willy Duncan (!) says it may be necessary to hang Lincoln and Seward and Greeley hereafter, but our present duty is to sustain Government and Law, and give the South a lesson.[10]

Nor was this northern diarist alone in his opinion. However, some were fearful of the consequences. And Greeley, still uncertain of his place in the crisis, temporarily turned his newspaper over to Charles A. Dana, who possessed the military experience which the editor lacked. Meanwhile, Greeley retired to his Chappaqua farm, there suffered a self-inflicted knee injury, and recovered from it slowly.

While Greeley was away, during the weeks of late April and early May, Dana shaped the fiery editorial policy of the *Tribune;* however, as his letters indicate, Greeley approved the militant policy at this time. Furthermore, the editor, "booted and spurred," did not make a very imposing figure.[11] He told Dana and others that Lincoln was still too conservative and too conciliatory, that the President should have called for 500,000 men instead of the 75,000 which he asked for on the day following the surrender of Fort Sumter. From this moment onward for several months, Greeley overlooked and failed to understand either military strategy or enrollment problems; he declared repeatedly that Lincoln could have used half a million men immediately and successfully, crushing the southern "rebellion" before it actually began.[12]

Almost without hesitation, the *Tribune* began its "On to Richmond" banner headlines, and Greeley, furious at Lincoln's apparent inactivity, went to Washington to visit the President. He found him "obstinate" and openly "undisturbed" at the secession crisis. Greeley returned to New York, joining his assistant Dana in a daily editorial demand that the northern armies march "Forward to Richmond." [13]

Greeley also attacked the attitude of the border states, failing utterly to comprehend Lincoln's policy of winning border-state support for the Union cause. For example, Mayor George William Brown of Baltimore declared that the *Tribune* editor with characteristic vehemence and "severity of language," attacked the "proceedings of the city authorities" on April 19, when they acted in regard to the Sumter crisis. Greeley "scouted the demands of the mayor and his associates, whom he designated as Messrs. Brown and Company," and, much to the horror of Lincoln, he insisted that, "practically on the morning of the 20th of April, Maryland was a member of the Southern Confederacy, and that her Governor spoke and acted the bidding of a cabal of the ablest and most envenomed traitors." [14]

Mayor Brown declared that it was true that the city of Baltimore "then and for days afterwards was in an anomalous condition which may be best described as one of armed neutrality." However, the mayor denies emphatically that "in any sense it [Baltimore] was, on April 20, or at any other time, a member of the Southern Confederacy." [15] These vicious attacks by Greeley upon the attitude of Maryland in general, and of Baltimore in particular, placed Lincoln in an almost impossible position.

In his next virile attack upon the North and upon Lincoln's weak policies, Greeley declared that the loss of the Norfolk navy yard was an unnecessary surrender. The editor wrote that "Capt. Paulding might have held his position a week, and that week would have brought at least 30,000 men to his aid." [16]

Secretary of the Navy Gideon Welles, who harbored no kind feelings for the *Tribune* editor at any time, bristled at this attack, and responded in these words, defending the administration and its policies:

> Not thirty thousand men reached imperiled Washington in one week, in response to the call of the President by proclamation, aided by all the state authorities, and official and individual effort, zeal, and influence; and such as came in obedience to that national call were indifferently provided with arms, munitions, and supplies, backed though they were by the Federal and State governments. If [Greeley] is to be believed, a larger army

would have gathered on an appeal from the Commodore to save the navy yard, than came to defend the National Capital on the official call of the President. What thirty thousand men could have done, had they gathered in Norfolk in a week, towards defending a place in the enemy's country, without batteries or shore defenses of any kind, without engineers to construct them, without resources, with no commissariat or quartermaster's supplies, are matters not clearly explained by the critical Greeley. It is doubted if Greeley could have got that number of men at Norfolk, to say nothing of their equipment and supplies, when the President, with all the power and energies of the country, gathered no such number in that brief time at Washington to defend the capital of the nation. . . . Greeley . . . declares: "Thus ended the most shameful, cowardly, disastrous performance that stains the annals of the American Navy." [17]

Welles wrote in the light of subsequent revelations that the naval performance could be condemned as shameful, but hardly as cowardly. The Union was not prepared for Virginia's decision to secede, explained Welles; besides, for months Greeley had "been urging in the *Tribune* that the Southern States should go in peace. . . ." Until the storm actually burst, neither Greeley nor Congress appears to have been prepared for it. Nevertheless, concluded Welles, bitterly, "Greeley might have saved the navy yard through proper presentation of facts in his journal," but Greeley deluded himself and endeavored to close the eyes of the nation.[18]

From this time forward, Welles struggled to see that Lincoln did not succumb to the influence of Greeley. However, the editor was only beginning his "On to Richmond" campaign. On May 19, he wrote thus to Lincoln:

> . . . The intelligence that the war for the Union is to be prosecuted with emphatic vigor, and that the traitors are to be thrown back from Washington in every direc-

tion causes general rejoicing here. We feel that the struggle thus prosecuted cannot be of long duration. All are
confident that the result will justify our fondest hopes.

The one drawback on the general satisfaction is the
existence of wide-spread complaint and heart-burning
with regard to the acceptance of this regiment and the
rejection of that and the other.—These men have volun-
teered to defend the country on its own terms, they cannot be made to see why they should not be taken. The
report that *all* who are efficient and ready are henceforth to be accepted, rejoices every loyal heart. I trust
that report is well-founded; if it is not, I pray you to
make it so at the earliest moments and thereby gratify
millions beside.[19]

Lincoln read this letter carefully, doubtful that Greeley could
be trusted but hoping that he could properly translate into
words the public pulse of the nation. Lincoln endeavored to accept volunteers as rapidly as they could be processed, and he
was, at this time, inclined to hearken to Greeley's words and to
urge action upon the military branch of the government, before
that branch was properly prepared to attack the enemy.

In early June, a smart cavalry skirmish at Fairfax Court House
killed and wounded a few men. Washington saw its first prisoners of war—"Virginia boys who were taken to the Navy Yard."
They did not seem to realize their position, as the Washington
Star observed, but were entirely unconcerned, having "a jolly
time with cards." The country had grown wildly impatient for
news of a decisive battle, and such insignificant skirmishes, high-
lighted by the capture of a few unconcerned "rebel" prisoners,
brought loud demands for immediate action from the whole
northern press. Richmond had been made the new capital of
the Confederate States of America, and the "rebel" Congress
was to meet there on July 20. Horace Greeley had already sent
out the cry "Forward to Richmond" ringing through the North.
Now he suggested that the federal armies should prevent the

South from convening its Congress at Richmond. Such military action would "break the back of the Rebellion," and such action should be taken at once.[20]

But Lincoln would not move in June. Greeley insisted that "old" Winfield Scott and "policy-minded" William H. Seward deserved the blame for this disastrous hesitation. He talked freely of his problems to a ministerial companion:

> During my summer vacation [writes Moncure Daniel Conway, in 1861] I was continually preaching and lecturing on the theme that filled all minds [the Civil War, and the problems of military victory and emancipation of the Negroes]. On my way to Newport, R.I., to preach for my dear friend Charles T. Brooks, I travelled with Horace Greeley, who had recently [seven years before] dissolved political partnership with Seward and Thurlow Weed. Greeley denied earnestly any ill will toward Seward, but said he had no faith in him as a minister.
>
> "Seward has and always must have a *policy;* a policy is just what we don't want. We want manliness."
>
> He was haunted by fear of a restoration of the slave power. "We may wake up some fine morning and find the Democratic party wheeled around and united on some base and ruinous concession for peace." I found that the pain and responsibility of editing the *Tribune* were telling on him sadly. . . .[21]

Lincoln's failure to heed his demands immediately, although the President was at this time considering Greeley's advice, also pained the editor deeply, wounding his political pride. "Richmond was not yet fortified," Greeley told Lincoln. "It was accessible by both land and water." The North held Fortress Monroe and should have captured Richmond long before the Confederate Congress assembled there. "Forward to Richmond" should have been the immediate war cry, not of the press and the people alone but of the federal government as well. Instead of "energy, vigor, and promptness," instead of "daring decision,"

Greeley thundered, "we have in our councils weakness, irreso-
lution, hesitation, and delay." "Our forces are permitted weeks
of dissipation," when they should be sent forward immediately,
under one command.[22]

As the encampments in the environs of Washington—some in
the very halls and grounds of the Capitol itself—began to fill,
bulge, and overflow with sturdy recruits, the temper of the leaders of northern opinion took a sharp change. Suddenly, Greeley's
cry of "On to Richmond" was echoed from every quarter. However, the *Tribune* still directed the bandwagon parade, now actually serving as a somewhat reputable public index. Everyone,
including Greeley himself, had forgotten his February and March
editorials—"Let the erring sisters depart in peace"—everyone, that
is, except Lincoln. Therefore, it was with sad surprise that the
President read Greeley's June and early July editorial leaders—
"Are not two more than one?" "And have we not the two to
our enemy's one?" "What dullards and laggards our generals
must be to delay for a day or an hour!" [23]

This rising of public opinion, sparked by *Tribune* editorial
fires, began to press heavily upon Lincoln and Winfield Scott.
Efforts were made to precipitate a battle.

Finally, this pressure won, and Greeley, at least indirectly,
had his way. By direction of the President, the still reluctant
General of the Army, Winfield Scott, commanded his subordinate, Irwin McDowell, to advance. Thus, Greeley's "On to
Richmond" cry was translated from the heavy-leaded columns
of the *Tribune* to the straggling columns of the ninety-day mili-
tia. Hence, tirade was turned into tragedy.[24]

Greeley had assumed command of the armies, and for once,
Lincoln acquiesced in the directions of his pressing adviser of
the press.[25] The armies advanced; the first Battle of Bull Run
followed. It ended in the northern defeat—a stampede which
has become legendary. Almost immediately, Greeley received the
full brunt of national criticism, because he had been the foremost exponent of the "On to Richmond" policy. The phrase was
associated with him, and it was declared that he had been the

author of it. Greeley never admitted that he deserved this criticism, writing in defense of his policy and of himself:

> The war cry, "Forward to Richmond!" did not originate with me; but it is just what should have been uttered, and the words should have been translated into deeds. Instead of energy, vigor, promptness, daring, decision, we had in our councils, weakness, irresolution, hesitation, delay; and, when at last our hastily collected forces, after being demoralized by weeks of idleness . . . were sent forward, they advanced on separate lines, under different commanders; this enabling the enemy to concentrate all its forces in Virginia against a single corps of ours, defeating and stampeding it at Bull Run, while other Union volunteers, aggregating nearly twice its strength, lay idle near Harper's Ferry, in and about Washington, and at Fortress Monroe. Thus, what should have been a short, sharp struggle, was expanded into a long desultory one; while those whose blundering incapacity or lack of purpose was responsible for those ills, united in throwing the blame on the faithful few who had counseled justly, but whose urgent remonstrances they had never heeded.[26]

This statement of his part in the "On to Richmond" policy and of its failure from military blunders and presidential inabilities is at least partially, if not wholly, unreliable. Yet Greeley made it sincerely and in bitterness; it seemed to him that Bull Run was his Waterloo.

Not only did he upbraid Lincoln and Winfield Scott, as well as almost every other northern leader, but Greeley suddenly decided that Charles A. Dana was entirely responsible for the militant policy which the *Tribune* had been pursuing. When the South unexpectedly sent northern troops "running for cover," Greeley sent Dana seeking other employment. He then began to doubt whether the North could ever be victorious, and he halfheartedly apologized in the *Tribune* for its fiery policy, himself disclaiming any part in that policy.[27]

Meanwhile, the Battle of Manassas had swung public opinion from a feeling of joyous confidence to one of grim determination. Stocks fell. The circulation of the *Tribune* slipped to a new low. The populace of the North, angered and mortified at the results of Bull Run, blamed Greeley, Lincoln, Winfield Scott, and the Cabinet indiscriminately. Greeley, enduring more of the nation's abuse than he felt he deserved, filled his columns with editorials which, after exonerating himself, blamed the defeat upon inefficient preparation by the administration, and demanded a fresh supply of generals and Cabinet members who would impart a much-needed vigor to the prosecution of the war. As the days following July 21 and 22 brought new and more vehement whiplashes of popular condemnation, however, the editor quailed before the onslaught, again proffering repentance, first for Dana's and eventually for his own part in bringing on a premature battle, promising to bar all future criticisms of military movements from his columns. This reformation was ephemeral, but Greeley's mercurial nature had suffered a hard blow. He confided to friends that, for weeks after Bull Run, he was unable to sleep, tormented by fears of "a disastrous war and a disgraceful peace." [28]

If all did not agree with the troubled editor that the war would end in a northern defeat, everyone knew, after Manassas, that the winning of the conflict would be no easy three months' affair.[29] As for Greeley, he had lost all hope. After seven sleepless nights, with insomnia beginning to bear a telling effect upon the editor, he wrote of his problems to Lincoln, not asking for consolation but giving advice and pouring out condemnation. Whatever Greeley could find to say in defense of his "On to Richmond" cries, no possible justification could he give, or even suggest for this letter to Lincoln which he penned in a state of absolute hysteria and delirious fear, after the first Battle of Bull Run. It seemed to him that the Union cause was irretrievably lost, and he was even ready to consider an armistice looking to the end of a war that had scarcely begun. A more horrifying and less comforting letter than the one which Greeley addressed to the President from New York on Monday, July 29, can hardly be imagined.[30] It ran as follows:

> This is my 7th sleepless night—yours, too, doubtless; yet I think I shall not die, because I have no right to die. You are not considered a great man, and I am a hopelessly broken one. You are now undergoing a terrible ordeal, and God has thrown the gravest responsibilities upon you. Do not fear to meet them. Can the rebels be beaten after all that has occurred, and in view of the actual state of feeling caused by our late awful disaster? If they can, and it is your business to ascertain and decide, write me that such is your judgment, so that I may know and do my duty. And if they *cannot* be beaten, if our present disaster is fatal—do not fear to sacrifice yourself to your country. If the rebels are not beaten, then every drop of blood henceforth shed in this quarrel will be wantonly, wickedly shed, and the guilt will rest heavily on the soul of every promoter of the crime.
>
> Yours in the depths of bitterness,
>
> HORACE GREELEY [31]

This was the second hysterical letter Lincoln had received from the editor of the *Tribune*. The first had come the preceding December, when Greeley was caught in the web of peaceable secession but was advising Lincoln not to compromise—to sacrifice himself, the party, and anything else necessary to avoid another "disgraceful" surrender to the southern slaveholders. Lincoln disregarded this second letter, just as he had disregarded the first one. Furthermore, he vowed that, although he had yielded to Greeley's personal and editorial pressure in ordering the Battle of Manassas, he would not yield to the editor of the *Tribune* again. He did not reply to Greeley, as the editor had commanded him to do. He kept his own counsel, and Greeley spent more sleepless nights.

However, Greeley had been correct in one of his very hys-

terical statements. Lincoln was not considered a great man. Moreover, it may be that Lincoln's nights had been as troubled as
those spent by the editor in absolute insomnia. "Can the rebels
be beaten?" This question was passing through the minds of all
the nation's leaders—all but one of them, the leader of leaders
soon to be. The calm loo' on his face the Sunday evening when
he heard the message of defeat, brought to him by Seward, told
plainly enough what his answer would be to Greeley, had he
written it. The rebels could be beaten, and would be beaten.
He must be the incarnation of the thinking and the feeling of
all of his people; and he did not despair of the Republic. The
Union could be preserved and would be, though hell itself, accompanied by Greeley, rose up in arms against it.[32]

Although Greeley was heartbroken at the Manassas catastrophe, despite the defeat about which he had written so disparagingly to Lincoln, the editor found some small consolation
among those friends who sympathized with him and who, unlike Lincoln, wrote to him in this hour of trial. Among these
friends one discovers Moncure Daniel Conway, a man who felt
that he understood Greeley's peculiarities, who endeavored to
comfort the "scapegoat" of Bull Run. He tells of his efforts and
of Greeley's disheartening reply, thus:

> The advance was made, the Bull Run disaster followed,
> and Horace Greeley was made the scapegoat.
>
> Knowing Horace Greeley well, I felt the injustice of
> the public fury against him, and, on hearing that his
> health had broken down under the denunciations,
> wrote him a long letter, to which came the following
> answer:—
>
> New York
> Aug. 17, 1861
>
> MY DEAR CONWAY,—I have yours of the 13th. I have been
> very ill, and am yet too weak to work, yet am doing so
> because I must. I scarcely slept at all for a week; now
> the best I can do is to get two or three hours' uneasy

oblivion every night. But I hope I shall mend. The *Tribune did* suffer considerably by the truth told by Warren, etc., about the want of purpose and management at Washington, and I think would have been ruined had I not resolved to bend to the storm. I did it very badly, for I was all but insane, yet I hope all will yet be well with us. You see that everybody is now saying that we were right originally with regard to Scott, etc., and that the Cabinet ought to be reconstituted. My strong objection to the attack on the Cabinet was that it would [because of the momentary fury against the *Tribune*] keep them in when they want to go out. No President could afford to have it said that a newspaper had forced him to give battle and then turned out his Cabinet because he lost that battle.

My friend, the hour is very dark; but I have not lost my faith in God. If this people is worthy to fight and win a battle for Liberty and Law, that battle will be won; if they are not, I do not see that there is any more a place for so weak and poor an instrument as I am. . . .[33]

This letter evidences Greeley's ghastly pessimism. It also shows, however, that by this time, some weeks after the tragedy, much of his old egoism and self-assertion had returned. He is ready again to dictate policy, just as he had dictated it prior to Bull Run. For, as this letter indicates, he still privately believed himself to be in the right.

In the *Tribune* of July 20, the day preceding the Battle of Manassas, Greeley had written, "In addition to developing the best talent of officers who had any to develop, it was equally essential to dispose of the hopelessly incompetent—and their name was legion." With his usual penchant for criticism, the editor had publicly advocated and highly recommended "(1) examinations for all officers; (2) transportation to training camp immediately after enlistment; (3) reservation of the right to place men in other regiments than those which they originally choose; (4) making recruiting officers responsible for completing regiments they have started." [34]

Each of these items suggested by Greeley before Bull Run, and advocated after he had somewhat recovered from his illness, was aimed at a current abuse. In fact, his suggestions for once seem applicable to the existing situation. Furthermore, actions which Greeley thus recommended would allay a certain amount of very potent but excusable discontent. The first of Greeley's suggested items for military reform is of special interest, since it was just a step in advance of a provision enacted by the Congress two days later, and which provision, already in the process of becoming law, may have been the source of Greeley's inspiration. In the Army Act of July 22, 1861, provision was made for a military commission in each military department to examine all officers in volunteer regiments and to remove all officers adjudged incompetent. No officer, however, was to be removed without the approval of the President. [35]

Sorrow over the defeat at Manassas prevented Greeley from rejoicing when some of his more sensible military recommendations were enacted by Congress and accepted by the President. On July 29, the Congress authorized the federal government to enlarge the regular army to 42,000 men. Such a setup, it may readily be seen, afforded both the President and the governors of the various states an extensive appointive domain. Frequently, state executives appointed those who "would produce the most agreeable consequences at the next election-time." That is, the spoils system prevailed. Nor was it different with the federal executive. Congressmen or congressional delegates gave Lincoln the names of those whom they wished appointed as brigadiers, as major generals, and as lesser officers. Such a policy, as one might naturally expect, resulted in the appointment of many misfits and in a constant struggle over military patronage from political sources. It was to remedy some of this misapplied patronage and to remove some of these misfits that Greeley recommended improvements in the existing military system. "The people know," a correspondent had written to the editor of the

Tribune, "that it takes long to organize an army—longer to discipline it to those qualities which make veterans and insure victories—longer yet to discover the true commanders from among the crowd of egoists, peacocks and place hunters," with which "the volunteer system is apt to oppress a great military movement." [36]

Although Greeley sometimes insisted that he agreed with this statement, although he often struggled to improve the system of recruiting and training volunteer armies and officers, he was never patient enough to wait for this system to produce an efficient commander. He criticized almost every general Lincoln ever employed. In fact, there was only one whom he really honored as a great general; that was John C. Fremont.[37]

Apart from the disaster at Manassas Junction, the West offered the Union most of its excitements, its joys, and its sorrows during those first months of the war. Even as John M. Forbes, a radical New England industrialist, truly prophesied, "Lowering clouds in the West portended a gathering storm" in May, 1861. In the very center of the swirling gusts of this onrushing storm stood the romantic figure of General John C. Fremont, commander of the Department of the West. Lincoln invested the defeated presidential candidate of 1856 with this important and highly explosive office in the early summer of 1861. The general, a dramatic figure to the public by reason of his western explorations, journeyed to his headquarters in St. Louis amid ringing applause which echoed and reverberated throughout the whole North. From all sides came confident predictions that the dashing "pathfinder" would give the country action, and that Missouri would soon be cleared of all Confederates and southern sympathizers.

Powerful political elements had combined their forces to secure this substantial appointment for a man with scanty military training and experience. Horace Greeley pointed out to Lincoln the political advantages offered to the administration through the bestowal of high military office upon the Republican Party's first presidential candidate. Gustave Koerner, leader of the antislavery German population of the Mississippi Valley, assured Lin-

coln that the selection of Fremont, known to be opposed to slavery, would unite his area of the country in support of the war.
Furthermore, the popular Blair family—the father being the unofficial adviser of the President, one son being in the Cabinet,
another being the chieftain of the Republican Party in Missouri
—had selected Fremont as their political cat's-paw and had, assisted by Greeley, convinced Lincoln of the advisability of choosing the pathfinder to head the armies of the West.[38]

On August 13, 1861, the readers of the New York *Tribune*—
by means of Greeley's correspondents in the field—were gratified
at last with these headlines: "Important from Missouri—The
Rebels Repulsed Again—They Fly to the Woods—General Lyon
Endeavors to Draw Them Out." [39] The dispatches which were
the basis of such headings had come from Franklin and Jefferson
City and were dated the preceding day, August 12. The following day the *Tribune,* which had numerous "able" correspondents covering the battles in the West, had headlines still more
arresting: "Great Battle in Missouri—Defeat of the Rebel Forces
—A Splendid Union Victory—General Lyon Killed." Beneath
these headlines the readers discovered that "all this had been
done . . . by eight thousand troops against twenty-three thousand rebels." Then the headline writer prepared the jubilant
reader of the North for the bad news by informing him that
Colonel Franz Sigel, who had succeeded to command when
General Nathaniel Lyon had been killed, had "very coolly returned to Rolla." [40]

The *Tribune* then received another news dispatch, this one
filed in St. Louis on the afternoon of August 13. It began bluntly:
"Rumors are current in the street, in which some reliance is
placed, that General Lyon's command in the South-West has
been totally routed by the rebels." Secessionists, the message continued, received the news the night before, word having been
brought to Rolla by a very eager messenger who had killed no
fewer than four horses in a mad ride from Springfield. Official
dispatches were believed to be in the hands of General Fremont,
but as nothing had been divulged, the Union men entertained
apprehension for the safety of the army.[41]

Horace Greeley's reporter was well informed. Fremont had received the bad news officially in time to wire the Secretary of War on August 13. This wire contained the facts of Lyon's death and of Sigel's subsequent withdrawal to Rolla. Fremont and his wife, both then on good terms with Frank Blair, urged immediate aid from Secretary of War Simon Cameron, from Postmaster-General Montgomery Blair, and finally from Lincoln himself. Meanwhile, Greeley's correspondents continued to supply his *Tribune* with news of further disasters, albeit the correspondents' reports appear to have been somewhat different from and actually more authentic than the imaginative statements sent by the eager yet fearful Fremont.[42]

Lincoln, however, did not follow Greeley's accounts of the western campaign with any thought of their accuracy. Instead, he read with disgust and pain the telegrams and letters from Fremont and his wife, deploring the fact that he had again listened to Greeley, together with others, and that he had appointed this California hero to a task for which he was unequal.

If Lincoln did not read Greeley's newspaper, the soldiers did, at least when they were afforded the rare opportunity of doing so. Newspapers were read by the men in uniform until the words had become illegible and the paper had been worn out completely. Newspapers even became articles of exchange when the Union soldiers were on enemy soil. Wisely anticipating this need for printed material by the soldiers, and correctly evaluating the propaganda power which would accrue from such action, the New York Tribune Company at the beginning of the war made a standing offer of a dozen free copies of the *Daily* and of the *Weekly Tribune* to the colonel of each regiment throughout the period of the war, if they would only keep the publishing company informed of their forwarding address.[43]

This would have been an extremely large contract to fill had general advantage been taken of it. Moreover, one is inclined to wonder whether the results of this generosity had anything to do with Greeley's later anxiety to bring the war to a hasty close.[44]

Even in August and September, 1861, Greeley desired that the war might be brought to a hasty close. Again misjudging his acquaintances and poorly evaluating their abilities, he felt that John C. Fremont must be the man to defeat the "rebels" in the West. Could Fremont prove himself a great leader, he would vindicate the trust Greeley had placed in him, and he would prove to Lincoln the validity of Greeley's advice. Unfortunately, however, Fremont did not live up to his part of the bargain. In addition to certain failures, besides making certain rather ridiculous pleas and grandstand plays for Lincoln's special aid and attention, the pathfinder issued a proclamation freeing the slaves in Missouri. Lincoln, pursuing a policy of conciliation toward the border states, ordered that Fremont withdraw the proclamation; the general, who had been loudly applauded for his action by many abolitionists and radicals, now numbering Greeley among them, refused to do so. In desperation, the President decided to remove Fremont, after reprimanding him and nullifying his emancipation declaration. As a precautionary measure, in a vain effort to allay hostile opinion, Lincoln sent Montgomery Blair as an emissary to inform Governor John A. Andrew of Massachusetts and the newspaper editors, Horace Greeley and William Cullen Bryant, of the reasons for the dismissal of the western general. Then, on October 24, he sent General Samuel R. Curtis a letter containing two enclosures: one to Fremont, relieving him of his command; the other to General David Hunter, appointing him to Fremont's place.[45]

When Montgomery Blair called upon Greeley to tell him of Lincoln's plans, he found the editor, recovered from his Manassas disease, firmly ensconced in the camp of the violent antislavery radicals—a follower of Salmon P. Chase, Charles Sumner, and the other Jacobin leaders. With the removal of Fremont an accomplished fact, these radicals could scarcely contain themselves. As soon as the November election returns were in, they burst forth in new demands for vigor and speed in conducting the war, and with more open avowals of their antislavery aims. Leading in the cry, Horace Greeley declared openly that no reconstruction of the Union would be worth having at the cost of slavery.[46]

Despite the fact that Montgomery Blair had warned him of

Greeley's attitude, Lincoln appeared disappointed to find the pacifist editor firmly in the ranks of the emancipationists, the abolitionists, and the fiery northern radicals. But Greeley was there. He continued to uphold Fremont, also. Shortly after the general had been relieved of his command, he and his wife journeyed to New York because the pathfinder had no new assignment. He and his wife were guests of honor at an immense and impressive dinner given by Henry Ward Beecher; the diners included—according to the *Tribune* of December 8, 1861—"a large (and distinguished) representation from the pulpit." [47] Greeley still thought highly of Fremont's military record in Missouri, and the deposed general felt complimented by the *Tribune* comment regarding the Beecher dinner that "the vestibule of the Astor House continues to be thronged with persons anxious to see the 'Pathfinder.' " [48]

During the remainder of this autumn of 1861, while Lincoln endured the gibes and the public wrath of the supporters of Fremont, the country began to murmur at the continued inactivity of the military forces. All eyes were on the banks of the Potomac, where General George B. McClellan drilled and paraded his magnificent army in the balmy autumn weather. The press, its martial ardor temporarily repressed after the northern defeat at Manassas, again shouted for an offensive movement. The *Tribune,* forgetting its pledge, no longer mindful of its loss of subscriptions, the editor having forgotten his broken and bleeding heart, again sent forth the cry "Onward to Richmond." In fact, the once penitent Greeley demanded that McClellan hurl his entire army at the foe before winter began and further operations were prevented. The radical press, led by Greeley, who associated the reprimand and the removal of Fremont with Lincoln's Sewardizing policy of compromise and mildness, demanded, called for, and clamored to have a military offensive directed in the East by McClellan or some "more able" general. However, this time the President was determined not to be rushed into hasty action; as is well known, he learned by his past experiences. Therefore, he assured McClellan that there would be no military advance because of political pressure. Greeley's cries went unanswered. His influence remained ineffectual.[49]

Nevertheless, Lincoln hoped that he might win Greeley over to a support of the administration, for he knew the tremendous power wielded by the *Tribune*. On the matter of co-operation between the President and the editor of the *Tribune*, Lincoln prepared himself to make certain negotiatory steps. In November, 1861, two unusual unofficial advisers called upon the President. One was James R. Gilmore, a friend and correspondent of Greeley's; and the other was Robert J. Walker, former Mississippi citizen, one-time governor of the territory of Kansas and general lobbyist and adventurer. Both Walker and Gilmore, as advisers to Lincoln, suggested that they might serve as mediaries between the President and the editor of the *Tribune*. The program would work in this fashion: Lincoln would give to Walker certain information concerning the inner workings of the federal administration; Walker, in turn, would transmit this information through Gilmore to Greeley for the use of the editor and for the guidance of his editorial policies along administration lines. Quite possibly, although no proof of it exists, the initial idea for this co-operation was Greeley's, although Lincoln had been for some time groping to find a suitable mediary—one who would reliably transmit secret information to the editor of the *Tribune*. Gilmore, who knew Greeley much better than did either Lincoln or Walker, formulated the first steps in the elaborate plan. During his interview with Walker and Gilmore, the President accepted Gilmore's idea readily, writing a supposedly confidential letter to Walker that might be shown to Greeley as a means of inaugurating the program. This is the letter which Lincoln gave to Walker, but which was meant for Greeley's eyes: [50]

DEAR GOVERNOR [WALKER]:

I have thought over the interview which Mr. Gilmore has had with Mr. Greeley, and the proposal that Greeley has made to Gilmore, namely, that he [Gilmore] shall communicate to him (Greeley) all that he learns from you of the inner workings of the administration,

in return for his [Greeley's] giving such aid as he can
. . . and allowing you (Walker) from time to time to
use his (Greeley's) columns when it is desirable to feel
of, or forestall, public opinion on important subjects.
The arrangement meets my unqualified approval, and
I shall further it to the extent of my ability, by opening to you—as I do now—fully the policy of the Government—its present views and future intentions when
formed,—giving you permission to communicate them
to Gilmore for Greeley; and in case you go to Europe I
will give these things direct to Gilmore. But all this must
be on the express and explicit understanding that the
fact of these communications coming from me shall be
absolutely confidential,—not to be disclosed by Greeley
to his nearest friend, or any of his subordinates. He will
be, in effect, my mouthpiece, but I shall not be known
to be the speaker.

I need not tell you that I have the highest confidence
in Mr. Greeley. He is a great power. Having him firmly
behind me will be as helpful to me as an army of one
hundred thousand men. That he has ever kicked the
traces has been owing to his not being fully informed.
Tell Gilmore to say to him that, if he ever objects to my
policy, I shall be glad to have him state to me his views
frankly and fully. I shall adopt his if I can. If I cannot,
I will at least tell him why. He and I should stand together, and let no minor differences come between us;
while we both seek one end, which is the saving of our
country.

. . . This is a longer letter . . . than I would have
written for any other man than Horace Greeley. . . .[51]

This letter of November 21, 1861, neither the first nor the
last such letter for Greeley's benefit, is enough to give evidence
that Lincoln could have handled the editor, had Greeley been
a man of ordinary emotions and mentality. As has been written truly:

His [Lincoln's] dealings with a hostile press are enough to prove him a diplomat. He admits the powerful Greeley—a man whose support was almost indispensable, and a man who had not been won over during a personal interview in Springfield—to a knowledge of all the plans of the government, on the understanding that Greeley shall open his newspaper to the advocacy of the governmental policy. . . .

This epistle, very carefully worded in such a way that the recipient ["Governor" Robert J. Walker] would be able to show it confidentially to the great journalist, was an attempt at mental bribery and corruption. If it was not more than half successful, this redounded to the credit of both parties.[52]

Reading the letter addressed to Robert J. Walker but meant for him, Greeley momentarily acquiesced in Lincoln's policy of moderation and mildness. Although such co-operation was not to endure forever, despite the fact that the President's formula of mental bribery only half succeeded, Lincoln was permitted a moment of respite in December, 1861, during which time he could prepare his annual message to Congress, and be thankful that, for the moment, Greeley appeared to stand with him.

CHAPTER SEVEN

Columns of Criticism

With the political, military, and foreign situations what they were in December, 1861, the preparation of a message to Congress was not a simple task. Of the Trent affair Lincoln said not a word, and he handled the slavery question conservatively and cautiously. Since this message was delivered only a short time after the beginning of co-operation between the President and the *Tribune,* it brought forth strong commendation from Horace Greeley. However, Lincoln remarked that the editor stood with him only about half the time, and he felt that Greeley's words—"each weighing about a ton"—would still praise him and his policies only occasionally. His assumption was correct, for after commending heartily the President's annual message to Congress, Greeley found it necessary to remind the chief executive that, in certain basic particulars, he was inferior to Jefferson Davis and the Confederate regime at Richmond. Noting that Davis had recently sent a message to the "rival conclave" in Richmond, Greeley reported that Davis was "quite commonly presumed to be the abler of the two" men, that he was certainly the better grammarian, that he could "use the English language with decided perspicuity and force." [1]

Then, in further discussing Jefferson Davis's message, Greeley "dropped some blockbusters" for the benefit of Lincoln. The Confederate President's address had been "truculent, sanguinary, demoniac," while Lincoln was not moved even by such an "unseemly display of rage and malignity to use harsh inculpations." Finally, congratulating the President on his "appropriate" message of December 3, Greeley commended the address for its brevity and asserted that it would be universally and intently read. He quoted the section dealing with slavery and with slaves, remarking that "the spirit of this is admirable, and will command general approval." [2]

Two days later, on December 5, in a still more conciliatory mood, Greeley editorialized upon Lincoln's message once more, setting forth in strong terms the presidential contention that the "sole real objective of the war" was the maintenance of the Union and the authority of its government, and stating emphatically that there should be no question of arming fugitive slaves until all white volunteers were effectively equipped. "We lack evidence," Greeley wrote, after reading the Lincoln dispatches which had passed through the hands of Robert J. Walker and James R. Gilmore, "that the material exists for Black regiments of Unionists, any more than of Indians, that would be worth their cost." [3] Furthermore, Greeley continued by blasting Simon Cameron's ill-timed fugitive-slave proposal with volley upon volley of editorial grapeshot. Seeing this, and temporarily despairing of Greeley's newspaper support, the Jacobins took Cameron into their fold as one who would make war according to their formula. The Confederate government, despite the appealing nature of Lincoln's mild statements and Greeley's editorial support, made use of much anti-Union sentiment in the crucial border states; and the editor of the *Tribune,* not fathoming the President's all-important border-state policy, remained silent on this score, in spite of Lincoln's desire that he co-operate with him.[4]

At home and abroad the political situation remained tense. Greeley's support of the administration remained on a quasi-wholehearted basis, principally because of the two Republican factions in New York State and because it appeared to contemporary observers that Seward held the chief advisory post in the President's Cabinet.

"I dislike to make changes in office as long as they can be avoided. It multiplies my embarrassments," Lincoln wrote to W. Jayne, February 26, 1864. But the American political game as played in Lincoln's day—and before and ever since, with some modifications—demanded changes in public office, and still more changes. Theoretically it was contended that the war for the Union had transcended political parties and factions within those parties. No longer should the nation be divided between Republicans and Democrats and Constitutional Unionists, between Weedites and anti-Weedites. Henceforth, preached some, there should be but two parties—the "party of union" and the "party of disunion." Nevertheless, the number of Democratic federal officeholders displaced by Republicans in the year following the firing on Fort Sumter may be considered a criterion for the period; if it is, it would indicate that the Republicans had no plans for keeping pace with the demands of the times and for maintaining peace with northern or southern Democrats. Party labels still meant the difference between employment and seeking a new position.[5]

In this connection, one may examine that rich mine of government jobs, the New York Custom House. That portion of the Democratic press which supported Lincoln's Unionist cause appealed to the President not to remove Democrats from office for partisan reasons, pleading that the traditional rule of "to the victors belong the spoils" be abandoned for the duration of the war. This appeal was of little avail, however, for the struggle between the Weed and the anti-Weed Republicans to gain control of all patronage continued unabated. Thirty-five inspectors were removed from the custom house in late October, 1861, and several days later came word that "the heads of the clerks under the last administration were to continue to drop off quietly."[6] Although he was now supporting Lincoln's general policy, Greeley continued to strive in his effort to have all such vacancies filled with anti-Weed Republicans. And, despite the fact that he had expressed confidence in Greeley, even after admitting the editor to be a "great power," Lincoln usually divided the posts equally between the Greeley faction and the Weed faction, or actually gave more appointments to the political followers of Seward and Weed.

In the New York Post Office it was much the same story. In the spring of 1862, Lincoln made room there for another follower of Seward and Weed, Abram Wakeman, who was to be postmaster of the metropolis. Upon hearing of the appointment, the ever-jealous Greeley began to regret his co-operation with Lincoln. "Wakeman," the disgruntled editor complained bitterly, "is mere clay in the hands of the potter, Weed." [7] It was clear now, if it had not been before, that, although Lincoln might whisper "sweet nothings" in Greeley's ear, Weed undoubtedly held the upper hand in New York politics, and the men he recommended more often received rewards of patronage than did the officeseekers suggested by the editor of the *Tribune.*

Originally, Greeley had felt no sympathy for those "base men" who sought offices as political rewards for scanty service to an "often corrupt" political party. However, as time passed, the reforming editor began to tolerate such men and even to hold them in high esteem. In fact, Greeley himself became one of those "base men" who sought political office as a reward for scanty service. Thurlow Weed, in commenting on what he considered to be Greeley's basic change of attitude in regard to officeseekers and a personal desire to occupy a public office himself, records that—

> In later years . . . [Greeley] not only became tolerant of office-seekers, but some of the most impudent and worthless of the tribe entrenched themselves strongly in his confidence and favor. It is a fact equally mortifying and instructive, that Mr. Greeley during the last ten years of his life was the dupe and victim of political adventurers, men so universally discredited that their shame would pass current with nobody else. And yet, while sufficiently distrustful of others, Mr. Greeley's con-

fidence in sharpers involved him in frequent political entanglements and subjected him to serious pecuniary losses. . . .

In looking back through a vista of nearly forty years, I find myself seriously perplexed in endeavoring to understand Mr. Greeley's true character. While all I saw and knew of him in early life inspired feelings of confidence and admiration, there was very much in later years to occasion surprise and regret. I can account for this change . . . only by attributing [it] to a cause which has worked men's downfall in all ages of the world. Ambition, while under the subjection of reason, is laudable; but when it breaks bounds and o'erlaps itself, the consequences are disastrous.[8]

Before Weed set down this opinion of Greeley in his memoir, he had doubtless rehearsed it well by telling it to Lincoln many times. It is clear that Lincoln possessed similar doubts concerning Greeley's stability; that, during his first term, he would not consider the editor as a possibility for a Cabinet post or for any other appointment; and that he proposed the plan of issuing private governmental information to Greeley with grave reservations, knowing that the editor was already placing himself in the camp of the radicals, and hoping thus to divert the vacillating editor for a moment from his ideas of a speedy prosecution of the war and an immediate emancipation of slavery.

If Lincoln actually hoped to hold Greeley in hand for more than a few months, he hoped in vain. The announced resolution of the radicals to force emancipation upon the government by congressional enactment as a war measure alarmed the moderates. It was not the function of Congress, insisted Lincoln's supporters, to define the purposes of the war. Senator Jacob Collamer, veteran Vermont Republican, summed up their views in an interview at Boston, on his way back to Washington: ". . . war is not a business Congress can engineer. It is properly *executive business,* and the moment Congress passes beyond the line of providing for the wants of the government, and deciding the purposes of the war, to say how it shall be conducted, the whole thing will prove a failure." [9]

Conservative appeals, however, did not shake the radicals in their determination to call the administration to account for its conduct of the war. By December, 1861, their accumulated grievances against the President had become too powerful to be shunted aside by any arguments for party regularity. They were resolved that not the preservation of the Union and the authority of the federal government but emancipation must be the principal, the "sole real" objective, the one paramount reason for fighting the war.

In early 1862, Greeley, who had been in a conciliatory mood for months and had been following the administration lines of policy, again deviated from his established course and thundered for the immediate and absolute destruction of slavery. Emancipation, he insisted, must be proclaimed without delay, as a measure of military necessity. "It is high time that we had either war or peace," suddenly shouted the momentarily muted editor; "and a contest in which we guard and protect our enemies on their most exposed and critical point is not war. . . . It is at best but one of those sham fights so current of late on the Potomac." [10]

Lincoln was disgusted. He had too many enemies in Washington already, and he did not need another in New York. When on December 2, 1861, Greeley had declared that the majority in the Republican Party were in accord with the sentiment of his paper, that the sole purpose of the war was "preserving the integrity of the Union and vindicating the rightful authority of the Government," Lincoln had devoutly expressed hopes that Greeley had abandoned the camp of the Jacobins. But the editor had added, cautiously: "What we do demand and insist on is that, as the efforts and sacrifices of the Nation are not to be perverted to the overthrow of Slavery, so *they shall not be rendered ineffective or fruitless by anxiety to uphold and perpetuate Slavery*." [11]

At the time, Greeley admitted that his position was merely one of expediency, but he emphatically did not believe that there were "true and hearty Unionists" who would refuse to fight for the Union if Negroes were allowed and invited to do so.[12] As December gave way to January, Greeley began again to hear the voice of the radicals, and he decided that it was high time that the Negroes be allowed to fight beside the other true and hearty lovers of the Union—high time that emancipation be everywhere proclaimed as a doctrine which motivated the continuation of the war to a successful, if not a speedy, conclusion.

As the year 1862 dawned, the radical abolitionists expressed publicly a revolting disgust for Lincoln's cautious border-state policy. Not many of the developments of 1861 had been to their liking; therefore, they began the new year with a new determination to destroy slavery, to rid the nation of the dangers of southern domination, and to control the South after the war had been won. Thus, the "lure of loot" infused a crusade whose banners bore the words of freedom.

On the day after New Year's, Horace Greeley lectured in Washington, and Abraham Lincoln, Secretary of the Treasury Salmon P. Chase, and half of the members of the Congress heard him proclaim that the real objective of the war must be the destruction of slavery. The audience, fully packed with an abolitionist majority, applauded loudly each time the editor repeated that slavery's destruction was the "sole purpose of the fight," and it gave vehement approval to the orator's assertion that the rebels had no right to own anything. This, continued Greeley in explanation, was Andrew Johnson's opinion—the enunciation of a patriot and the wisdom of a statesman.[13]

According to a *Tribune* correspondent, someone in the government had asked Lincoln if he would attend this lecture. He replied, quickly: "Yes, I will. I never heard Greeley, but I want to hear him. In print every one of his words seems to weigh about a ton; I want to see what he has to say about us."[14]

It did not take the President long to discover what Greeley had to say about him and his associates. He attended the lecture at the Smithsonian Institution, and saw, with amazement, that when Greeley spoke of the destruction of slavery being the "one sole purpose of the war," he looked directly at the Presi-

dent, as if he were removing from print all the words of commendation which had poured forth from his pen in reference
to Lincoln's December 3, 1861, message to Congress. Lincoln sat
on the platform with Gideon Welles, the Connecticut Yankee
who had absolutely no admiration for the editor of the *Tribune,*
with Edward Bates, who had been Greeley's choice for President in 1860, and with Salmon P. Chase, who was, like Greeley,
now a full-fledged member of the radical clan and a possible
opponent for Lincoln in the race for the Republican nomination in 1864. When most of the audience stood up and joined
in wild cheers at Greeley's pronouncements, Lincoln sat still on
the platform with an impassive face. After the lecture was over,
he remarked casually, according to George W. Julian: "That
lecture is full of good thoughts and I would like to take the
manuscript home with me and read it over carefully some Sunday." [15]

As we have seen, for months Lincoln had been striving to obtain something resembling co-operation from Greeley. Now, in
this speech of January 2, he received an open affront from the
erratic editor. Lincoln was puzzled and dismayed. He asked
Homer Byington, a New York *Tribune* correspondent in Washington, "What in the world is the matter with Uncle Horace?
Why can't he restrain himself and wait a little while?" Byington replied that one man did not write all that appeared in the
Tribune, hoping thus to calm the perturbed President. "Well,"
retorted Lincoln, "I do not suppose I have any right to complain; Uncle Horace agrees with me pretty often, after all; I
reckon he is with us at least four days out of seven." [16]

Of course, Lincoln exaggerated here, as he sought in his mind
for some means of bringing Greeley back into the realm of moderation. However, he knew that one man who had been seated
on the platform with him during the lecture approved Greeley's
every statement. This man was Salmon Chase. And as early as
May, 1862, long before the editor himself had thought of Chase
as a presidential possibility, even before he had made his in-
credible proposal that Chase be given the command of the Army
of the Potomac, Chase found reason to court Greeley's favor and

to congratulate him on his now vigorous antislavery policy. Obviously enough, the ship of state floundered in troubled waters, thought Chase; he was outnumbered in the Cabinet, and therefore he sought support from Greeley. Since the editor could easily become an anchor to windward, the Treasury Secretary wrote to him, informing him that two lucrative Treasury clerkships were vacant and that they would be filled upon Greeley's recommendations. In the next sentence of the missive, the secretary, already preparing himself for the role he hoped to play against Lincoln in but two years, took occasion to thank Greeley for the "generous and disinterested support" of his paper in the past and during the present trying months.[17]

Greeley approved of Chase's vigorous manner, but he failed to comprehend the shadows and the delicate hesitations found in Lincoln's early 1862 antislavery policy. These delicate shadings and this halting manner toward the problem stand forth clearly in a letter which Lincoln addressed to Greeley on March 24, 1862, and which he carefully marked "Private." Freedom for the slaves should be urged "persuasively" on the South, not "menacingly." He was "anxious," "a little uneasy," somewhat groping in his straightforward, confidential, revealing missive to the man who had written him again, demanding that he emancipate the slaves immediately and that he employ them to fight "against the rebels." As he always did, Lincoln carefully phrased his reply to the great editor, to the man whose support he so earnestly needed, so fondly desired. Thus, he wrote privately:

Your very kind letter of the 16th to Mr. Colfax, has been shown to me by him. I am grateful for the generous sentiment, and purpose, expressed toward the administration. Of course I am anxious to see the policy proposed in the late special message, go forward; but you have advocated it from the first, so that I need to say a little to you on the subject. If I were to suggest anything it would be that as the North are [sic] already for the measure, we should urge it *persuasively,* and not *menacingly,* upon the South. I am a little uneasy about the

abolishment of slavery in the District, not but I would
be glad to see it abolished, but as to the time and manner of doing it. If some one or more of the border-states
would move first, I should greatly prefer it; but if this
can not be in a reasonable time, I would like the bill
to have the three main features—gradual—compensated
—and vote of the people—I do not talk to members of
Congress on the subject, except when they ask me—I am
not prepared to make any suggestion about confiscation
—I may drop you a line hereafter. . . .[18]

Lincoln wanted Greeley to be with him on his policies. He
reached out for Greeley's help and influence again in this letter. He took care on the principal pressing issue to reveal his
mind fully, even with its awkward corners, to Greeley. Could he
have Greeley with him, he remarked, each man could do more
for the country. But Greeley missed his rare opportunity, not
seeing that by co-operation rather than by opposition he could
best serve his own interests as well as those of the Union he
loved.[19]

Although the radicals were pleased in early 1862 to hack
away the secondary appendages of slavery, such victories only
magnified their great fundamental purpose—to bring about the
emancipation of all the slaves in the southern states. In July,
when McClellan had stumbled back from Richmond and the
nation was momentarily appalled by his astounding defeat, the
Jacobin chiefs thought they saw a chance to accomplish their
objective under the guise of military necessity. Charles Sumner
went to Lincoln immediately, urging him to issue a proclamation of emancipation on July 4 in order to make the day "more
sacred and historic than ever." And Seward noted apprehen-
sively in a letter to Charles Francis Adams, in London, that the
radicals were demanding an edict of universal emancipation as
a war measure. Enthusiastically in the *Tribune*, Horace Greeley,
having thrown away Lincoln's letter of March 24, cried that
"emancipation by weakening the Confederacy would insure a
speedy, overwhelming triumph for the Union." But Lincoln

turned his usual irritating deaf ear on the radicals and to the noisy Greeley.[20]

Just a year before, the editor had told his friend Moncure Daniel Conway that Seward was a "worthless minister" because he possessed a policy. Now, Greeley filled the columns of his *Tribune* with demands for an antislavery policy, with orders that Lincoln dismiss the "proslavery generals who control the Union armies." A proclamation of emancipation, the editor predicted, would "lift the nation right off its feet, and surprise it into one unanimous yell of enthusiasm." [21] Privately, Greeley remarked that he did not intend to abate his vociferous efforts until emancipation was a reality.

Furthermore, he joined with the war governors in this summer of 1862 in demanding that the Negroes be allowed to fight for the North. The draft and the new levies weighed heavily upon the war-weary people and the harassed governors and men of the press. More and more of the governors and newspaper editors began to listen to another proposal for securing men to meet the military's endless demands—the proposal that Negroes be used as soldiers. Governor John Albion Andrew of Massachusetts, after the July 3, 1862, call, growing worried as he saw the best youth of his commonwealth slain on the battlefield, turned plaintively to Senator Sumner. "Is not a Negro, good enough for them, good enough for us?" he asked. And Horace Greeley echoes, "Shall we love the Negro so much that we lay down our lives to save his?" [22]

It was at this time, with the cries for emancipation and for the use of Negro troops growing stronger in every quarter, but nowhere more so than in the *Tribune,* that Lincoln called in James R. Gilmore to see him again, reminding him of the arrangements which had been made for private governmental information and planning to reach Greeley by way of Robert Walker and Gilmore. After talking of this old scheme for some moments with Gilmore, the President disgustedly remarked, "I infer from the recent tone of the *Tribune* that you are not always able to keep Brother Greeley in the traces." Gilmore responded that he had handed the editor many memoranda sent on by Walker, but that it had not done much good. Thereupon, he had taken the liberty of showing Walker's dispatches to Greeley's managing editor, Sidney Howard Gay, and this had softened Greeley's wrath on several occasions.

"What is he wrathy about?" asked the President. Gilmore retorted that the war was "going too slow to suit Greeley, and worse yet, the administration was not attacking slavery as it should." Moreover, Gilmore hinted to Lincoln that it was rumored in the *Tribune* office that Greeley was writing an appeal to the country that would drive the President into action.[23]

Making mental note of this rumor, Lincoln asked, "Why does Greeley not come down here and have a talk with me?" Gilmore declared in reply that such an interview had been proposed, since the editor had visited the President before, but that in this case Greeley had haughtily demurred. He even remarked cagily that he would not allow the President to act as an advisory editor of the *Tribune*.

"I have no such desire," exclaimed Lincoln. "I certainly have enough now on my hands to satisfy any man's ambition. Does not that remark show an unfriendly spirit in Mr. Greeley?" In reply, Gilmore doubted that Greeley intended to appear unfriendly, for he still maintained a strong personal regard for the President. However, McClellan's failure at Richmond and the administration's do-nothing slavery policy troubled the *Tribune* editor, since for years his paper had been a "big gun for the antislavery propaganda." Now the abolitionists were striding forward in larger numbers than ever with a fresh fury of attack, and Greeley, ever interested in the welfare of enslaved human beings, did not wish to be left behind.[24]

Gilmore's explanation did little to satisfy Lincoln, nor did the former's words make him think any more highly of Greeley. Certainly the editor did not hold him in high personal regard, and his refusal to talk matters over with the President, construe it as one might, was an exceedingly unfriendly, perhaps a hostile, gesture.

Back in New York, Horace Greeley, whose editorial abilities had gained so much from his great and warm personal qualities, was hard at work on what he believed to be an edict from the people. Although he had been intense in his pursuit of many goals, he was never more absorbed than when he advocated freedom for the slaves and the employment of Negro troops. He knew that the Jacobins stood behind him, and considering himself to be a true democrat, he believed the masses always to be with him. Hence, before he had completed his remonstrance to Lincoln, he entitled it "The Prayer of Twenty Millions," because he felt certain that many people stood behind him, praying his prayer with him. If he wished Lincoln to proclaim emancipation, doubtless so did twenty million others—people who read his paper and believed his words. Such was his egotism.[25]

On August 13, 1861, General John C. Fremont had issued his proclamation, as commander of the Department of the West, freeing the slaves in Missouri; without hesitation, Lincoln had revoked the proclamation, then dismissed Fremont when he would not submit, in order to save the border states for the Union. Later, General H. J. Hunter, in command of the Department of South Carolina, Florida, and Georgia, declared those states under martial law and the slaves in them free (May 9, 1862). Despite the fact that the retraction of Fremont's proclamation had produced a definite feeling of bitterness in a certain substantial segment of the northern population, Lincoln also revoked Hunter's order. Then he answered the delegates sent to him by northern clergymen to pray him to declare slavery at an end in the southern states by refusing their prayers. Although Greeley had originally been incensed by Lincoln's remanding of Fremont's order, his ardor had somewhat cooled in the months of November and December, 1861. However, as has been indicated, by May of 1862, Greeley was again loudly beating his editorial drums for emancipation. Therefore, when Lincoln revoked Hunter's order and when he refused to heed the prayers of a large body of northern clergymen, Greeley raved and roared in the columns of the *Tribune*. As he prepared his "Prayer of Twenty Millions"—a scorching attack to be delivered against the administration in the heat of summer—the editor could not find public epithets suitably reprehensible to heap upon Lincoln's head. Furthermore, he gloated that the President would be unable to "revoke" his open letter from the people of the North as he had so unceremoniously revoked the orders of Fremont and Hunter. This prayer would be answered with action—with emancipation.[26]

Already Greeley felt that he had won one point, although his influence had had little to do with Lincoln's decision. On July 22, 1862, just one year after the first Battle of Bull Run, all of the national commanders were ordered to employ as many Negroes as could be used advantageously for military and naval purposes, paying them for their labor and keeping a record as to their ownership, "as a basis on which compensation could be made in proper cases." Thus, events were creeping along toward a true statement of the great problem, without which it would never be solved, when Horace Greeley, having completed what he considered to be his masterpiece, published it in the columns of his New York *Tribune,* on August 19–20. It was his "Prayer of Twenty Millions." After condemning the President, it exhorted him not so much to general emancipation as to an execution of the existing laws, which, it declared, would free immense numbers of slaves belonging to men who had taken up arms against the government. It was impassioned and powerful; no one can deny that. But one passage will serve to indicate this:

> On the face of this wide earth, Mr. President, there is not one disinterested, determined, intelligent champion of the Union cause who does not feel that all attempts to put down the rebellion, and at the same time uphold its exciting cause, are preposterous and futile; that the rebellion, if crushed out to-morrow, would be renewed within a year if slavery were left in full vigor; that the army officers who remain to this day devoted to slavery can at best be but half-way loyal to the Union; and that every hour of deference to slavery is an hour of added and deepened peril to the Union.[27]

On July 13, Lincoln had decided to prepare some sort of emancipation proclamation, and through the summer days of heat and fury in Washington he worked on it quietly. He had it almost completed on August 20, unknown to Greeley, when the latter accused him of excessive proslavery sentiments. Further, in his two-column attack of bitterest innuendo, Greeley talked directly to the President, accusing him of "ignoring, disregarding, and defying" the existing laws already enacted against slavery.[28] "We complain," screamed the half-insane editor, "that the Union cause has suffered and is now suffering immensely from your mistaken deference to rebel slavery." [29]

With heartfelt sorrow, Lincoln read Greeley's bitter denunciation of his administration. He knew it would further damn him in the eyes of the people. He heard the cheers of the radicals. Yet he determined not to be influenced, not to be stampeded by it. He would not listen to Greeley as he had before the first Battle at Manassas. If the North would win what could be considered a victory, he would issue his proclamation. Otherwise, he would wait. Nevertheless, he must answer Greeley, answer him as effectively as he had answered Fremont and Hunter and the northern ministers. And he must do it through Greeley's own medium—the press. Therefore, he carefully prepared and worded an official statement, which he placed in the Washington *National Intelligencer,* for August 23, 1862. The document he produced in answer to Greeley's "prayer" challenges comparison with the "state papers of all times and all countries, for its lucidity and its courage." [30]

Perhaps anyone save Lincoln would have found it difficult to answer Greeley at all; and Lincoln's answer was not one in the sense of being a refutation. Nevertheless, it exhibits his view of the question, and is "perhaps as fine a piece of literature as was ever penned by anyone in an official capacity." [31]

[August 22, 1862, Executive Mansion, Washington]

. . . I have just read yours of the 19th, addressed to myself through the New York *Tribune.* If there be in it any statements or assumptions of fact which I may know to be erroneous, I do not now and here, controvert them. If there be in it any inferences which I may believe to be falsely drawn, I do not, now and here, argue against them. If there be perceptible in it an impatient and dictatorial tone, I waive it in deference to an old friend whose heart I have always supposed to be right.

As to the policy I "seem to be pursuing," as you say, I have not meant to leave anyone in doubt. I would save the Union. I would save it the shortest way under the Constitution. The sooner the national authority can be restored, the nearer the Union will be "the Union as it was." If there be those who would not save the Union unless they could at the same time save slavery, I do not agree with them. If there be those who would not save the Union unless they could at the same time destroy slavery, I do not agree with them. My paramount object in this struggle is to save the Union, and is not either to save or to destroy slavery. If I could save the Union without freeing any slave, I would do it; and if I could save it by freeing all the slaves, I would do it; and if I could save it by freeing some and by leaving others alone, I would also do that.

What I do about slavery and the colored race, I do because I believe it helps to save the Union; and what I forbear, I forbear because I do not believe it would help to save the Union. I shall do less whenever I shall believe what I am doing hurts the cause, and I shall do more whenever I shall believe doing more will help the cause. I shall try to correct errors when shown to be errors, and I shall adopt new views so fast as they shall appear to be true views.

I have here stated my purpose according to my view of official duty; and I intend no modification of my oft-expressed personal wish that all men everywhere could be free.[32]

Thus perfectly did Lincoln sum up his position. And, in general, although the radical Jacobins could not quell their cries for action, his words helped to steady many very ordinary people who had been unreasonably shaken by Greeley's blistering attack. Lincoln soothed many nerves, made many other persons angry, made a fool and laughingstock of Greeley. The editor, however, did not realize that he had been so thoroughly bested, so outstripped at his own game. His influence was not worth the price of one of his papers in Lincoln's house. He even tried to answer the President's superb missive; but his garbled words made his position only more embarrassing. True, the radicals still supported him, Chase still upheld him for his own personal reasons, and the editor still supported the Jacobins in their demands that Lincoln act. But, generally speaking, Lincoln had taken on Greeley at his own game and had bested him.

Consequently, one may easily compare Greeley and Lincoln as the representative exponents of the two policies currently followed in 1862. There was, first of all, in their personal relations at this time a fundamental lack of sympathy. They simply could not see things alike. Lincoln knew men; Greeley did not. Lincoln had a keen sense of humor; Greeley had none. Indeed, the two men, in 1862, had almost nothing in common, except that each wished the vast majority of the people to understand and to follow his policy. The *Tribune,* although it did not exert so powerful a force in formulating public opinion as it had during the seven years preceding the war, was still a far-reaching influence. It gave expression to the thoughts rising in the minds of many earnest men and women. No one knew this fact better than Lincoln, who, in stating his policy in a public dispatch to Greeley, complimented the editor and those for whom the *Tribune* spoke. Lincoln's words received the widest publicity, and were undoubtedly read by virtually every literate Northerner.[33] Yet the President knew that his victory had been a small one, that Greeley's letter, although it might not represent the prayers of twenty million people, expressed more than the mere rantings of one hostile editor. Many in the Union desired military action; many more desired emancipation for the slaves.

Realizing that, in order to save the Union, some of the slaves must be freed (at least theoretically) and some must be "left

alone," the President, with real reluctance and deep sorrow, at
last squarely faced the problem of emancipation without the
correlative plan for the removal of freed Negroes from America.[34] He had prepared his proclamation after deciding definitely
to act, on July 13, and he had informed his Cabinet of the plan.
Nevertheless, the President waited for a propitious moment. At
last, on September 17, the battle of Antietam occurred, when
Robert E. Lee and his Confederate forces invaded northern
territory. Although the result of the battle was a victory for
neither side, it seemed to Lincoln that the North could claim
enough of a victory for him to keep his bargain with God and
release his proclamation. This he did then on September 22.[35]

When Greeley, who had so long been clamoring for this public statement of policy and decision, first saw the document—a
paper which actually bore none of his influence—he remarked
joyously: "Henceforth and forever we shall be free people." [36]
But even he was obliged to admit, shortly thereafter, that it had
been issued in advance of public opinion, not behind it, as he
had claimed for so long. And this fact was speedily borne out
by the victories of the Democrats in many of the elections in the
northern states in the autumn of that same year. Proof that
Postmaster-General Montgomery Blair had prophesied aright lay
in these election returns; the Democrats were now able to say
that the war was a war against slavery and not a war to save
the Union. Lincoln's August 22 letter lost some of its force after
the September 22 emancipation proclamation. The Democrats
gained political power. Everywhere it was said that the Civil
War was being waged solely to manumit the slaves. Lincoln was
troubled. Greeley should have exulted, but, as usual, he complained, blaming the administration for the Democratic victories
and for the military failures and inactivity.[37]

However, the President had more problems than merely those
connected with the matter of emancipation. The constant warfare of the irreconcilable antislavery men on General George B.
McClellan brought on a Cabinet crisis in the summer of 1862.
Up to the time of the appointment of Edwin M. Stanton as Secretary of War, on January 16, Benjamin Wade and Zachariah

Chandler and their ardent Jacobin followers, though constantly
sniping against the "young Napoleon," had found little popular
or official support for their anti-McClellan campaign. Chase, it
is true, had early embraced their side, but he was not an effective
party intriguer and enjoyed little personal influence or prestige
in the White House. He was already laying plans for the presidential succession, and undoubtedly his alliance with the Jacobin
leaders and his antagonism to McClellan—of whom at first he
had been a warm defender—were explained in large measure by
this ambition.

In Stanton, on the other hand, the radicals discovered a far
more adroit and useful ally. Their exultation at his elevation
knew no bounds. The Jacobin press, led, of course, by Greeley's
Tribune, hailed Stanton's promotion to the Cabinet as the beginning of a new day. "There is a very general agreement,"
wrote Greeley with confidence, "that the appointment of the
new secretary means business. . . . No man ever entered upon
the discharge of the most momentous public duties under more
favorable auspices, so far as public confidence and support can
create such auspices." Moreover, "here is the man who would
know how to deal with the greatest danger then facing the country—treason in Washington, treason in the army itself, especially the treason which wears the garb of Unionism." [38]

Yet, once again, Greeley's predictions were doomed to original disappointment. Stanton had been in the Cabinet almost
eight months when the President issued his watered-down emancipation proclamation. McClellan was still in command. In the
autumn, Greeley lamented that the war dragged on, that the
eastern and western generals were absolute failures, and that
Lincoln's proclamation had simply "freed the slaves where his
word meant nothing, but in the regions where he could have
unlocked their shackles, he took care that they should remain
in chains." In addition, the President had not preached and
still was not preaching the abolition gospel; he "had deliberately
refrained from declaring emancipation as a purpose of the war."
He had justified it as a military necessity, and in that way alone.
With increasing vigor, Greeley attacked the feebleness of form

and the exception of areas from the operation of the proclamation. He demanded that the President "furnish a further proof of his zeal for freedom." [39] And when the Democrats carried many of the elections, with McClellan still in power and Stanton having "fallen down" in his responsibility, the editor again wept for his bleeding country.

When the voting citizens of New York State, rebelling against the emancipation proclamation, the growing power of the federal government, and the increasing radicalism of the Jacobin elements within the Republican Party, elected Horatio Seymour as the Democratic governor, Greeley became incensed. Again he insinuated that Lincoln was to blame for the New York tragedy. Had he been fair in his treatment of the anti-Weed elements in the state, this tragedy would never have occurred. But the editor misinterpreted the signs of the times. Many voters felt discontented at the way in which the Republicans were prosecuting the war. And Horatio Seymour found himself to be the newly elected chief executive of the Union's most populous state and in a position to capture the leadership of the state-rights forces—a leadership that might well place him in the White House two years hence. To the task of crystallizing, organizing, and inspiring the opposition, Seymour brought an incorruptible integrity and a scholarly intellect. Lincoln, beholding the rise of this man with well-placed apprehension, saw another ogre facing him from the Empire State. Shortly after the Democratic upsurge, therefore, being in lowly mood because of Greeley's incessant press attacks, the President told Weed that Seymour had greater power for good than did any other man in the country. He could bring the Democrats into line, defeat the Confederacy, and save the government. "Tell him for me," wrote Lincoln to Weed, "that if he'll render this service to his country, I shall cheerfully make way for him as my successor." [40]

However, Seymour decided to disregard Lincoln's proposal, of which the frightened and inconsistent Greeley had no knowledge, and to make his inaugural a ringing denunciation of the tendencies of the day—a combined attack upon Lincoln and the moderates as well as upon Greeley and the radicals. This he

did. He launched into· a condemnation of the war on both political and economic grounds, declaring that the central and
western states had abandoned Lincoln because he had abandoned his border-state policy and his adherence to states' rights.
Furthermore, interspersed through his political and economic
dissertation, and illustrating his exposition, were the new governor's comments upon the unconstitutionality of the emancipation proclamation, arbitrary arrests, and conscription.

The address became a sensation. The Indiana Legislature
acknowledged Seymour as its leader; border-state governors commented approvingly. Many journals hailed it as the enunciation
of a brave new doctrine. But Greeley, who had, almost incessantly, been condemning Lincoln for some of the identical crimes
charged to him by Seymour, eschewed all rationality and common sense and denounced the address as "dexterous dishonesty,"
concocted of "cowardice, drunkenness, and masked disloyalty,"
delivered by a demagogue.[41]

When Lincoln read these comments, he was utterly con-
founded. Greeley was still attacking him daily, but he was also
condemning Seymour in the same inane language. At this point,
recalling how the editor had attacked each of his generals, almost
all of his policies, and also his skillful enemies, Lincoln decided
that Greeley and his national influence ought to be counter-
acted by some means. He had at hand no solution. Nevertheless, he hoped that the editor's incessant attacks on everyone
from Buell to Seymour to Halleck to McClellan would eventually open the eyes of the public to his inconsistency and his inability to think clearly.

In reference to Major General Don Carlos Buell, Greeley
had been unusually critical. For the *Tribune* had carried a Cincinnati dispatch, of February 7, 1862, which spoke freely of the
"inefficiency and uselessness of General Buell." Solely at his
door, ran the item, rested the responsibility for the chance the
enemy had had to fortify Bowling Green. Then, when the
northern troops took Fort Henry and Fort Donelson, the unruly
editor of the *Tribune,* unable to evaluate properly a first-rate
achievement, editorialized, on February 8: "A few more events

such as the capture of Fort Henry, and the war will be substantially at an end." He had still been gloating on February 14, when he told of a letter found at Fort Henry, which had been written by a spy from Paducah and which contained six pages of minute descriptions of "gunboats, armaments, and the like, but which did not give the strength of our land forces, because, thanks to the prompt and rapid movement of General Grant, nobody in Paducah could learn it." [42]

Such statements had been typical of Greeley's military gloatings and glumness throughout 1862. However, Greeley refused to admit that any of his editorial elaborations upon military events or faltering generals had been in the slightest degree inaccurate.

Tribune correspondents had sent Greeley news from Fort Henry of Lieutenant S. Ledyard Phelps, who, as a naval officer, had led a group of wooden gunboats up the Tennessee River and had "found the Union sentiment strong" in the South. Greeley editorialized quickly: "Old men, young children, youths, women, and maidens, turned out to greet the flag they had so long known only in dishonor and under insult. . . . They wept tears of exultation, and brought gifts of their substance to the friends who represented the Government they love." [43]

After lauding Burnside's success at Roanoke, and noting that reinforcements were moving to Hunter at Leavenworth for his anticipated operation, Greeley had continued his exaggerations: "The cause of the Union now marches on in every section of the country." "Every blow tells fearfully against the rebellion." "The rebels themselves are panic-stricken, or despondent. It now requires no very far-reaching prophet to predict the end of this struggle." [44]

Moreover, Greeley, praising the new Secretary of War in connection with the victories at Fort Henry and Fort Donelson, had cried exultantly: "To Edwin M. Stanton, more than to any other individual, [is due the credit] . . . for these auspicious events." However, Stanton quickly denied himself this honor, and was later grateful that the confused, erratic editor did not associate the defeats of 1862 with his person.[45]

Meanwhile, the gloom which had settled over the Confederate commanders after the Henry-Donelson disasters began to lift. Greeley, however, still hoped for a speedy victory, but Lincoln, who obtained his war information from sources other than the *Tribune,* remained more practical.[46]

Thus, in general, did Greeley begin his series of condemnations of Lincoln's generals. Don Carlos Buell was "inefficient," and Edwin M. Stanton, not General U. S. Grant, had accomplished the unusual victories at Forts Henry and Donelson. Greeley, during 1862, had also lashed out at a number of naval officers and had condemned General Henry W. Halleck for his flagrancies and failures. That summer, the new situation in Tennessee and Kentucky heightened Lincoln's deep concern which had initially developed after George B. McClellan's retreat to Harrison's Landing on the James River. He became anxious, "almost impatient," to have Major General Halleck in Washington, despite the fact that the western commander had been enduring the gibes of many radicals and many editors, including Greeley. "Having due regard to what you leave behind, when can you reach here?" the President asked. Halleck replied that Grant had just arrived from Memphis, and that he expected to leave in two days, on July 17. Before departing, Halleck revealed an aspect of his nature which Greeley had, through his correspondents in the field, never been privileged to see; the major general addressed a confidential note to William Tecumseh Sherman, in which he declared sadly: "I deeply regret to part from you. . . . I am more than satisfied with everything you have done. You have always had my respect, but recently you have won my highest admiration. Good-bye, and may God bless you." [47]

However, toward his successor—another of Greeley's habitual editorial targets—there was no unbending. Grant indicates in his *Memoirs* that little was said to him about his future operations; yet Halleck had given him a helpful appraisal when he acknowledged that it was not in Grant's nature to be stampeded. It seemed to Greeley that neither man could be stampeded.

Then Halleck departed, telling Sherman he had studied out

and could finish the campaign in the West, but that he did not understand and could not manage affairs in the East and had no desire to be involved in the quarrels of Edwin Stanton and George McClellan. However, no appointment to high office that had been consummated up to that time stood more clearly upon past accomplishments than did Halleck's, in spite of the fact that he had endured so much of Greeley's public criticism, based almost solely upon the movement against Corinth. The radical-minded editor, hearing of Halleck's new elevation, continued to complain bitterly of the major general's order of the preceding November, which had barred escaped slaves from all of the army camps. It seemed to him that, in choosing generals, Lincoln had no judgment at all. Whether it was Halleck or McClellan, the President could not find a suitable general, one who loved the Union cause. At length, however, Greeley was forced to concede in the favor of the President and the general that "General Halleck is a thoroughly educated soldier; he has large natural capacity; he has brains enough to detect and profit by his own errors." [48] It was not easy for the editor to make such admissions, and this one he made with reluctance, after he saw that his influence upon Lincoln's military appointments, if he had ever possessed any, was waning.

Returning to Greeley's idol in the Cabinet, Edwin M. Stanton, one finds that he spent most of the months of 1862 in a desperate effort to make "McNapoleon" fight or get out of the army. He had prepared an elaborate intrigue in February, shortly after Lincoln had named him to the War Secretaryship, which he had hoped would end McClellan's career. However, the scheme had exploded before it ever had come to fruition. But with its collapse, the secretary had begun work on new plans to remove his most detested army commander. Being a master of the art of propaganda, he turned to this method to weaken McClellan in the public opinion. General Grant, appearing out of obscurity, had just achieved the capture of two enemy forts, Henry and Donelson, in Tennessee, and the great majority of the people, hungry for a military success, hailed the new general as a public benefactor and hero. Stanton seized the opportunity to add his voice to the chorus, and at the same time to administer a slap to McClellan.

The eager but thoughtless Greeley, his own radical aide, almost foiled his patiently developed plans by heralding him, instead of Grant, as the Tennessee victor. Stanton had to silence Greeley's inappropriate babbling, while knifing McNapoleon in the same operation. Consequently, on February 19, he addressed a letter to the *Tribune* for public consumption, ostensibly to announce officially the Tennessee victories and to assure Greeley that he had not been responsible for them. But actually, after extending the nation's congratulations and public gratitude to Grant, the Secretary of War closed his missive with a superb piece of innuendo. He contrasted, by implication, the action and the success in the West with the inactivity and the emptiness in the East. The letter accomplished its mission. Taking Stanton's lead, Greeley immediately forgot that he had been praising the War Secretary for the western achievements, forgot Grant altogether, and lashed out at McClellan with a virile verbal assault. The editor charged that McClellan wanted to prevent any decisive military action in the East in order that he might bring about a peace without victory, a peace which would preserve slavery, so that he himself might be elected President with southern support.[49] In fact, Greeley, urged on by Stanton, continued his attack upon McClellan until the general was at length removed by a disheartened and discouraged Lincoln.

After nine months of anti-McClellan propaganda, stirred up and served principally by Greeley in his *Tribune,* Lincoln determined, under his own will, to dismiss McClellan, hoping despondently that such action would please the radical Jacobins and would lessen some of the tension. The Democratic victories in the autumn, coupled with the unpopularity of his emancipation proclamation both among radicals and moderates, directed Lincoln in the course of some forward action. McClellan must go.[50]

On November 5, 1862, the general was dismissed. Exultantly, Greeley crowed to his radical friends and to his patient readers, "God will save us yet." He even added, "At the last hour [Lin-

coln acted]—too late to save his friends, but not too late, we
trust, to save the country." [51]

But this was not all that Greeley had to rejoice over in early
November, for on October 24 Lincoln had removed Don Carlos
Buell, one of the editor's most prominent targets, replacing him
with William S. Rosecrans, a general whom Greeley and the
radicals had long favored for this western position. Momentarily,
Greeley and the Jacobins were delighted with the President's
judgment. They praised him for realizing at long last that the
war must be fought by Republican generals whose hearts were
in the cause. The elated Greeley cried, "Be patient a very little
while, and all the 'augurs that won't bore' will be served as Buell
has been," as McClellan has been.[52]

With these two generals out of the way, Greeley and the
Jacobins in Washington breathed more easily. These two singular men had commanded the two largest armies in the nation,
and nightmares in which they marched their troops upon Washington to establish a Democratic dictatorship had unnecessarily
but mercilessly plagued these radical minds. At last, it seemed
to Greeley, in spite of the ordeal of the autumn Democratic
victories, despite the odiousness of Horatio Seymour in New
York State's executive mansion, and in spite of the many northern military failures and hesitations, the catastrophes had at last
borne fruit. Lincoln's mild policy toward the South and toward
slavery had been instrumental in precipitating these catastrophes,
but they had caused Lincoln to see the radical light and to remove Buell and McClellan. [53] It would have surprised the editor
to know that his reasoning was again fallacious and that he had
not motivated Lincoln's movements. The President was not a
radical.

In fact, Lincoln took some definite steps to minimize Greeley's influence upon other people, already determined that he
himself would not yield to it. One of these steps again proved
Lincoln's sagacity and his bucolic belief that "fire must be fought
with fire." In 1861, John W. Forney had founded the Washington *Sunday Morning Chronicle* as a weekly newspaper in which
the administration could set forth some of its views, with par-

ticular reference to the army personnel and the politicians who made Washington their headquarters. In November, 1862, the very month in which the President removed McClellan, not at Greeley's insistence but at his own behest, Lincoln suggested to Forney that his paper be made into a daily. This was done. Thenceforward, the views of the administration, particularly upon military matters, were indirectly set forth in the Washington *Daily Morning Chronicle*. It is said that Lincoln made this suggestion and then had it carried out in order that the daily paper might counteract the influence of Greeley's anti-administration New York *Tribune*. For the President remarked that he feared the adverse influence that Greeley's paper might have upon the Army of the Potomac. By this time, Lincoln had given up all hope of co-operation with Greeley, and was striving to counteract his dangerous influences in every way possible.[54]

In November, 1862, with Buell and McClellan gone, the radicals now had hopes for Lincoln's eventual salvation. Therefore, they took the next necessary step, demanding that he make his Cabinet an integral unit, entirely radical or entirely conservative, instead of adhering to that polymorphic conglomeration of divergent views and personalities. "The country is in no condition to tolerate divided counsels," proclaimed Horace Greeley, leading in the cries for action. When Lincoln did not immediately respond, the Jacobins renewed their attack upon Seward, to them the most unspeakably disgraceful member of Lincoln's advisory board.[55]

That Seward had supported McClellan almost to the day of his deposition was common knowledge. Furthermore, he had opposed emancipation and even now was attempting to dissuade the chief executive from that policy. Then, in December, another charge was hurled against him—that he had once been known to be a great antislavery advocate, and that he had now added to his other vices those of an apostate. Moreover, the blatantly published dispatches to Charles Francis Adams, which Greeley was enabled to read in December, 1862, seemed to verify this latest charge. Therefore, one need look no further, it was declared, for the influence that had persuaded Lincoln, every time a patriotic general like Fremont or Hunter had issued a proclamation freeing the slaves in his military district, to issue orders revoking the decree. The Jacobin press, led by Greeley, teemed with denunciations of Seward, his policies, and his influence upon the President. The time had come to rid the government of this incubus once for all.[56]

Leading the parade which was to precede Seward's political funeral, the writers of the New York *Tribune* denounced the Secretary of State for his "shallow smartness" and for the "coldness, alienation, and almost open hostility which the incompetent cunning of our Secretary has exerted in our regard in almost every quarter." [57] Of course, Greeley directed his writers, poured venom into their pens, concurred in their statements, and directed the entire attack of wholesale Seward denunciation.

Lincoln had made no move to comply with these Jacobin demands by the end of the year. Consequently, in January, 1863, Greeley again loudly demanded a unified Cabinet, one which believed in emancipation. He even made a trip to Washington, openly telling his friends that he was going "to see about getting Seward kicked out" of the government. He did not call on Lincoln at all. Instead, he worked among his congressional friends and his fellow intriguers of the press. He left happily, assuring everyone that the evil genius would be removed within a week. Local political bosses and newspaper correspondents had encouraged him in his endeavor to oust Seward and were to continue his work after he returned to the *Tribune*. And, in fact, step were taken to fulfill his prophesied results. Congress caucused on January 17. House Republicans tried to inject some radical blood into the Cabinet by force. Nothing was accomplished, however; and, on January 20, in anger, these Republicans decided not to admit to Congress any representative elected to that body from any southern state in which the President should attempt to reconstruct a government by military authority, on the assumption that such representatives would be upholders of slavery. Nevertheless, these Jacobins and Greeley found, to their dismay and discomfiture, that Lincoln remained unmoved, that he was determined to adhere to his own policies, and that he intended to maintain his array of divided advisers.[58]

Meanwhile, Greeley and his radical friends still had military headaches, even with the removal of McClellan and Buell. The Army of the Potomac had been placed under the command of Major General Ambrose E. Burnside, and he was putting it on the march, for a change. The general-in-chief and the commander of the engineer brigade did not appreciate the way in which Burnside had put the army over the road, moreover. But the newspaper correspondents were at first enthusiastic, while the subordinate officers evaluated the feat properly. From Falmouth, on November 18, came this dispatch:

> "Napoleon once told me," says Jomini, "that he knew no method of conducting a war except to march twenty-five miles a day, to fight, and then to encamp in quiet." Burnside begins like a believer in that policy. Whatever his other qualities, he is at least very much in earnest. He has already inspired the army to a marvelous extent. Officers [are] wont to believe that a great command cannot move more than six miles a day, and accustomed to our old method of waiting a week for the issue of new clothing or a month for the execution of an order to advance, rub their eyes in astonishment. . . . We have changed our base from the Manassas Railroad to Aquia Creek and the Rappahannock. *We have marched from Warrenton forty miles, in two days and a half.*[59]

Thus wrote a *Tribune* war correspondent to Greeley, and the editor temporarily exulted. Another reporter for his paper wrote some days later that "time was everything with Burnside." He "was promised, when he left Warrenton, that the pontoons should be here before him, via the river. This delay may cost us thousands of lives, and prolong this campaign several weeks." [60]

When he received this dispatch, the editor's joy began to fade. Furthermore, several references in the detailed descriptions of the advance indicated that Burnside had expected to gain considerable reward from his rapid march, and that he had

thought there were definite advantages in fighting at Hanover
Junction. In addition, the dispatch revealed the blunders "made
by the High Command," blunders for which payment could be
expected in terms of the loss of many lives. Greeley exploited
this knowledge, using it as ammunition for criticizing not Burnside, not the army, but Lincoln and the distressed administration.[61]

Payment came. Late in December, 1862, gloom had settled
heavily over the nation, particularly over the federal capital.
The appointment of Burnside as McClellan's successor had failed
to help the political situation at Washington, as has been seen.
The soldiers under McClellan, furthermore, since they liked
the general, attributed the change to Cabinet interference and
hence did not enter with enthusiasm into Burnside's plans, especially those which involved marches of twenty-five miles a
day.[62] At Fredericksburg, the army failed signally, casting the
country into deeper gloom, spreading over all the Union a
blanket of deep despair.[63] Congress *knew* that the President was
badly advised by his Cabinet; as we have seen, the demand for
change grew apace. But Greeley had been unable to remove Seward or to dictate military policy to the chief executive. The
gloom, it seemed, lay heaviest upon the editor, although he had
no means of reading the sorrow in Lincoln's heart. In desperation, he suggested to the President that the latter appoint Robert J. Walker as Secretary of State. After all, Walker had once
served with Gilmore as a mediary between them, and Walker
was "probably the greatest American who had ever lived since
Benjamin Franklin." [64] With a weary smile and a half-despairing
gesture, Lincoln also disregarded this advice, kept Seward in
his Cabinet post, and sought elsewhere for a new general.

Lincoln did not find a satisfactory general to succeed A. E.
Burnside after he had slaughtered the northern boys at Fredericksburg. However, with great reluctance, the President placed
Joe Hooker in command of the eastern armies. He did it only
because he thought it wise at the moment to endeavor to placate
the radicals, so that Seward might retain his Cabinet post.
Hooker had intrigued long and diligently to secure the com-

mand of the Army of the Potomac, and he had mouthed much about dictators, looking in Lincoln's direction. On January 26, 1863, he succeeded to Burnside's post, and the following day Lincoln wrote him a fatherly letter, similar in character and tone to many of the fatherly letters he had penned and would yet pen to his erratic opponent Greeley.

> I have heard, in such a way as to believe it, of your recently saying that both the army and the government needed a dictator. Of course it was not for this, but in spite of it, that I have given you the command. Only those generals who gain successes can set up dictators. What I now ask of you is military success, and I will risk the dictatorship.[65]

Greeley's Washington correspondent crowed that Hooker's appointment meant "forced departure from the armies of the half-loyal, half-hearted, heavy and slow generals." Greeley himself predicted that Hooker would uproot from among the generals the "pro-slavery subservience to West Point traditions, of indifference to the cause of the Republic," which, he insisted, had paralyzed the Union's military efforts thus far.[66]

But again Greeley's predictions failed. He had misjudged Hooker, but Lincoln had not. May, 1863, and Chancellorsville— Joe Hooker was defeated by the forces of Robert E. Lee. When the *Tribune* editor heard the news, he again despaired. He reversed his militant "Forward to Richmond" cry, and wrote pensively: "We must all exercise patience. We strongly hope to have the pleasure of diffusing joyful intelligence before the end of the week." [67] Unfortunately, the end of the week brought no joyful intelligence, and Greeley's attempt at patience was not long-lived.

He had been hopeful, he declared falsely, as long as there had been any room for hope. But when the end of that week and of the next came and went without substantial change, he cringed in print at the thought "that the finest army on the planet had been defeated by an army of ragamuffins." [68]

Lincoln himself, doubting Hooker's ability, had hoped that

some good might come of the eastern campaign. But at last he received the bad news of Chancellorsville at about the same time Greeley did, in the form of a laconic telegram from Dan Butterfield. He read it, and his sallow face turned ashen-gray; to a caller he said, as if dazed, "My God! what will the country say?" [69]

As the days passed into weeks, it slowly became evident that the country, even with Greeley over the *Tribune,* had nothing to say. The depression which had followed Fredericksburg did not openly reappear, except in the heart of a certain newspaper editor who was preparing himself for the day when he would write his own obituary in blood. [70]

Then came Gettysburg and Vicksburg, with the summer granting joy to some hearts, mellowness to others. Not to Greeley. He continued to criticize the administration during the summer, desiring peace but finding none.

CHAPTER EIGHT

Longing for a Leader

Once, during this critical period, a committee of men induced the President to examine a newly invented repeating gun, the peculiarity of which was that it prevented the escape of gas. After due inspection, Lincoln remarked casually: "I believe this really does what it is represented to do. Now, have any of you heard of any machine or invention for preventing the escape of gas from newspaper establishments?" [1]

Lincoln, however, had great respect for the press. He often complained of the injustice of Greeley's criticisms and of the false light in which they placed him before the country. It seemed almost as if Greeley's opposition to his policies annoyed him more than did anything else during the war. Once, with great earnestness his friend Chauncey Depew suggested, "Why don't you publish the facts in every newspaper in the United States? . . . The people will then understand your position and your vindication will be complete."

"Yes, all the newspapers will publish my letter, and so will Greeley," replied Lincoln. "The next day he will comment upon it, and keep it up, in that way, until at the end of three weeks I will be convicted out of my own mouth of all the things he charges against me. No man, whether he be private citizen or President of the United States, can successfully carry on a controversy with a great newspaper and escape destruction, unless he owns a newspaper equally great with a circulation in the same neighborhood." [2]

Truly, Lincoln respected, at times almost feared, Greeley. He determined from the outset to listen to him; but he soon learned to avoid his advice. He kept Greeley's letters, even the most hysterical ones, and he read them often. He was a methodical president, and Greeley's missives had their place in his method of administering a nation.

Noah Brooks, who would have become private secretary to the President in his second term had Lincoln lived, and who always enjoyed a position of confidence at the White House, recorded his impressions on the matter thus:

> Naturally, Mr. Lincoln was methodical in his habits; he was scrupulously exact in all the details of his office, and his care for written documents was sometimes carried to an extreme. . . . In his office in the public wing of the White House was a little cabinet, the interior divided into pigeonholes. The pigeonholes were lettered in alphabetical order, but a few were devoted to individuals. Horace Greeley, I remember, had one to himself. . . .[3]

As the years of 1862 and 1863 dragged slowly by, as Lincoln filed away Greeley's many missives in his special pigeonhole, answering but a very few of them, the editor himself believed and even publicly stated that Abraham Lincoln was serving his only term in the White House. The President, he told his friends and readers, was too informal to head the complex machinery of government. Besides, beneath Lincoln's outward inefficiency there lay a more fundamental fault: his aim was wrong. He was an idealist, in the sense in which the practical man uses that term; his hope of reconciling the South without a decisive victory was futile, and in pursuing it he was surrendering the weapons upon which control of the South must rest. Gazing at the stars, his feet stumbled over the obvious and endangered the precious burden he was carrying.

Equally was he unsatisfactory to all radicals, who, like Greeley, were the real idealists, following stars. With a weak, at times a mawkish, sentimentality where persons were involved, Greeley thought that Lincoln failed to grasp the serious, God-given duty of his age. His actions and his words proved him a laggard on the paramount subjects of freedom and equality. If one were to accept the editor's August 20, 1862, estimate, the President was the twenty million and first person to be converted to the need for and the doctrine of emancipation. Lincoln had professed to prefer gradual emancipation to immediate emancipation; his proclamation had borne out his statement of profession. He preferred a gradual winning of the war in order to save the Union. He talked only of saving the Union; and as 1862 passed and 1863 turned toward autumn without any recession in the blood-letting, Greeley found Lincoln to be too sentimental about the Union. He would be a gradual leader of his people, and the impatient Greeley was no gradualist.[4]

Lincoln felt that if Greeley and the radicals would only give him time, he could work out most of his problems. However, Greeley incessantly meddled in political as well as in military affairs. When he could not go to Washington himself, he used his correspondents there to initiate difficulties. Particularly was this true in the connection of the President's numerous Cabinet crises. In December, 1862, for example, Chase was in a real dilemma. Together with Greeley, he had freely condemned the conduct of the war, and his relations with Seward scarcely permitted formal conversation. All this the Senators knew, and consistency demanded that he join them in their persistent attacks upon Lincoln and his mild military policies. On the other hand, ethics demanded that he remain loyal to the group of which he was a member. It seemed that he must do as Seward had already done, tender his resignation; therefore, on the morning of December 20, he called on the President with Stanton to support him and delivered his notice of withdrawal from Lincoln's advisory council. Holding both the resignations of Seward and Chase, Lincoln availed himself of the ample opportunity which this singular occurrence afforded him. He refused the resignations of both men, and each leader had to acquiesce in order to maintain his prestige, while the two factions had to consent in order to retain their respective leaders. By December 21, Seward had agreed to remain in the Cabinet if the President insisted; the following day, Chase did likewise, and the Cabinet crisis had formally ended.[5]

The whole affair was then published in the *Tribune,* with Greeley, dissatisfied as he was with affairs, intruding his opinion that both Chase and Seward should have resigned.[6]

Although this crisis had thus ended before Christmas, Greeley continued to wrangle about it in the *Tribune* for months, vehemently urging Seward into some overt act which would precipitate the next revolt of Cabinet personnel. When Seward did make the cutting but imprudent declaration that the "extreme advocates of African slavery and its most vehement opponents are acting in concert," Greeley smarted at the insult. He retorted that Seward was guilty of insubordination, that he had been sending dispatches without showing them to the President for approval or rejection. Henry J. Raymond, as usual, replied for his friend in the *Times,* declaring that not one dispatch, "not merely and exclusively formal and technical in its character," had been sent to any foreign minister without the approval of the President, and that this statement was made on the authority and by the permission of the President and of the Secretary of State.

This was a flank attack which Greeley had not anticipated— Lincoln supporting Seward and Raymond, and deliberately declaring his public statements to be erroneous. Further, it indicated that the *Tribune* editor had undertaken a most gratuitous task. Nevertheless, Greeley maintained that the exception was so broad that it was virtually a confession of guilt. This was a pointless and a fallacious statement, and the editor knew it. He was strong in a single charge, but his enemies were more resourceful; Lincoln was beginning to combat him in his own medium, on his own ground. On February 27, 1863, Raymond wrote that, "I think that before the matter is ended I shall put Mr. Greeley into an awkward position." [7] And he did. For more than two weeks after February 20, the *Times-Tribune* feud continued over this matter. Then it subsided, but Greeley had lost the round. He took up other objections to Lincoln and Seward as the year 1863 progressed, but none of them proved very rewarding.

Early in 1863, Congress was divided into hostile factions. We have already seen that the Cabinet was by no means a harmonious body. The loyal press of the country was bitter and arrogant in its criticisms of the administration; Greeley's condemnations did not stand alone, even though Raymond generally worked for Lincoln, endeavoring to keep certain papers in addition to the *Times* on the chief executive's side. In the army there were mutterings of discontent, with Hooker referring to Burnside as a "butcher" and then turning into an excellent example of a butcher himself, and with many lesser soldiers desiring the return of McClellan to command. An old officer was arrested for saying that the Army of the Potomac with "Little Mac" at its head should "clean out Congress and the White House." [8]

Many had despaired that the North could ever win the war. Greeley, as we have seen, was among these. In private conversations, which were reported to Lincoln, he declared that Chase, at that instant his favorite statesman, should long ago have been placed at the head of the Army of the Potomac. If this had been done, the "war would have been over by now," he cried. Also, he talked publicly of the possibility of using foreign intervention to end the stalemate, as he considered it. [9] With his "shallow mentality," under the stress of the war approaching an attitude rivaling the bizarre, he thought of taking matters in his own hands. Distrusting Lincoln, since the latter had bested him in the exchange of letters in the summer of 1862, beginning with the above-mentioned "Prayer of Twenty Millions," and always a sentimental pacifist at heart, he had become firmly set upon the idea of obtaining peace at almost any price. He entered into some sort of secret correspondence with Clement Vallandigham and other opponents of the war.[10] Then, he approached the French foreign minister, M. Henri Mercier, urging him to initiate some form of foreign intervention involving both Great Britain and France or France alone—some intervention which would drive Lincoln into bringing an end to the war.[11] Greeley conducted several interviews with Mercier, begged him to initiate a correspondence with Lincoln and Jefferson Davis, told him that the people would gladly welcome any foreign mediation which "should look to a termination of the war." "I mean to carry out this policy and bring the war to a close," Greeley confided to Mercier and to many of his *Tribune* friends; "you'll see that I'll drive Lincoln into it." [12] But again Greeley failed.

The finality of the British Cabinet decision in November, 1862, relative to proposals of mediation or intervention was not accepted at the moment by Greeley or some other eager pacifists, although the time was soon to come when its permanence would be proved. The British press was full of suggestions that the first trial might more gracefully come from France, since that country was presumed to be on more friendly terms with the United States. Others, notably John Slidell, at Paris, held the same view; and, on January 8, 1863, Slidell addressed a memorandum to Napoleon III, asking separate recognition of the South. The following day, Napoleon dictated an instruction to his ambassador, M. Henri Mercier, offering friendly mediation in courteous terms, but with no hint of an armistice or of an intended recognition of the South. Meanwhile, Mercier had again approached Lord Lyons, British minister at Washington, alleging that he had been urged by Greeley to make an isolated French offer, but that he felt this to be contrary to the close harmony hitherto maintained in Anglo-French relations. Lyons did not wish England to intervene, and Mercier expressed interest and concern about his government attempting to mediate alone. However, he approached the Secretary of State with the note he had received from the French government; but Seward quickly declined the offer, Lincoln feeling that any open acceptance of offers of mediation would be an overt recognition of the Confederate States. Mediation by foreign dignitaries, foreign diplomats, and foreign powers was the last thing that Lincoln wanted. Again he and Greeley were at odds, and once again Greeley was left outside the government door, his plans foiled, his ideas disregarded, his dreams shattered.[13]

At every point the policy which Lincoln had somehow set in motion with painful foresight and labor was working, but it was working very slowly. He saw that many months of struggle and blood and patience might separate him from the completion of his task—the preservation of the Union. Many months—and in less than a year there would be a presidential election, and he might be obliged to leave his task unfinished. He did not hesitate to say frankly that he wanted the opportunity to finish it. Among the leaders of his party were a few conservatives who, in the autumn of 1863, supported Lincoln in his desire for a second term, but there were more who doubted his ability and who were secretly looking for an abler man to replace him.

Meanwhile, a strong and open opposition to his re-election had developed much earlier in the radical wing of the party. The real cause of this opposition was Lincoln's unswerving purpose to use emancipation merely as a military and a propaganda measure, not as a means of satisfying the earnest abolitionists. The earliest active form which this opposition took was under the direction of Horace Greeley. By the spring of 1863, having become thoroughly disheartened by the slow progress of the war and by the meager results of what he considered to be an almost worthless and meaningless emancipation proclamation, he began to look in every direction for someone to replace Lincoln the following year. Eventually, he settled upon General William S. Rosecrans, a western commander, who at that moment was the most successful and most popular general of the army in the public eye.[14]

After consulting with a number of Republican leaders, Greeley decided that someone should go to Rosecrans and sound him concerning the possibility of his becoming the Republican standard-bearer in 1864. James R. Gilmore, who wrote radical propaganda material under the pseudonym of Edmund Kirke and who, as we have seen, was a good personal friend of Greeley's,

was chosen for this mission. As he recounts in his *Personal Recollections,* the extent of the discontent with Lincoln was enormous. For when he departed on his way to talk with Rosecrans,
Greeley gave him letters from "about all the more prominent
Republican leaders except Roscoe Conkling, Charles Sumner,
and Henry Wilson." [15]

Greeley's idea was, as he instructed Gilmore, to find out, first,
if Rosecrans was "sound on the goose"—sound on the antislavery
policy—and, secondly, if he would consider the nomination to
the presidency. If Gilmore found Rosecrans satisfactory, Greeley
boasted that he would force Lincoln to resign, put Hannibal
Hamlin in his place, and compel the latter to give Rosecrans
the command of the whole army. Although these statements were
utterly insane, Greeley believed then that, with Rosecrans heading the entire army, the war could be finished promptly, and
the general would naturally be the candidate for the Republicans in 1864.[16]

Gilmore went on his mission. Rosecrans seemed to fulfill
Greeley's two qualifications—soundness on the antislavery question and proper political attitude. Finally, the informal ambassador laid his case before the general. Rosecrans immediately
declined the honor. "My place is here," he insisted stoutly. "The
country gave me my education and so has a right to my military
services." [17]

Gilmore brought the news of the general's refusal back to
Greeley. Again the editor's plans had been foiled. Soon, however, news came of Rosecrans's failures. He was disgraced in the
public eye, and Greeley thanked his political stars that nothing
had come of the mission.[18]

Many factors motivated Greeley's decision, in 1863, to search
for a new Republican candidate for 1864, one who could and
would outshine Lincoln in the popular mind and hence replace
him as the party's standard-bearer. Among these factors were
Lincoln's failure to answer most of Greeley's impassioned epistles,
the fact that when the President did answer the editor he invariably bested him at his own game, and the failure of Lin-

coln to consult him on any of the Cabinet or other political
appointments, as well as all of the military appointments, including the selection of generals for both the eastern and western campaigns. Another factor which disturbed the editor's
equilibrium was the problem of the draft. The Confederate
States stole a march on the Union by the passage of an early
conscription act. The full significance of this law coming to the
North at about the same time that news was arriving of the
victories of Lee over McClellan, in 1862, caused it to be received
with emotions ranging from admiration to anger and disgust.
By some specious type of reasoning, the editor of the New York
Tribune considered that a "dirty and ignoble" trick had been
played upon the Union. In a curiously inaccurate and horrifying ill-reasoned statement, he explained the causes for the necessity of calling more men in the North as the result of this southern conscription act.

> It [the federal government] had men enough three
> months ago, as things then were, to have broken the
> back of the Rebellion. But the traitor chiefs, realizing
> their extremity, took the last desperate step that usurpa-
> tion and tyranny could devise. They ordered a levy *en
> masse* of all the Whites and Mulattoes in the South be-
> tween eighteen and fifty-five years of age, and sent their
> myrmidons into every county and neighborhood to en-
> force the decree.[19]

Greeley took care to insert this odious editorial in his paper
on July 4, Independence Day, 1862; from that point forward
into early 1863, he openly cursed the South for its conscription
act, lamented the fact that this caused the North to need more
men, but refused to support any program for Union conscription. He continually placed Lincoln in a distinctly disadvan-
tageous position, because the northern military situation was
growing desperate in late 1862 and early 1863, especially after
the Fredericksburg slaughter and the other concomitant disasters. Finally, therefore, in March, the North passed a con-

scription act, further antagonizing an already half-crazed *Trib-une* chief.

On the political front as a whole, the developments of 1863 were not propitious to the Lincoln administration. In March, there came simultaneously the conscription law and the *habeas corpus* act, both of which Greeley began to condemn with vigor. As to the *habeas corpus* law, it soon became evident that, while not restraining arbitrary arrests as intended, it did contain an indemnity feature by which federal officials committing wrongs upon citizens' rights within a state were exempted from existing judicial penalties. The *Tribune* thundered against the injustice of both acts; in regard to conscription, the editor, now growing in importance as the pundit of the radical Jacobin North, declared with cold bitterness:

> It is folly to close our eyes to the signs of the times. The people have been educated to the idea of individual sovereignty, and the principle of conscription is repugnant to their feelings and cannot be carried out except at great peril to the free States. . . .[20]

Lincoln could have reminded the erratic editor that, on August 9, 1862, after having printed the bombastic editorial against conscription on July 4, as a tribute to American independence Greeley had remarked that, since the South had inaugurated the whole affair, it would be perfectly honorable for the North to pass a conscription act, thus giving the "Confederacy and the southern sympathizers" within the Union "a bowl of the same soup." [21] But Lincoln said nothing. He had even been informed by some of his advisers that, by the spring of 1863, Greeley was an ardent supporter of all of the essential features which would compose the soon-to-be-passed enrollment act. But his informants were in error, or the editor again changed his mind and altered his position.[22] As soon as the act was passed by Congress and signed by the President, Greeley became its arch rival. Throughout the country in those early days of conscription Greeley rioted with the rest of the bewildered and imbittered North.

The law was poorly framed and poorly administered; it became a favorite theme of denunciation, not only by those who felt as Greeley did, but also by liberal Democrats and supporters of individual liberty.[23]

In addition to complaining publicly through the *Tribune* about the conscription act and its poor functioning qualities, Greeley wrote to Secretary of War Edwin M. Stanton, outlining his disgust with the act and the public disfavor with it:

> . . . The people have been educated to the idea of individual sovereignty, and the principle of conscription is repugnant to their feelings and cannot be carried out except at great peril to the free States. . . . The entire system must be changed. . . . Drafting is an anomaly in a free State; it oppresses the masses. Like imprisonment for debt . . . it must and will be reformed out of our system of political economy.[24]

Greeley added, fallaciously, that "if the pay in the army were raised from thirteen to twenty or twenty-five dollars, or even, if necessary, thirty dollars a month, the army would be filled." [25]

It is now agreed that Congress, during the Civil War, possessed the constitutional right of conscription, but this point was disputed during the 1860's. To Greeley, it seemed that Lincoln and his administration had concocted the formula, copying certain disgraceful southern ideas, to weaken the Union's morale even further and to ensure a northern defeat. Convinced that Lincoln had utterly subjugated himself to the prevarications of Seward and the distasteful influence of Weed, Greeley abandoned himself to an orgy of criticism which abated only as the summer of 1863 wore on into autumn.[26]

As his attacks upon the draft act grew less vociferous and venomous, Greeley began to pursue a quite ambiguous policy toward the whole affair. An example of this lay in his advice—in the *Tribune* of August 8, 1863—in reference to the employment of substitutes in the conscription. Apparently, in all sincerity, the inconsistent editor wrote quaintly:

If you are drafted, and can possibly leave your business, Go. If you cannot, send your substitute—the best man whom money will obtain. If you cannot possibly get one, pay the commutation. But pay $500 for a substitute rather than $300 as commutation—if for no other reason than that, if you send a substitute, you cannot be drafted again while he continues to serve in your stead; whereas, if you commute, that suffices only for this draft, and leaves you clearly liable to the next, if a next there shall be.[27]

Those who opposed the draft had formerly felt themselves to have a friend in Greeley. But after August, 1863, he wavered from one side to the other, sometimes, as above, advising the citizenry to comply with the law and not to commute unless this proved to be absolutely necessary, and at other times attacking the "Enrollment Act" as a traitorous piece of legislation fit only for "Southern aristocrats." Fortunately for the Union, Lincoln remained aloof from Greeley, who was still searching for a suitable candidate to replace the President, and adhered to his own counsel.

In the elections of 1863, the Republicans, having campaigned diligently throughout the North, remembering the huge Democratic sweeps of the preceding autumn, carried every state but New Jersey, "which does not count," *Harper's* explained exultantly. The conservatives interpreted the results as a popular ratification of the administration's policies, now "fairly and squarely endorsed by the people." To the amazement of all of the radicals, Greeley, who had strangely modified his attacks upon the conscription act and who had not made a personal unkind remark against Lincoln since the latter had proclaimed in a few but memorable words at Gettysburg the thoughts of a war-weary but determined "nation under God," agreed publicly with this statement of the moderates. Suddenly, with almost no forewarning (certainly Lincoln was not prepared for it), Greeley began rather confusedly to accept administration policies as they had been fixed, not by his influence but by Lincoln's hand. To be sure, there were no real words of praise for Lincoln's utterances as yet, as there were to be shortly; yet the *Tribune's* silence in regard to the victories at Vicksburg and at Gettysburg, in appraisal of the Gettysburg address, with reference to the President's reconstruction policy, was an anthem new to the ears of Lincoln and his followers. When the results of the autumn elections were announced, Greeley even urged his party to forget its factional differences and to follow the President's leadership unitedly.

However, the startled Jacobins, who openly cursed Greeley's waywardness while Lincoln chuckled contentedly, viewed the astonishing Republican successes at the polls in an entirely different light. To them it appeared that the people had placed a permanent seal of approval upon their radical war program; emancipation was at last safe from any popular attack. Greeley was out of the fold for a time, but he would return. He always had. Let the war drag out for a few more bloody months; let him finally fathom the truth that Gettysburg and Vicksburg had not brought the South entirely to her knees. He would soon be among the ranks of the radicals once more.[28]

At this time the Union began to face the difficult problem of reconstruction, with the rift between Lincoln and the radical Jacobins growing ever deeper. In midsummer, 1863, the Jacobins began to ponder this problem from their point of view. Charles Sumner hoped that one of the Gulf states, possibly Florida, could be inducted into the Union under congressional supervision, with an entirely new state constitution in which slavery would formally be abolished. This would be a controlling precedent for the admission of other states. The radical press sent up trial balloons in every direction in order to test public sentiment concerning this vital problem. Who should direct the process of readmission?—Congress or Lincoln? What conditions should and "must" be imposed upon the "conquered states"? Emphatically newspaper editors declared that only loyal men should be permitted to participate in the restored southern governments, and that Congress alone had the right and the authority to decide whether representatives and senators elected from the recon-structed states were entitled to their seats.

However, in this radical press campaign to drum up sup-port for their plans and for their violent program, the Jacobins noticeably missed the powerful voice of the *Tribune.* Greeley was still honeymooning with the administration. Publicly he an-nounced that he favored a speedy re-establishment of the Union with absolutely no harsh measures of punishment for the de-feated southern people and for the beaten and penitent south-ern states. To the utter horror and complete disgust of the radicals, he proclaimed boisterously that he wished to entrust the difficult task to Lincoln.[29] It would require a greater length of time than they had anticipated for the erratic editor to re-turn to his former belligerent policy of condemning each and every administration-sponsored program.

Meanwhile, the President, rejoicing at Greeley's momentary, albeit unsolicited support, prepared to take another dangerous step. On December 8, 1863, he took a portentous plunge against most of the leaders of his own party, sending to the Congress a special message containing a copy of a proclamation, already issued, irrevocably committing the executive to a general plan of reconstruction. He announced, as the conditions necessary for the recognition of a state, three preliminaries: first, "the com-pletion of an organization by persons who," secondly, "have sub-scribed to the Constitution of the United States, and," thirdly, "who have pledged themselves to support the acts and proclama-tions promulgated during the war with reference to slavery." [30]

Greeley, being in Washington at this time, listened atten-tively to this first portion of the message and was quite thor-oughly satisfied with it, although the Jacobins winced in many instances with horror. Greeley had not come to see the Pres-ident, and he did not visit him; however, he did glory in the conscientiousness of this special message, as it further dealt with the status of individuals by prescribing an oath to be used in states lately "in rebellion," pledging the person taking it "to support the Constitution of the United States, and all acts and proclamations put forth during the war relating to slavery, except such as had been formally repealed." This oath might be taken by all men except high military and civil officers of the Confederate States and others who had resigned civil or military positions in the United States "to take part in the rebellion, or who had unlawfully treated Negroes in the United States service who had been taken prisoners." To all persons taking this oath, full amnesty for past offenses was granted. This section particularly appealed to Greeley's fancy, and he was well pleased.[31]

As the editor leaned forward in his seat in the congressional hall, he heard the message continue, declaring that "whenever, in any rebellious state, a number not less than one tenth of the voters at the presidential election of 1860 should desire," having taken the oath, "to reconstitute their state, they should have the power to do so, and thereupon return to the old relations with the Union." Furthermore, the proclamation recognized that the admission to seats in the federal Congress of persons elected as senators and representatives rested entirely with Congress, being clearly outside the executive control. While thus laying down "for rebellious states" a method for returning to their allegiance, "it must not be understood," the message concluded, "that no other possible mode would be acceptable." [32]

Moreover, the President also reviewed the situation in the war up to this point, citing the acceptance which his proclamation of emancipation had met at last, as well as the justification and the growing approval of the employment of Negro soldiers, the lessening of the proslavery sentiment in the border states, the favorable change in the feeling of Europe.

Finally, Lincoln maintained that his action was authorized by the federal Constitution or by special statutory laws, and thus he ended this historic statement of his mild but exceptional reconstruction policy. John Hay, who was on the floor of Congress when the message was read to the assembled multitude, recorded that the approval seemed unanimous, although, of course, the true state of feeling was far different from that. Actually, the Jacobins thought the whole Lincoln program despicable; but Horace Greeley, having listened with rapt attention to the entire address, cried to those around him that the speech was "devilish good." [33]

This statement of Greeley's that the speech was "devilish good" bears close scrutiny. Almost every item mentioned by Lincoln in the prepared speech had been opposed at one time or another by the erratic editor. He had fought against Lincoln's border-state policy, declaring that it was merely a means of condoning the evil practices of slavery. He had demanded that the President proclaim emancipation; and, when the proclamation was issued, he condemned it from beginning to end. Instead of desiring Europe's support of the northern cause, he had asked M. Henri Mercier to intervene in American affairs in behalf of obtaining a speedy peace or a suitable armistice of some form or character. Now he upheld and glorified all of Lincoln's policies, policies which he had daily, weekly, monthly endeavored to thwart. He even upheld the President's mild reconstruction policy—but soon he would be less commendatory of that.

The war dragged on interminably. The year 1864 arrived. There was everywhere a deep impatience with Lincoln's slow and conservative methods. Radical Republicans and antislavery leaders grew daily more angry at what they deemed his dilatory tactics in dealing with the slavery question, as well as with the potent problem of reconstruction. Indignation, too, was rampant because Lincoln had given so many high commands to men who were not strong in their antislavery feelings and expressions. There was widespread criticism also, and not only on the part of the Democrats, of his permitting the arrest and exile of the bitter Ohio "copperhead," Clement L. Vallandigham. This was attacked as "a violation of the Constitution, and of the right of free speech." Greeley, who had himself corresponded with Vallandigham on several occasions with reference to effecting "an honorable peace" between the two warring sections, disapproved heartily of Lincoln's decision, a decision which he had by no means dictated and in which he, as a true pacifist at heart, did not concur. As the days of 1863 turned the calendar to 1864, Greeley found his heart again weary of war, weary of the war President. Republican factionalism grew steadily, and James G.

Blaine lamented that the rifts could not be extinguished, even amid the agonies of war.[34]

Behind all of this endless wrangling was the natural disappointment at the seemingly infinitesimal progress which had been made in the suppression of the "rebellion," after the expenditure of such vast sums of money and the loss of so many thousands of lives. In January, feeling that this money and these lives had been spent in vain, that the South might yet defeat the Union, Greeley did what the radicals had been patiently waiting for him to do: he reversed his position once more. He was at odds with Lincoln again.[35]

One of the reasons for Greeley's abandonment of Lincoln in the beginning of 1864 lay in the fact that the President had ignored the editor's praise of his reconstruction policy. Greeley had not been rewarded for his brief support in any way. Furthermore, Lincoln was gradually turning to look for advice from the influential family of Blairs. Many evidences of intimacy between the President and the Blair family existed at this time. Lincoln's frequent trips to Silver Springs, the access of the Blairs to his private rooms, the President's crossing Pennsylvania Avenue for chats with Montgomery at the Blair "mansion," the sight of Montgomery's children playing on the White House lawn with the Lincoln boys—these affairs were common knowledge. They aroused to fury the anti-Blair element, the abolitionists and the violent radicals, who howled against Lincoln's association with this powerful clan of moderates. Greeley railed against the Blairs now, although he had once worked with them to boost Edward Bates for the 1860 presidential nomination, despite the fact that he had once associated himself with them in order to secure for John C. Fremont the appointment as commander of the Department of the West. Now, the Blairs were "a dangerous family"; they had "got Lincoln completely under their thumb." He joined the Chase following and denounced the entire family as a group "of Maryland serpents." If Lincoln would take directions from such a family, Greeley would find himself another presidential candidate.[36]

In his search to find a suitable radical for president, Greeley

at last landed upon Salmon Portland Chase. The editor could
not support Lincoln's renomination, "for," he insisted, "I
wanted the war driven onward with vehemence, and this was
not in his [Lincoln's] nature" to do. Moreover, in late December,
1863, he was beginning already to fear that Lincoln's "easy
ways," which he had praised three weeks before, "would allow
the rebellion to obtain European recognition and achieve ultimate success." [37] Thus he played upon the fears of the people.

Actually, during December the political front was rumbling
with threats of upheavals to come, and Greeley felt the impending turmoil. He was jealous of Lincoln's leanings toward the
Blairs, Seward, Weed, Bates, and other moderates. Had Lincoln
turned to him, given him a high political position, consulted
him daily for advice, he too might have become a conservative.
However, Lincoln held him at arm's length; instead of asking
his advice, he sent him communiques of government plans and
programs fourth-hand. Lincoln would show him no personal
kindness. Chase had. Perhaps, if he were placed in the presidency,
Chase would confide in him, ask his advice, appoint him to an
important office. Chase should be his choice.

In Washington, the radical Jacobins were discussing a Cabinet
housecleaning again, demanding the resignations of the two
prominent moderates, Montgomery Blair and Edward Bates. It
was rumored that fifty members of Congress had signed a peti-
tion to Lincoln asking for the dismissal of the Postmaster-General. The Chase boom, secretly sparked by new northern and
eastern forces, began to gather strength, to the anxiety of administration leaders. On the day after Lincoln had announced
his reconstruction policy, Chase's supporters in Washington
had held a meeting to discuss ways of pushing their candidate's
cause. It seemed to the Treasury Secretary's friends that Greeley
was almost ready to bolt into their camp. Certainly a little kindly
persuasion might send him and his *Tribune* into their midst.[38]

As for Chase himself, no prodding was necessary to kindle
his ambitions to take Lincoln's place in the White House. This
strutting master of the Treasury Department was a quadrennial
candidate for the presidency before and after 1864. Convinced

that he was of larger political stature than the Illinois lawyer "who had sneaked the nomination from him" in 1860, Chase had entered the Cabinet blissfully confident that the voters would yet recognize his transcendent abilities and call him to the office he was born to fill. As early as 1862, he had begun to make plans to take over Lincoln's work, and his friends had started constructing a political organization then. As we have seen, he courted the favor of Greeley from time to time, using the great propaganda machine built up by his ally, Jay Cooke, to sell national bonds and to advertise his financial and political merits. By the spring of 1863, he let it be known that he was in a receptive mood, and his friends openly suggested him as an excellent successor to Lincoln. Soon the elements of dissatisfaction within the party clustered around his candidacy. A few editors and many pint-sized political bosses tendered him their substantial endorsements. Privately, leaders like James W. Grimes, Oliver P. Morton, James S. Wadsworth, and others of similar note assured him of their support. In the autumn of 1863, after the Rosecrans fiasco, while he was verbally supporting the administration, Greeley began a private correspondence with Chase, in which he flatly informed the Treasury Secretary that he was his first choice to receive the Republican nomination the following year.[39]

In January, 1864, with the brief love affair between his paper and the administration ended, Greeley was breathing affection for Chase, as well as for John C. Fremont, in his columns. Furthermore, he recommended that the Republican Convention, scheduled for early June, be postponed until late summer. By that time, he hoped, all of the enthusiasm for Lincoln would have cooled, and the radicals could name their own nominee.[40]

In early February, however, Greeley was reluctant to go as far in backing Chase as he had gone four years earlier in backing Bates. A member of the "Committee of Five" working for Chase's candidacy in New York State, Judge James W. White, endeavored to force Greeley to bring the *Tribune* to the unqualified support of Chase. The editor reluctantly refused, declaring that, should he make his paper more partisan than it already was, he and his partners would sustain a financial loss they could ill afford to bear. Judge White took this to mean that, if the proper financial guarantees were made, the *Tribune* would become the organ of the committee. Thereupon, he conferred with his finance committee and procured sufficient aid to assure the owners of the *Tribune* against loss. When he took this news to Greeley, the latter was still reluctant, finally altogether refusing Judge White's appealing proposition.[41]

At about this same time, in mid-February, Greeley sounded a Joshua ram's-horn blast that he trusted would send Lincoln's Jericho walls toppling. He employed the same editorial techniques against Lincoln which he had used successfully against Seward four years before. He began by praising the President, declaring that he had "well discharged the responsibilities of his exalted station," having been "patriotic, honest, and faithful," so that the "luster of his many good deeds will far outlive the memory of his mistakes and faults." Secondly, Greeley admitted, in italicized words, that "*Lincoln is the first choice, for the next Presidential term, by a large majority of those who have thus far supported his Administration and the War.*" It would be strange, indeed, if this were not true, continued Greeley. Then, to clarify his point, he remarked:

> In the fearful ordeal through which we have passed, his place has necessarily and uniformly been first in the thought of the loyal millions; his name first, after God's, in their prayers. To say that, knowing far more, they think more of and feel a warmer attachment to him than to any other living man, is only saying that he has not proved an utter disappointment and failure.[42]

These sentences, read once, read twice, and then a third time, would not lose a peculiar lurking light, perhaps of personal jealousy and malice, perhaps of something else, something more akin to hatred. The editorial virtually insisted that the people would have loved any war president, that what they loved now was not Lincoln but a president who had not proved "an utter disappointment and failure." But this was not enough to satisfy the hate-hungry Greeley. He set down his doubts concerning the second-term endorsements given to Lincoln by several state legislatures:

> The loyal masses, not having begun seriously to think of the prospective Presidential contest, have not yet fixed upon someone else to succeed him in his high position. (Did Lincoln so overtop all other candidates that no others should be considered?) We answer in the negative. . . . Heartily agreeing that Mr. Lincoln has done well, we do not regard it as at all demonstrated that Gov. Chase, Gen. Fremont, Gen. Butler, or Gen. Grant, cannot do *as* well.[43]

In addition, Greeley declared that he favored the "salutary One Term principle," and summed up his arguments acidly:

> We freely admit Mr. Lincoln's merits; but we insist that they are not such as to eclipse and obscure those of all the statesmen and soldiers who have aided in the great work of saving the country from disruption and overthrow.[44]

On February 22, 1864, Greeley published an editorial similar to this masterpiece. Some considered that it favored the President. Actually, it was a thinly veiled mass of propaganda aimed at destroying any portion of Lincoln's popular pedestal that might still exist. Then, on February 23 and 24, the *Tribune* carried editorials openly favoring Chase's candidacy. At this time the Pomeroy intrigue was cleverly unearthed, and Greeley wrote that the circular by Samuel C. Pomeroy was authentic, that it reflected no ill repute and no discredit upon the excellent statesmanship of Salmon P. Chase.[45]

In actuality, by the end of February, 1864, despite the fact that he had staunchly refused the offer of financial assistance from Judge James W. White in return for openly supporting Chase and Chase alone, Greeley was the most ardent and the most positive and helpful journalist aiding Chase in his campaign to receive the Republican nomination for President or for any other office. The eccentric editor evidently regarded his idol qualified to fill any official role. Earlier, as we noted, Greeley had made perhaps his craziest proposal when, half-insane at the sluggish progress of the war, he had ordered Lincoln to make Chase commander of the Army of the Potomac. On September 29, 1863, the erratic "ink-slinger" (as he called himself) had written morosely to the Secretary of the Treasury: "If in 1864 I could make a President [not merely a candidate], you would be my first choice." [46]

Chase had then responded with an effusive letter of thanks, remarking incidentally that there were two well-paying clerkships vacant in the Treasury Department, into which he was willing for Greeley "to put a couple of his friends." Greeley had responded warmly; since that day, the two men had corresponded, waiting for 1864 and convention time.[47]

As February ended and March began, Greeley was certain that Chase would make the party's best presidential choice. Chase concurred in this belief. However, the skillful Lincoln managers proved to be too clever for Greeley once more. They outmaneuvered him, his paper, Chase, Pomeroy, and the entire organization backing the Treasury Secretary. During January and February, while Greeley was gloating about his new candidate and his new president, while he was writing defamatory editorials concerning Lincoln, while he was filling his columns with calumniations, the Lincoln managers were working through local, city, county, and state organizations and caucuses to ensure the nomination for Lincoln in the first ballot when the Republican convention met in Baltimore in early June. By the first part of March, the Chase boom had boomeranged. Chase's chances were insignificant if not hopeless. Seeing this at last, the Secretary of the Treasury asked Greeley and his friend James Garfield whether or not he should withdraw from the running. They advised him to do so. And as he did, he lamented the fact that America had lost a great opportunity for his services, while Greeley wept for himself, for his Jacobin associates, and for his country.[48]

With many self-commiserations, Greeley reluctantly resigned

himself to four more years of Lincoln. To a friend, Mrs. R. M. Whipple, he confided wearily:

I am not at all confident of making any change [in the presidency]; but I do believe I shall make things better by trying. . . . There are those who go as far as they are pushed, and Mr. Lincoln is one of these. He will be a better President . . . for the opposition he is now encountering.[49]

In line with this reasoning, Greeley continued his vigorous support of the radicals throughout March, and afterward, despite the fact that he had advised Chase to withdraw from the race. Both the *Tribune* and William Cullen Bryant's New York *Evening Post* continued to clamor for a postponement of the Republican Convention to some date in late summer—perhaps in September. On March 11, the *Tribune* publicly regretted the announcement that Chase had absented himself from the running, while, at about the same time, Greeley commented privately to a friend that "Lincoln is not out of the woods yet," adding that he would "keep up a quiet but steady opposition and, if we should meantime have bad luck in war, I guess we shall back them [Lincoln and his managers] out" before the convention "has adjourned." [50]

Greeley pursued his policy of opposition on almost every possible line between March and June, 1864. Furthermore, although his opposition was steady, it was not always quiet. Inevitably, he would entangle himself in military or naval affairs. And during this period he again crossed the path of and considerably angered the Navy Secretary, Gideon Welles. The squabble arose over S. F. Du Pont, a controversial naval officer, whom Lincoln classed in the same category as George B. McClellan— a misfit, "not nearly so fortunate an appointment as D. G. Farragut." [51]

In early 1863, this naval officer had been sent to menace the port of Charleston. He had proved incompetent and had utterly failed in his mission, finally declaring to Gideon Welles that he did not favor the policy of attack at all, despite the fact that

he had originally desired it, eagerly seeking the opportunity to
carry it out successfully. On April 7, 1863, he was ordered home
by Welles and Lincoln, and he returned to Delaware to "nurse
his wounds." Many Northerners now thought him deranged,
and he was replaced by Farragut, in the minds of the populace,
as a naval hero.[52]

Determined to justify the position and the action taken by
the administration, Secretary of the Navy Welles made a docu-
mentary report against Du Pont, which was supposed to be published and carried in all of the newspapers in order to clarify
the administration's decision in regard to the Charleston fiasco.[53]

As usual, Greeley took a partisan view, favoring Du Pont
with illogical fervor, vociferously opposing and condemning the
administration for its actions. In fact, the editor refused to publish the abstract of the report against Du Pont in the *Tribune*.
As this report was made public in April, 1864, Greeley endeavored to place Lincoln in a bad light through it, just prior to
the June assembling of the Republican Convention. He distorted
the truths in the case, and although he failed to weaken Lincoln's position materially, he brought down upon his head the
wrath of many administration supporters. On Friday, April 15,
Welles wrote bitterly in his diary that, "without ever looking
at the facts, Greeley has always vigorously endorsed Du Pont
and had his flings at the Navy Department." [54]

Greeley's intrigues failed. In early May, a large group of
radical Germans from St. Louis, as well as a representative number of abolitionists from New England, realizing that Lincoln's
enterprising managers had already captured for him the nomination at Baltimore, attempted to form a third party and
nominate John C. Fremont in a convention to meet at Cleveland. The important party bosses stood coldly aloof from the
movement, and it finally collapsed. However, certain significant
Republicans, among them John A. Andrew of Massachusetts
and Horace Greeley secretly urged forward this Fremont move,
hoping thereby to foil the plans of Lincoln and his astute backers. But, as June approached, all political signs seemed to point
in the direction of Lincoln's renomination. Greeley, feeling that

America lacked a leader in her President, certain in his heart that the Union must have a leader to survive, despaired.[55]

Lincoln's renomination had been assured because his managers were quick to read the signs of the times and to test the velocity and the validity of every anti-Lincoln movement. The editors actually had the same grievances against Lincoln which the radical politicians displayed; they had advised him to follow certain policies, and, too often, he had disregarded that advice. As an editor and a journalist, Greeley had given Lincoln the most voluminous amount of advice possible; as a wary man, not quite sure of his position but ever sure of himself, Lincoln had disregarded it. As June, 1864, approached, Greeley grew still more hostile toward the administration, but Lincoln's managers did not quail under fierce editorial attacks. Through state conventions, party caucuses of all sizes and types and varieties, through gatherings of every political shape and description, through meetings of the Republican members of Congress and of the state legislatures, Lincoln and his astute political supporters laid the groundwork for their convention victory. Clubs and societies were persuaded to make public endorsements of the President, while many legislators overstepped bounds in fighting for the renomination. Greeley found himself utterly outweighed.

During the last week in May, he tried again to halt the convening of the Republican delegates at Baltimore. "It's a mistake," he cried. "To nominate a candidate so early would expose the Union party to a dangerous and possibly successful flank attack." However, the Lincoln managers well knew that Greeley's proposal to postpone the convention was, in itself, a flank attack designed to give the radicals sufficient time to align themselves in proper order behind another, a "stronger" candidate.[56] No one listened to the editor's last-minute suggestions. He was impotent, his words unheeded.

It was at this time that Greeley again, in desperate struggles with his own soul, journeyed to Washington, not specifically to see Lincoln but merely as an exercise for his troubled brain. He called at the White House, talking there with the artist who

was painting the President's portrait. The story of his call is
vividly recorded by the conscientious portrait painter:

> About the first of June [1864] I received a call from the
> Hon. Horace Greeley, who was temporarily in Washing-
> ton. Very near-sighted, his comments upon my work,
> then about half completed, were not particularly grati-
> fying. He thought the steel likenesses in his book, *The
> American Conflict,* were much better. I called his atten-
> tion, among other points, to a newspaper introduced
> in the foreground of the picture, "symbolizing," I said,
> "the agency of the 'Press' in bringing about *Emancipa-
> tion";*—stating, at the same time, that this accessory was
> studied from a copy of the *Tribune.* Upon this his face
> relaxed. . . . Knowing that he had not been friendly
> to the renomination of Mr. Lincoln, it occurred to me,
> in my simplicity, that if I could bring them together, an
> interview might result in clearing up what was, per-
> haps, a mutual misunderstanding of relative positions,
> —though I had never known Mr. Lincoln to mention
> the name of the editor of the *Tribune* otherwise than
> with profound respect. Leaving my visitor in front of
> the picture, I went to the President's office to inform
> him of the presence of Mr. Greeley in the house, think-
> ing that he might deem it best, under the circumstances,
> to receive him below stairs. In this, however, I "reck-
> oned without my host." He looked up quickly, as I men-
> tioned the name, but recovering himself, said, with un-
> usual blandness, "Please say to Mr. Greeley that I shall
> be *very* happy to see him, *at his leisure.*" [57]

Apparently this calm remonstrance informed the artist, Francis B. Carpenter, that Lincoln would be *very* happy to talk with
the editor, if and when the editor himself desired an interview.
At this time the hostile Horace Greeley did not desire one, and
the two men therefore did not meet.[58] In about a week the Republican National Convention met in Baltimore, and Lincoln
was renominated. As far as New York Republicans were con-

cerned, the Weed faction ruled the day. Greeley remained on the outside, an unwelcome guest.

For chairman of the Union National Committee, the organization corresponding to the Republican National Committee today, the Baltimore convention—on June 9—selected Greeley's arch foe, Henry J. Raymond, delegate and committee member from New York, friend of Seward and Weed, editor of the powerful and influential *Times,* the counteracting force to Greeley's *Tribune.* Raymond's selection was a distinct victory for the conservative, or Seward-Weed, forces over the radical, or pro-Chase, faction among Empire State Republicans. Consequently, scarcely had Lincoln been renominated (to the horror of the now impotent Greeley), hardly had the convention adjourned, when a lively press battle developed between Raymond's *Times*—mouthpiece of the Weed interests and of the Union Party in New York —and the *Tribune* and the *Evening Post,* which the moderate William Cullen Bryant had relinquished for a time to the editorial whims of Park Godwin. Little came of the ensuing press battle, however, except that Greeley's influence seems to have been further weakened. Actually, this was merely a small phase of that larger and more vehement national struggle between radical Jacobins and moderate conservatives—a struggle that often, prior to Lincoln's death, threatened to split his party into irreconcilable splinters, and that proved such a nightmare to the President.[59]

It is not surprising that the editorial in the *Tribune* of June 9, 1864, announcing Lincoln's renomination, held forth scant hope for party harmony and unity during the rigorous campaign that lay ahead. Although Greeley's New York strength had been severely curtailed by his factional encounters with Seward and Weed, it must be remembered that the *Tribune*'s greatest source of power lay outside its own home state, in the middle states and the old Northwest. Even in 1864, it would not be incorrect to say that the *Tribune* was the leading Republican organ in the nation. And the *Tribune* frankly regretted the renomination of Lincoln, in spite of the fact that it "accepted the result as inevitable" and as "unquestionably representing the will of the party voter." "That the President has made grave mistakes in the prosecution of our great struggle," the editorial declared, "all are aware; that he has *meant* to do wrong, nobody believes. We cannot but feel that it would have been wiser and safer to spike the most serviceable guns of our adversaries by nominating another President" and thus "dispelling all motives, save that of naked disloyalty, for further warfare upon this administration." Once more, Greeley was knifing Lincoln in the back; the President might be renominated, but it was not too late to initiate a boom for a "more serviceable" candidate, forcing Lincoln to withdraw in favor of a "sure winner." Therefore, in full earnestness, Greeley concluded his editorial thus:

> We believe that the rebellion should have lost something of its cohesion and venom from the hour in which it was known that a new President would surely be inaugurated on the 4th of March next. . . . All that is of the past. The will of the great majority of the Unionists has been heard and it says, "Let us have Abraham Lincoln as our President for another term." We bow to their decision, and ardently hope that the result may vindicate their sagacity and prove our apprehension unfounded.[60]

Thus, the campaign progressed, without Greeley's active support, but with his active, secretive, deceptive intrigues in an effort to replace Lincoln with another candidate.

On July 18, Lincoln called for 500,000 additional troops to serve for one-, two-, and three-year periods. All of the discontent which had been prophesied by Lincoln's advisers broke forth upon the announcement of this call. The awful brutality of the war dawned upon the half-stunned nation as never before. A feeling of revulsion against the sacrifice of the nation's youth developed and would not abate. All of the complaints which had been urged against Lincoln both by radical Republicans and by McClellan Democrats broke forth afresh. The draft was discussed in terms which made it sound like the arbitrary whim of a tyrant. It was everywhere declared that the President had violated constitutional rights and prerogatives, personal liberties and guarantees, freedom of the press, and rights of asylum. To the New York *Tribune,* he had been guilty of all the abuses of a military dictator. Further, public criticism was freely made of his treatment of peace overtures. It was declared that the Confederates were anxious to make peace, that they had taken the first steps, but that Lincoln was so bloodthirsty that he was unwilling to use any means but brute force to end the conflict. Up to this time, Greeley had generally, with a few exceptions, demanded his "Forward to Richmond" policy involving a vigorous prosecution of the war. Except for a year filled with qualms over the legality and righteousness of the conscription laws, Greeley had incessantly supported the idea of calling and using a sufficient number of men to bring a military victory which would ring down the curtain on the bloody conflagration. However, opposed as he was to Lincoln's renomination, Greeley now led the criticisms, condemning the President as a military dictator and a tyrant thirsty for blood. He berated the President for the July 18 call. He called for peace; he utterly forgot an incident two months before which had impressed itself indelibly upon the mind of Lincoln.[61]

In May, when Greeley had been agitating for a postponement of the Republican, or Union, convention and for the nomination of a vigorous presidential candidate, one who would bring the war to a close with a decisive military victory, Senator John Dawson had proposed, in the Senate chamber, that the North should "tender the olive branch of peace as an exchange for the sword." Greeley had ridiculed the idea and suggested that Dawson, without waiting for his congressional colleagues to adopt his resolution, should set forth at once on a private mission to the camp of Robert E. Lee "with a whole cart-load of olive branches." "Some good may come of it," the editor chortled; "Mr. Dawson may possibly be treated as a spy." [62]

Shortly thereafter, in the same month, when peace was proposed in a resolution by a member of the Congress of the Confederate States, Greeley editorialized, cryptically: "Speaking generally, it is safe to say that if there had been any foundation other than the unconditional surrender of the Confederacy, upon which to build it, we would have had peace long ago." But, he continued, "the quarrel is a mortal one . . . and there can be no peace the terms of which are not dictated and enforced by the Congress of the United States." [63]

On June 10, in answer to a Democratic attack upon the administration for refusing to allow a Confederate gunboat to bring Alexander H. Stephens to Washington, Greeley wrote vehemently and in his most warlike style:

> The naked truth lies here: Up to this hour the rebels have never been ready or willing to treat with our government on any other footing than that of independence; and this we have not been inclined to concede. When they (or we) have been beaten into a willingness to concede the vital matter in dispute, negotiations for peace will be in order—and not till then.[64]

Unfortunately for Lincoln and his administration, Greeley was still erratic, even more erratic than he had been earlier in the war. In July, he was prone to forget his statements of May and June. Furthermore, in the month after Lincoln's June 8 renomination, the condition of the Confederate States seemed to grow steadily more hopeless, as the lines of the federal forces under Grant's management were tightened around the South. Naval successes along the Atlantic and the pressure from every direction on the land made themselves felt gradually, even in the very heart of the Confederacy. Significantly, talk in the North about the possibility of securing peace by some type of compromise grew more and more common, particularly after the July call for additional military manpower. The horrors and the miseries of war were dwelt upon with greater persistence as the hope of finally crushing the "rebellion" became more reasonable. At length, two Confederate emissaries, Clement C. Clay of Alabama and Jacob Thompson of Mississippi, former Secretary of the Interior under James Buchanan, journeyed to the

Canadian border and appeared near Niagara, from which point they placed themselves in direct communication with the erratic but patriotic editor, Horace Greeley. Knowing that he was still fuming about an absolute northern victory, they yet hoped to plant seeds of doubt in his heart and mind, through which they might gain access to the presence of Lincoln.[65]

The spread of the 1864 peace movement, both North and South, was an inevitable expression of a war-weary and heartsick population. When Horace Greeley was willing to associate himself prominently with such an endeavor, the attention of the whole North was focused upon the subject. Vindictive though he was in his abolitionism and in his denunciations of the South, Greeley possessed in his spectacular makeup more than a small trace of pacific idealism. On learning from a self-constituted envoy named W. C. Jewett of the Colorado territory on July 5 that "two ambassadors of Davis and Co. are now in Canada, with full and complete powers for a peace," and being advised that "the whole matter [could] be consummated by me, you, them, and President Lincoln," the editor of the *Tribune*, eager for peace but craving no personal connection with a possibly unpopular negotiation, referred the matter to Lincoln, as in fact he should have done.[66]

However, in his usual bombastic fashion, Greeley wrote to the President, on July 7, lecturing him soundly and at considerable length concerning his unfortunate policies in the past, and again telling him specifically what he should do in this situation. First of all, he asked that Lincoln grant safe conduct to these two emissaries in order that they might reach Washington, and there discuss with the President terms for establishing a peace. Secondly, Greeley delivered his vehement lecture in the severest terms upon which he could rest his virile pen:

> I venture to remind you that our bleeding, bankrupt, almost dying country longs for peace—shudders at the prospect of fresh conscriptions, of further wholesale devastations, and of new rivers of human blood; and a widespread conviction that the Government and its sup-

porters are not anxious for peace, and do not improve proffered opportunities to achieve it, is doing great harm now, and is morally certain, unless removed, to do far greater in the approaching elections.[67]

Finally, in closing his attack, the editor, always confident of his great wisdom, submitted to the President a basis for conducting negotiations, the first two items of which were the restoration of the Union and the abolition of slavery. Feeling that Greeley was deliberately attempting to place him in an impossible position so that he might be forced to withdraw from the presidential race, Lincoln again bested Greeley at his own game by turning over the entire affair to the editor, permitting him to wallow in his own mire.[68]

The chief campaign material in 1864, judging from the records of that day, seems to have been the events of the war and the desire in many quarters to establish peace at some reasonable price. While he was engaged in wrestling with Greeley over a two-month period, Lincoln drew up a secret document and asked his Cabinet members to sign it, sight unseen. When they had complied, he sealed it. After the election it was opened and found to commit them, in case of McClellan's election, to cooperate with the President to win the war before McCellan's inauguration, as Lincoln doubted that it could be accomplished by a Democratic Congress, because of the intense national pressure for peace. As matters stood in July, when Greeley prepared to leave New York for Niagara, Lincoln would not accept peace unless the Union could be saved, while Jefferson Davis still refused to consent to peace on any terms short of independence for the South.

Lincoln feared what Greeley might do at Niagara, as he pondered the problem of whether to send him or not.[69] Yet he hoped that, if the editor fell for the ruse, he would be quieted, muted, during the remainder of the campaign. As for Greeley, his heart was sad, because he felt that America still lacked a leader, that there could be no victory, and therefore that peace must be the only alternative.[70]

CHAPTER NINE

The Pathway to Peace

By July, 1864, Canada harbored a small group of bizarre personages assembled from the Union and from the Confederate States
of America. There were northern traitors and politicians, southern gentlemen and representatives, intriguers and conspirators
of unknown allegiance, Confederate soldiers escaped from Union
prisons, spies, adventurers, and an imbecile from Europe and
Colorado. They came for different motives and by different paths.
But suddenly the raveled threads of their separate purposes were
tied together by the unexpected arrival of Horace Greeley. His
presence united these diverse characters into a unified scheme
for peace negotiations of significant import.

The reasons that compelled Greeley to become a conspicuous
peacemaker must not be sought in the immediate situation of
June and July, 1864. That situation merely brought to the surface the fundamental forces which animated a personality that
has baffled both its contemporaries and posterity, a perplexity
occasioned by the contradictions of the man. He was, really, a
typical country boy, not in harmony with his surroundings;
Greeley maintained this sense of incongruity to the end of his
life. His contradictory character was fashioned by the narrow-

ness of his early life, a life filled with hardships and privations, coupled with a rapidly developed and dangerously heightened sensitivity of nature, so apparent in his reforming fanaticism to make "good from ill." [1]

The whole Civil War period was an unhappy one for Greeley, as we have already seen. It set at odds within his own mind irreconcilable desires and ideals. On the one hand, he had a profound abhorrence of warfare; temperamentally, he was a pacifist. As he was convinced of the perfectibility of man and the concomitant goodness of God, war seemed inexplicable and unrighteous to him. Therefore, when the prospect of civil war first confronted him, Greeley jumped to the nonresistant position. On the other hand, expediency whispered to him that it would be a better policy for the *Tribune* to be loyal to the North. But at the same time, this did not necessarily mean being loyal to Lincoln. Consequently, Greeley justified his position and the war itself only in terms of the abolition of slavery—a reform he had advocated for years.[2]

Gradually, Greeley progressed from pacifism and an advocacy of peaceable secession to the utmost extreme of Jacobin radicalism. He deliberately wrote his history of the Civil War, *The American Conflict,* to prove that the war was being waged for the principle of emancipation and not, as Lincoln had repeatedly asserted, to "save the Union." He was prostrate and almost insane after the first Battle of Bull Run; and when his measures were not adopted by Lincoln, he drifted back to a point of pacifism, working for foreign mediation to end the conflict, in early 1863. Chancellorsville—May, 1863—almost killed him. And July, 1864, bringing its northern military failures coupled with Greeley's political failures in losing the battle with Seward and Weed, in failing to influence Lincoln's policies or his defeat for the renomination, brought him to the brink of a mental collapse.[3]

Requirements of party harmony during the Civil War did nothing to still the quarrel between the Weed-Seward and the Greeley factions. Since neither combatant could obliterate the other, the battle between them waged without quarter. Weed accused Greeley of making monetary gains through illicit trading in southern cotton and characterized him as a fanatic, dazed, muddle-headed aspirant for office. The squabble spread from New York to Lincoln's doorstep. The President was annoyed by the frequency with which such complaints were referred to him, and he tried stubbornly to remain aloof; if action were forced upon him, he sought escape through compromise. Three years of this executive impartiality had filled Greeley with a fundamental distrust of Lincoln. Furthermore, Seward, Greeley's irritating enemy, was still Secretary of State and confidential adviser to the President. Rumor justly attributed to him the most influence of all the Cabinet members.[4]

This distrust, originating from the obscure roots of personal politics, was steadily increased in Greeley's mind and heart by Lincoln's conservative war and peace policies. Since the editor of the *Tribune* was as ardent an abolitionist as Benjamin Wade, Zachariah Chandler, and Thaddeus Stevens, he was distressed by the President's milk-and-water attitude toward slavery. Lincoln's every act had persuaded Greeley that he should not be renominated. However, in June, Lincoln had been selected to serve again; furthermore, in the same month Lincoln had filled a vacant New York custom-house post—a very lucrative office—with a powerful Seward-Weed conservative. These two events soured Greeley on Lincoln, determining the editor to upset the President's applecart in such a way that he would be forced out of the presidential race, so that an avowed radical might carry the Republican banner to victory.[5]

In early July, Chase, the radical mouthpiece for whom Greeley had carried a torch for many months, resigned from the Cabinet. Weed exulted at this "gleam of sunshine," while Greeley felt himself lost in a morass of despair. The administration was in open alignment with his foes; therefore, in early July he considered Lincoln wholly incompetent and an unsafe November candidate. A war conducted by such a leader—if the term could be stretched to include Lincoln at all—was certainly destined to failure. Then, as if to justify this tenet and to deepen his gloom, the military situation at that moment took a turn for the worse.

At the beginning of the year, the vacillating editor, in one of his rare bursts of optimism and enthusiasm, had envisaged "the Confederacy tottering to its downfall" and had prophesied the conclusion of the war by the first of July. By that day of prophecy in July the situation had altered noticeably from that of January 1. The rapid advances of Grant had changed into a slower progress; the number of casualties was horrifying. Cold Harbor and Petersburg promised an indeterminate stalemate. Then a brilliant and showy maneuver on the part of the Confederate States seemed to overturn for a brief instant the proper relations of the armies. Jubal Early spilled out of the Shenandoah Valley and wiped away the forces before him, momentarily thrusting a wedge between Washington and the North. To one looking at this situation today, the North's military position seemed secure, but not so to Greeley, publicly for war and a decisive northern military victory, publicly against Fernando Wood and the northern copperheads, publicly denouncing all peace offers.[6]

Greeley denied that the President had the power under the Constitution to treat with envoys from the Confederate States, asserting that "definite proposals of peace on satisfactory terms have never been made by Jefferson Davis" and calling for the continuance of the war "until they (or we) have been beaten into a willingness to concede the vital matter in dispute"—the matter of southern independence.[7]

In the secret places of the man's heart, however, these sentiments did not ring true. Once more Greeley was emotionally adrift. Any impulse was quite likely to push him in the direction which he had taken after previous disasters of the war—in the direction of peace. As a matter of fact, when he was writing his pro-war editorials in the *Tribune* in June and early July, he was already in correspondence, as we have seen, with an old friend, William Cornell Jewett, who on July 5 wrote to Greeley from Niagara Falls, telling him of the southern emissaries there.[8]

Upon receiving this news from this irresponsible and officious source, known to those who sneered at his lack of mentality as "Colorado Jewett," Greeley had wavered, and then toppled over the brink. The communication stated that "two ambassadors of Davis and Co." were in Canada, with full and complete powers for establishing a peace, and requested Greeley to come immediately to Niagara to talk with them.

Taking the matter seriously, Greeley had written to Lincoln a long and hysterical letter, urging that the offer be accepted and that someone (preferably not the editor) be sent to Niagara to discuss the terms of the proposed peace with the two emissaries. Lincoln, seeing in this incident an opportunity to demonstrate to the country the futility of peace negotiations, had immediately appointed Greeley himself as an informal ambassador to meet with the representatives from the Confederate States.[9]

On July 9, Lincoln sent this brief note to Greeley in response to the latter's hysterical missive of two days before:

DEAR SIR:

Your letter of the 7th, with inclosures, received.

If you can find any person, anywhere, professing to have any proposition of Jefferson Davis in writing, for peace, embracing the restoration of the Union and abandonment of slavery, whatever else it embraces, say to him he may come to me with you; and that if he really brings such proposition, he shall at the least have safe conduct with the paper (and without publicity, if he chooses) to the point where you shall have met him. The same if there be two or more persons. . . .[10]

Greeley apparently had never expected the turn of events as outlined in Lincoln's first letter on the subject. Jewett had insisted that Greeley come to Niagara Falls; now the President demanded that the editor go and discover whether the peace negotiators were frauds or true representatives of Jefferson Davis with adequate Confederate credentials. Greeley protested violently. Lincoln insisted that the editor carry out the mission, his only conditions being those to which Lincoln had consistently adhered—preservation of the Union and emancipation of the slaves.[11]

On July 13, Greeley wrote a powerful letter of protest to the

President, in which he endeavored to sidetrack the whole issue of the Niagara affair and of the emissaries. Still determined to place the editor in his proper relationship to the executive office, Lincoln wrote, from the executive mansion, on July 15, a letter worthy of note, preceded, on the same day, by this telegram:

> HONORABLE HORACE GREELEY, NEW YORK:
>
> I suppose you received my letter of the 9th. I have just received yours of the 13th, and am disappointed by it. I was not expecting you to send me a letter, but to bring me a man, or men. Mr. Hay goes to you with my answer to yours of the 13th.
>
> A. LINCOLN [12]

Lincoln had become fearful of Greeley's attitude in the matter; and despite the fact that, in his July 13 letter, Greeley had indicated that he was going to Niagara to see what he could do, the President felt that the editor needed John Hay's steadying influence at the scene. Knowing well by now the erratic nature of Greeley, Lincoln felt that he could not trust the journalist busybody even in this fiasco. John Hay left Washington on July 15, bearing this letter for Greeley:

> MY DEAR SIR:
>
> Yours of the 13th is just received, and I am disappointed that you have not already reached here with those commissioners, if they would consent to come on being shown my letter to you of the 9th instant. Show that and this to them, and if they will come on the terms stated in the former, bring them. I not only intend a sincere effort for peace, but I intend that you shall be a personal witness that it is made.
>
> Yours truly,
>
> A. LINCOLN [13]

John Hay also carried with him from Washington, when he departed at Lincoln's request, this paper, which was to be shown to Greeley and to the emissaries at Niagara in order to make certain that they understood the preliminary requisites to peace:

TO WHOM IT MAY CONCERN:

Any proposition which embraces the restoration of peace, the integrity of the whole Union, and the abandonment of slavery, and which comes by and with an authority that can control the armies now at war against the United States, will be received and considered by the Executive Government of the United States, and will be met by liberal terms on other substantial and collateral points, and the bearer or bearers thereof shall have safe conduct both ways.[14]

When Hay arrived in Niagara, he discovered that Greeley had been there for some time and that he had already bungled the entire affair by failing to show Lincoln's letter of July 9 to the emissaries and by utterly failing to mention that the two prime conditions of peace must be the restoration of "the whole Union" and the eradication of slavery from the South. Hay explained to the artificial commissioners the President's real terms, showing them the paper he bore from Lincoln. Immediately he learned what Greeley had not as yet fathomed—that the agents had absolutely no authority to conclude any agreement, that the whole episode was a disreputable fiasco. Therefore, Hay returned to Lincoln with the news and a few choice epithets for Greeley's head, while the latter returned to New York, determined that the correspondence between the President and himself should be published in full. Consequently, the Niagara peace conference, as it has been called since that day, fizzled out ingloriously, placing Lincoln in a more satisfactory light before the people and further evidencing Greeley as an emotionally disturbed, extremely muddled Republican newspaper editor.[15]

A close adviser of Lincoln's, Secretary of the Navy Gideon Welles, records in his diary for July 22, 1864, an interesting note on the Niagara peace conference, which seems to indicate that Lincoln's friends generally disapproved of his part in the whole affair but felt that he came out of it strengthened by the way in which he had handled Greeley in such a delicate political matter:

At the Cabinet-meeting the President read his correspondence with Horace Greeley on the subject of peace
propositions from George Saunders and others at Niagara
Falls. The President has acquitted himself very well—
if he was to engage in the matter at all,—but I am sorry
that he permits himself, in this irregular way, to be induced to engage in correspondence with irresponsible
parties like Saunders and Clay or scheming busybodies
like Greeley. There is no doubt that the President and
the whole Administration are misrepresented and misunderstood on the subject of peace, and Greeley is one
of those who has done and is doing great harm and injustice in this matter. In this instance he was evidently
anxious to thrust himself forward as an actor, and yet
when once engaged he began to be alarmed; he failed
to honestly and frankly communicate the President's
first letters, as was his duty, but sent a letter of his own,
which was not true and correct, and found himself involved in the meshes of his own frail net.[16]

This excerpt would appear to indicate that Lincoln's friends
now distrusted Greeley more than ever; and although they sometimes misinterpreted his confused efforts to secure peace as deliberate means of involving himself with the administration,
they correctly realized the troubles he had caused and was causing Lincoln.

Meanwhile, Greeley had decided that the entire correspondence in regard to the Niagara affair should be published.[17] Not
realizing that Lincoln had again bested him at his own game, he
hoped that, by publishing the correspondence during the course
of the campaign, he could so embarrass and weaken Lincoln
that he would be forced to withdraw from the canvass in favor
of a radical candidate. Greeley wrote to John Hay, asking whether
he might immediately publish the letters he had written to and
received from the President. In response, Lincoln, on Saturday,
August 6, sent him this telegram:

HONORABLE HORACE GREELEY, NEW YORK:

Yours to Major Hay about publication of our correspondence received. With the suppression of a few passages in your letters in regard to which I think you and I would not disagree, I should be glad of the publication. Please come over and see me.

A. LINCOLN [18]

On this same day, Gideon Welles recorded in his diary:

While at the President's Blair came in, and the President informed us he had a telegram from Greeley, desiring the publication of the whole peace correspondence. Both Blair and myself advised it, but the President said he had telegraphed Greeley to come on, for he desired him to erase some of the lamentations in his longest letter [the one dated July 7]. I told him while I regretted it was there, the whole had better be published. . . . The President thought it better that that part should be omitted.[19]

It appears that Lincoln worried a great deal over Greeley's lamentations concerning the blood-soaked, battered, and beaten state of the Union. He apparently decided to tell his advisers that he would permit Greeley to publish all of the correspondence, while at the same time he still urged the editor to omit certain of the most defamatory and degrading passages. Under date of August 9, Welles records in his diary:

. . . Alluding to the Niagara peace proceedings, the President expressed a willingness that all should be published. Greeley had asked it, and when I went into the President's room Defrees was reading the proof of the correspondence. I have advised its entire publication from the first moment I had knowledge of it. Whether it was wise or expedient for the President to have assented to Greeley's appeal, or given his assent to any

such irregular proceedings, is another thing, not necessary to discuss. Mr. Seward was consulted in this matter,
and no other one was called in that I am aware.[20]

On the other hand, it appears that Lincoln deceived Seward
and Welles, that he still held hopes of persuading Greeley
to suppress some of the most obnoxious passages. For on this
same Tuesday, August 9, Lincoln penned the following letter
to Greeley, enclosing the correspondence as it had been privately
prepared and printed:

> *(Private)*
> Executive Mansion
> August 9, 1864
>
> DEAR SIR:
>   Herewith is a full copy of the correspondence and
> which I have had privately printed, but not made pub-
> lic. The parts of your letters which I wish suppressed
> are only those which, as I think, give too gloomy an
> aspect to our cause, and those which present the carry-
> ing of elections as a motive of action. I have, as you
> see, drawn a red pencil over the parts I wish sup-
> pressed. . . .[21]

Greeley had not replied to Lincoln's invitation that he come
to Washington to discuss the correspondence and in particular
the parts which the President wished to suppress. And apparently
by August 9, because of firm Cabinet objections to the omission
of any part of the correspondence, the chief executive endeavored to prevent Greeley from making the journey by sending
the material to him with the places he wished suppressed carefully marked with a red pencil. Lincoln also endeavored to
soothe Greeley's ruffled nature and to explain his official position in regard to the Alexander H. Stephens escapade, closing
his letter of August 9 thus:

> As to the Alexander H. Stephens matter, so much
> pressed by you, I can only say that he sought to come
> to Washington in the name of the "Confederate States

navy," and with no pretense even that he would bear any proposal for peace; but with language showing that his mission would be military, and not civil or diplomatic. Nor has he at any time since pretended that he had terms of peace, so far as I know or believe. On the contrary, Jefferson Davis has, in the most formal manner, declared that Stephens had no terms of peace. I thought we could not afford to give this quasi-acknowledgement of the independence of the Confederacy, in a cause where there was not even an intimation of anything for our good. Still, as the parts of your letters relating to Stephens contain nothing worse than a questioning of my action, I do not ask a suppression of those parts.

Yours truly,

A. LINCOLN [22]

However, on the same day that Lincoln was writing this persuasive missive, Greeley, audacious and recalcitrant as he was, had refused to abandon his peace policy. On August 9, he wrote again to the President, in tones as hysterical, as exasperating, as despairing as before: "I beg you, implore you . . . to inaugurate or invite proposals for peace forthwith. And in case peace cannot now be made consent to an *armistice for one year*." [23]

When Lincoln received this letter, he considered that Greeley's case was hopeless and that any more words of persuasion on his part would probably fall upon deaf ears.

Meanwhile, in the South great concern and unrest had developed as a result of the Niagara peace conference and other peace movements in the summer of 1864. On August 25, therefore, Confederate Secretary of State Judah P. Benjamin wrote to James M. Mason in Paris, first describing the peace negotiations attempted between James R. Gilmore, Greeley's friend, and James F. Jaquess, both representing the Union, and Jefferson Davis, President of the Confederate States, and then alluding in this fashion to the Greeley fiasco:

It is deemed not improper to inform you that Messrs. C. C. Clay and J. P. Holcombe, although enjoying in an eminent degree the confidence and esteem of the President [Jefferson Davis], were strictly accurate in their statement that they were without any authority from this Government to treat with that of the United States on any subject whatever. We had no knowledge of their conference with Mr. Greeley, nor of their proposed visit to Washington, till we saw the newspaper publications.[24] A significant confirmation of the truth of the statement of Messrs. Gilmore and Jaquess that they came as messengers from Mr. Lincoln is to be found in the fact that the views of Mr. Lincoln, as stated by them to the President [Jefferson Davis], are in exact conformity with the offensive paper addressed to "whom it may concern" which was sent by Mr. Lincoln to Messrs. Clay and Holcombe by the hands of his private secretary, Mr. Hay, and which was purposely regarded by these gentlemen as an intimation that Mr. Lincoln was unwilling that this war should cease while in his power to continue hostilities. . . .[25]

The letter continues at great length in this same vein, constantly striving to overcome the feeling created by the Niagara peace conference that the South now desired peace. At the same time, this letter serves to indicate that Greeley's foolish actions in refusing to present Lincoln's terms to the so-called southern emissaries placed the President in an awkward position, making it appear to many in both North and South that Greeley's editorial accusations were quite correct, that he was so bloodthirsty that he had no intention of ending the costly conflict while he was chief executive.

One reads the apprehension of Secretary Welles in regard to the proposed publication of the Greeley-Lincoln letters as he confides in his diary on August 17:

They [these letters] place the President . . . at disadvantage in the coming election. He is committed, it will be claimed, against peace, except on terms that are inadmissible. What necessity was there for this, and, really, what right had the President to assume this unfortunate attitude without consulting his Cabinet, at least, or others? He did, he says, advise with Seward, and W. P. Fessenden, who came in accidentally, also gave it his sanction. [But] . . . Seward is a trickster more than a statesman. He has wanted to get an advantage over Horace Greeley, and when the President said to Greeley, therefore, that no terms which did not include the abolition of slavery as one of the conditions (would be admissible), a string in Greeley's harp was broken. . . .[26]

In actuality, Lincoln had cornered Greeley between two walls, both of which were impossible to climb. Formerly, the editor had demanded that the only purpose of the war was the abolition of slavery; now, when Lincoln declared that one of the prime conditions for establishing peace was the abolition of slavery, Greeley refused the condition as impossible, impracticable, and dangerous. At the same time, he continued to condemn Lincoln as a moderate lacking the qualities of leadership. And but nine short days after he had written Lincoln, on August 9, demanding that the President make or accept some immediate proposition for peace or inaugurate an armistice for one year, Greeley wrote bitterly, "Lincoln is already beaten. He cannot be elected. And we must have another ticket to save us from utter overthrow." [27]

Greeley hoped that this was true, that the story of the Niagara peace conference and his demands for the publication of the whole of the correspondence, including the disparaging passages in regard to the condition of the Union, would make it true.

But Lincoln did not intend to withdraw from the race, nor did he intend in any way to be influenced by a man in whom he had lost all faith, Horace Greeley. On August 19, these significant words appear in the diary of Welles:

Blair inquired about the Niagara peace correspondence. The President went over the particulars. [He] had sent the whole correspondence to Greeley for publication, excepting one or two passages in Greeley's letters which spoke of a bankrupted country and awful calamities. But Greeley replied he would not consent to any suppression of his letters or any part of them; and the President remarked that, though Greeley had put him in a false attitude, he thought it better he should bear it, than that the country should be distressed by such a howl, from such a person, on such an occasion.

Concerning Greeley, to whom the President has clung too long and confidingly, he said to-day that Greeley is an old shoe—good for nothing now, whatever he has been. "In early life, and with few mechanics and but little means in the West, we used," said he, "to make our shoes last a great while with much mending, and sometimes, when far gone, we found the leather so rotten the stitches would not hold. Greeley is so rotten that nothing can be done with him. He is not truthful; the stitches all tear out." [28]

Lincoln could not dissuade Greeley from publishing the whole correspondence; yet Greeley did not publish it all, and it was not published in his lifetime. Nevertheless, the Niagara peace conference and the correspondence connected with it had served to prove to Lincoln Greeley's untrustworthiness.

This strange conference, therefore, which ran over a considerable number of days and which was enveloped in a dark cloud of mystery, collapsed into nothingness, except for the publicity which it had wrought. When the newspapers did carry the story, when Greeley did publish a portion of the correspondence, it was evident to "people of sense" that the editor had been hoodwinked. It was evident, too, to those who thought a moment that Lincoln was willing to carry on peace negotiations if those points for which the war had been fought were yielded by the enemy. After these two truths dawned upon many northern people, all of the effectiveness of the peace cries was gone. And Senator James Harlan of Iowa, who, with other Republicans, appreciated thoroughly the cleverness with which Lincoln had disposed of the editor of the New York *Tribune,* remarked to Lincoln one day as both men stood together on the terrace of the White House, "Some of us think, Mr. Lincoln, that you didn't send a very good ambassador to Niagara."

"Well, I'll tell you about that, Harlan," Lincoln replied, affably; "Greeley kept abusing me for not entering into peace negotiations. He said he believed we could have peace if I would do my part and when he began to urge that I send an ambassador to Niagara to meet Confederate emissaries, I just thought I would let him go up and crack that nut for himself." [29]

If the controversy between Lincoln and Greeley over the Niagara peace mission had been the only one of its kind during the Civil War period, it would appear unique. But it was characteristic of Greeley to talk and to act intemperately, as a multitude of his precipitate, wishful-thinking procedures indicate. His expert editorship is not necessarily linked with good statesmanship or, as later turns out, with any great political leadership. [30]

However, all during the time of the Niagara peace conference in July, and the issue over the publication of the Lincoln-Greeley correspondence in August, the editor had again been intriguing with the supporters of Salmon P. Chase in an effort to form a new Union ticket headed by the ex-Secretary of the Treasury. From the day in early July when Chase resigned from the Cabinet, Greeley had mourned the loss of "one of the few great men left" in the government. To the editor, his idol Chase now loomed in stature equal to a Webster, a Clay, or a Calhoun. And from the moment of Chase's exit from the federal government, Greeley's name is linked with friends of the Ohio radical in numerous intrigues, plans, and programs to substitute Chase for Lincoln at the head of the Republican ticket as the only means of defeating the Democrats in November. [31]

It was for this reason that Greeley had been so eager to expose Lincoln to the wrath of the people in connection with the Niagara affair. However, once more Greeley had failed. During this summer of 1864, the heat of the sun could not compare with the heat of Greeley's criticism of the administration. First, he had wanted war, charging that Lincoln wanted peace without victory. Now, he proclaimed that he desired a peace or an armistice, condemning Lincoln as a warmonger and a bloodthirsty, cruel, heartless, disgraceful President.

Gideon Welles, who had never harbored any love for Greeley, thus sums up the editor's attitude toward Lincoln in 1864:

> The New York papers are engaged in a covert and systematic attack on the Navy Department,—covert so far as the Republican or Administration press is concerned. Greeley of the *Tribune* is secretly hostile to the President and assails him indirectly in this way. . . .[32]
>
> The *Tribune* is owned by a company which really desired to give a fair support to the Administration, but Greeley, the editor, is erratic, unreliable, without stability, an enemy of the Administration because he hates Seward, a creature of sentiment or impulse, not of reason nor professed principle. Having gone to extremes in the measures that fermented and brought on this war, he would not go to extremes to quell it. I am prepared to see him acquiesce in a division of the Union, or the continuance of slavery, to accomplish his personal party schemes. There are no men or measures to which he will adhere faithfully. He is ambitious, talented, but not considerate, persistent, or profound.[33]

Although in this estimate of Greeley and his efforts to influence Lincoln, the Navy Secretary evidences great sagacity and objectivity, despite his partisan position, he feels nevertheless that Lincoln has too often yielded to Greeley, as in reality he has not; for the diarist also declares, sadly, "I have regretted that the President should have yielded so much to Greeley in many things and treated him with so much consideration." [34]

If, indeed, Lincoln did yield to Greeley, particularly during this difficult 1864 campaign, as Welles suggests, the yielding was purely an outward sign, not manifesting the true inner feeling. Therefore, the facts prove Lincoln to be a diplomat, while in his heart he had by this time learned the true value of Greeley, no longer investing confidence in his "old shoe."

Many factors, military and political, served to weaken Lincoln's position in the campaign, in spite of the fact that he had, publicly and purposefully, bested Greeley in the Niagara affair. Greeley still had many subscribers to the *Tribune,* many readers, and many friends. True, many had sneered at the Niagara conclave, visualizing the naïveté and the nuisance value of the editor; nevertheless, many, longing desperately for peace, considered Greeley their hero, an honest pacifist, chagrined, deceived, and humiliated by a ruthless President.

Furthermore, three days prior to Lincoln's 1864 nomination, the Battle of Cold Harbor had been fought. This and other bloody reverses enshrouded the nation in gloom. Lincoln himself, as tragedy followed tragedy, despaired of his own re-election; his famous sealed memorandum of August 23, recording his belief that the administration would be defeated and pledging himself and his Cabinet to co-operate with McClellan to save the Union before the latter's inauguration, merely reflected the pessimism which affected most loyal citizens.[35]

With the possibility that both the regular and the bolting Republicans would drop their candidates in favor of another man, the hopes of Chase and his followers rose once more. News arrived in the middle of August, at probably the most despairing moment of the war, that a movement had been launched to persuade Lincoln voluntarily to abdicate his nomination, or, if he refused, to eject him forcibly from the contest. The insurrection possessed a far more formidable sponsorship than such a proceeding would seem to have deserved. Its leader was David Dudley Field of New York, whose brother, Stephen J. Field, Lincoln had a short time before appointed to the United States Supreme Court. Furthermore, Field's most active co-worker was that same George Opdyke whose name has several times appeared here as one of the chieftains of the anti-Weed-Seward faction of Republicans in New York State.

At a secret meeting in Field's New York home, on August 14, eminent representatives of politics, journalism, and the professions prepared a "call" for a convention to be held in Cincinnati, on September 18, in order "to consider the state of the nation, and to consecrate the Union strength on some one candidate, who commands the confidence of the country, even by a new nomination if necessary." [36] In addition, it was decided to send out questionnaires to all of the northern governors, asking them what they thought of this proposed convention and how they evaluated Lincoln as a presidential nominee. Surprisingly enough, most of the governors replied to this questionnaire, when it was sent out to them, indicating an expressed lack of confidence in Lincoln's abilities and in his qualities of leadership.[37]

Greeley was a close friend to David Dudley Field and a political associate of Opdyke. Consequently, he represented the *Tribune* in this important sabotage, assisting in preparing, printing, sending forth, and tabulating the questionnaires to the northern governors and planning with Field and others for the new September convention in which, it was believed, Lincoln could be replaced by another nominee. What Greeley privately thought of this whole intrigue may be seen in a letter which he wrote to George Opdyke some few days after the August 14 session in Field's New York home:

> Mr. Lincoln is already beaten. . . . And we must have another ticket to save us. . . . If we had such a ticket as could be made by naming Grant, Butler, or Sherman for President, and Farragut for Vice, we could make a fight yet. And such a ticket we ought to have anyhow, with or without a convention.[38]

Moreover, this was not the only group preparing to remove Lincoln from the race. Zachariah Chandler and Benjamin Wade were ready at last to force Lincoln from his coveted position at the head of the ticket. Their private plan was to organize a bolt of the party by the radical Jacobins, to detach most of Lincoln's support, and then place another candidate in the field. To these men, unaware of the secret meeting at Field's house and the quiet Chase boom among the Opdyke faction, the time was ripe for striking Lincoln at this point, just following the exposure of Greeley's peace fiasco. They felt that, among the radical Republicans, this incident had left the general impression that the President was willing to negotiate a far too generous peace, and that he intended to establish peace upon his own terms, without the advice or consent of Congress. Moreover, Grant had yet to achieve an important success in the East, and his sickening losses in "the Wilderness" had stunned the public momentarily.[39]

As usual, Greeley was the willing instrument through which the anti-Lincoln radicals worked. Therefore, on August 5, there appeared in the *Tribune* a communication signed by Benjamin Wade and Henry Winter Davis—the famous "Wade-Davis Manifesto." In essence, it was a detailed, withering, and malignant denunciation of Lincoln's reconstruction policy and his veto of the congressional bill passed in July. The radicals were jubilantly confident that this manifesto had set in motion a tremendous popular revulsion against Lincoln. They felt certain now that they could knock him from the race, either by appealing to him to withdraw for the good of the party or by nominating another candidate, as the Field-Opdyke forces proposed to do.[40]

However, the elation of the Jacobins—the Wade-Davis forces and the Field-Opdyke group—was unfounded, as they might well have realized had they studied the press reactions to the manifesto more carefully. Greeley, who served in both groups, actually helping to unite them after August 14 on the plan for calling the September convention, in editorial print would only go so far as to pronounce the manifesto a "very able and caustic protest." His caution did not seem to alarm the radicals, however; for, in private, he assured them of his utmost support. When in an editorial Greeley declared that he did not regret Lincoln's veto of the Wade-Davis bill, the Jacobins grew somewhat angry, but they made no comment, because they needed the aid of the *Tribune*.

Especially did they need this aid when most Republican newspapers saw fit to repudiate the manifesto in cold print. However, the Jacobin bosses, strangely blind to the signs of the times, blithely continued their plans to replace Lincoln with a radical candidate. Furthermore, the responses to the call for a convention, coupled with the governors' answers to their questionnaire, inspired real optimism. As August waned, Henry Winter Davis, John Jay, Benjamin F. Butler, Salmon P. Chase, Richard Smith of the Cincinnati *Gazette,* and Charles Sedgwick, with Horace Greeley, rallied round the radical program.[41]

However, the conspiracy soon tottered and was dealt a final blow by William Tecumseh Sherman. On September 2, news reached the North that Sherman had marched down Peach Tree Street, had captured Atlanta, had split the Confederate States hopelessly in two. Victory was rendered a virtual certainty. The country suddenly threw off its shrouds of gloom—gloom which had hung heavily as a mantle over the Union throughout June, July, and August—and went mad with joy. Lincoln and Sherman became popular heroes. The re-election of the rail-splitter was forecast by every portent, was predicted in every political sign. One by one the conspirators sneaked back into the fold. On September 6, Horace Greeley announced that he was supporting the "one true Union candidate, Abraham Lincoln." [42]

An interesting story surrounds Greeley's plunge to Lincoln's side, his leap upon the bandwagon. It may or may not be authentic, but it bears recording.

In New York State political affairs during the year of 1864, Greeley had allied himself with Reuben E. Fenton of Chautauqua County, an anti-Weed Republican. Lincoln, disturbed by Greeley's lack of support and even outright enmity, sought a way to lead Greeley back into the paths of righteousness, using Fenton as a contact, just as he had used Robert J. Walker and James R. Gilmore three years before.

Fenton had for an active agent George G. Hoskins of Wyoming County, who kept in touch with Greeley. Finding the editor chilly, Hoskins so reported to Fenton, who was then in Congress, and Fenton advised the President. The outcome was a direct invitation asking for a meeting, Lincoln, with his usual meekness, offering to make the trip to New York. In order to clarify matters, Lincoln wrote thus to Greeley:

DEAR MR. GREELEY:

I have been wanting to see you for several weeks, and if I could spare the time I should call upon you in New York. Perhaps you may be able to visit me. I shall be very glad to see you.[43]

This was in late August, shortly after the controversy over the publication of the Niagara correspondence and not long after the publication of the Wade-Davis manifesto and the meeting of the Field-Opdyke forces, with concomitant efforts to replace Lincoln as the Republican candidate in a September convention. Therefore, Greeley, still very hostile to Lincoln and actively working with his opposition, did not bother to reply to the letter asking for a meeting of minds.

When Hoskins dropped into the *Tribune* office to see how things were progressing, Greeley showed him Lincoln's courteous note, remarked that he had not answered it, and vowed that he would not. Hoskins urged a show of respect for the President, but Greeley was unmoved. His visitor then boldly advised that he, Hoskins, should act as a messenger by word of mouth. He proceeded to the White House and asked to see the President. Here is what is supposed to have occurred at the meeting between Lincoln and Greeley's independent emissary:

The doorkeeper . . . bade the caller take a seat and quickly disappeared. He returned in a moment or two, saying that the President, half-clad, was in the toilet shaving himself, but "he says if you will excuse his appearance, you should come up at once." Thereupon he led the way to the second floor and pointed to a half-open door. A slight rap brought the response "come in." As Hoskins entered, the President, clad in undershirt, trousers and slippers, put down the razor and extended his hand, saying, "Mr. Hoskins, I am very glad to see you. Take that chair," pointing to one near the entrance. The President . . . began at once to express his lifelong admiration of Mr. Greeley, asserting that he had been a constant reader of the *Tribune* since its

establishment, and that he regarded him [Greeley] as
the ablest editor in the United States, if not in the
world, and believed he exerted more influence in the
country than any other man, not excepting the President of the United States. He declared him the equal
if not the superior of Benjamin Franklin.

The mention of Franklin seemed to open the way to
business. "You know, Mr. Hoskins, that Benjamin
Franklin was the first postmaster-general and I have always regretted that I could not in 1861 appoint Mr.
Greeley to that office. But I have determined, Mr. Hoskins, if I am re-elected and re-inaugurated, to appoint
him postmaster-general. Seward wants to go to England,
and that will give me the opportunity. But, in any
event . . . I shall appoint him. He is worthy of it and
my mind is made up."

At this point, Hoskins, quite overcome with aston-
ishment at the President's frankness, asked if he was at
liberty to inform Mr. Greeley of his intentions. "Certainly," replied the President. "This is what I intended
to tell him if he had come himself. I shall not fail, if
God spares my life, to keep this solemn promise."

This seemed to close the interview, and . . . the
President . . . bade him convey to Mr. Greeley expressions of his high esteem.

Hoskins reached New York the same evening, and
going directly to Greeley's office conveyed the result of
his interview.

. . . Greeley asked, ". . . Hoskins, do you believe
that lie?" The latter asserted his belief . . . "I don't,"
retorted Greeley. . . . Thereafter Greeley remained silent . . . and Hoskins quietly retired. The next morning the *Tribune* blew the long wished for blast that
ended its languishing campaign. An editorial, nearly
two columns in length, closed as follows: [44]

"Henceforth, we fly the banner of ABRAHAM LINCOLN

for the next President. Let the country shake off its apathy; let it realize what is the price of defeat—a price neither we nor the world can afford; let it be understood how near we are to the end of the Rebellion, and that no choice is left us now but the instrument put into our hands, and with that we CAN and MUST finish it. . . .

"Mr. Lincoln has done seven-eighths of the work after his fashion; there must be vigor and virtue enough left in him to do the other fraction. The work is in his hands. We MUST re-elect him, and, God helping us, we will." [45]

Hoskins became speaker of the New York Assembly as a result of the state elections that autumn, and he often met Greeley during the course of the year. On April 14, 1865, they were together, and the editor, referring to the fact that the Cabinet had not been reconstructed or himself in any way recognized, burst out with, "Hoskins, didn't I tell you that was a lie?" In response, Hoskins promised to run over to Washington that very night and see what the trouble was. As he stepped out of the sleeper on the morning of April 15, he heard the clarion cry of a newsboy: "The President is assassinated! The President is dead!" [46]

Whatever his doubts may have been, however, Greeley supported Lincoln firmly, with fiery and vigorous editorials after he had once taken his stand. That he became deeply concerned is shown by a letter written to Moncure Daniel Conway, his friend and an abolitionist minister, who was in England at the time, writing special articles for the *Tribune,* reproving him for not coming home immediately to help in the campaign.[47]

While the *Tribune,* beginning on September 6 after Hoskins had his evening chat with Greeley, did all that it possibly could to "fly the banner of Abraham Lincoln," Greeley made stump speeches to advocate his re-election. And on September 24 the *Tribune* declared that "the only effective Peace Commissioners" were Grant, Sherman, Sheridan, and Farragut. Three days later it was repelled at the very thought of a cessation of hostilities in an effort to find peace. It cried, "An Armistice! The idea of one springs from folly or treason." [48]

Greeley had altered his peace policy again. No longer did the pathway to peace lead to Niagara; now, once more, it led directly to Richmond, and to military victory. Again the *Tribune* was militant. For two months it supported Lincoln in his hard-fought race against George B. McClellan. November came. Lincoln was re-elected. America's hopes rose; Greeley was temporarily satisfied, but scarcely exultant. Nevertheless, he believed that he might receive a Cabinet appointment this time. If he did, the ensuing four years might prove brighter than the four just passed.

When the congressional halls filled with senators and representatives in December, the atmosphere within the Republican camp resembled that of a marriage feast. Lovingly and with a proprietary manner the Jacobins caressed their idol, that "best of radicals, Abraham Lincoln, who had just emerged victorious from a savage struggle with the Copperheads because of Jacobin aid." Loudly and with an undertone of menace, meant for White House ears, the radicals proclaimed that the new Lincoln would carry forward to victorious conclusion the principles of Jacobinism.[49]

Lincoln's last annual message to Congress, delivered in December, 1864, seemed to corroborate their boasts. He called for a vigorous prosecution of the war and pledged that he would oppose any peace terms which did not include the destruction of slavery. He also advocated the passage of a constitutional amendment abolishing the institution, and repeated his unwavering support of the proclamation of emancipation which he had issued more than two years before.

Greeley, who was working on his interpretive history of the war, did not journey to Washington to hear the annual message. However, he read it with gusto, rejoiced in its statements of firmness. Momentarily forgetting that he had been the most ardent pacifist in America only six months prior to the issuance of this message, he declared it to be an excellent statement of his party's views. Further, he proclaimed the warfare between the radical Jacobins and the moderate conservatives to be forever at an end. This speeech, following in the wake of Lincoln's glorious campaign and heroic re-election, had made of his Republican Party one united phalanx.[50]

However, Greeley was destined for many new and sharp disappointments in the near future. First of all, the radicals and the conservatives soon found themselves at one another's throats again, much to the editor's horror. In the second place, military affairs had led to a new rift between Greeley and the administration. The Wilmington expedition inaugurated the disagreement, and Greeley's editorial haste and his fanatical loyalty to Benjamin F. Butler led Gideon Welles to write disparagingly in his diary on January 6:

> The papers are discussing the Wilmington expedition. Generally they take a correct view. The New York *Tribune,* in its devotion to Butler, closes its eyes to all facts. Butler is their latest idol, and his faults and errors they will not admit, but would sacrifice worth and truth, good men and the country, for their parasite.[51]

Greeley's latest idol, General Benjamin F. Butler, was subsequently dismissed, after the failure of the Wilmington expedition. Welles has left to posterity an enlightening comment upon this action and a three-way involvement of Greeley, Lincoln, and General U. S. Grant:

> . . . Much speculation has been had concerning the dismissal of General Butler. It was anticipated that, being a favorite with the extremists, his dismissal would create a great excitement, but it has passed off without irritation, almost without sensation. The quidnuncs and, indeed, most of the public impute his dismissal from the Army of the James to the Wilmington failure; but it will soon be known that General Grant desired to get rid of him. Butler's greater intellect overshadowed Grant, and annoyed and embarrassed the General-in-Chief. General Butler's farewell to his army is in many

respects skillful and adroit, but in some respects will
prove a failure [from the standpoint of propaganda
value].

. . . The New York *Tribune* has striven to warp
and torture facts to help Butler, regardless of others and
of stern truth. But the *Tribune* is unsupported. . . .

[Butler] is a suitable idol for Greeley, a profound
philanthropist, being the opposite of Greeley in almost
everything except love of notoriety.[52]

Although Welles, who hated the editor, misunderstood his
philosophy and his point of view in many respects, it is true
that Greeley in his *Tribune* supported Butler to an extent beyond all excuse or reason. At the same time, it appears that Grant
had much more influence over Lincoln in this matter than did
Greeley; Grant desired Butler's dismissal, Greeley begged Lincoln to retain Butler, and Butler was dismissed.

Thus, in January, 1865, Greeley was at odds with the President again. Nor was this a temporary affair. Other matters arose
which annoyed, irritated, and incensed the *Tribune* editor. One
of these, a matter in which he found himself violently attacking Lincoln's stand, concerned the Freedmen's Bureau. After two
congressional conferences and subsequent reports on the controversial Freedmen's Bureau which some congressmen wished
to be established in the South, the report of the second conference was adopted without division, on March 3, 1865. On the
same day, despite the strenuous efforts of Democratic opposition,
the bill was hurried through both houses and received the sig-
nature of the President.

The Freedmen's Bureau bill had had a hard struggle. It had
been opposed with bitterness and with determination. "It was
fought in public debate and in private conversation." [53] While
men like General William Tecumseh Sherman pronounced it
impracticable, Horace Greeley did everything in his power to
prevent passage of the bill and to discourage Lincoln from sign-
ing it. He endeavored to dissuade Charles Sumner from supporting it. In public editorial and in private missive, he had de-

nounced it. He asked congressmen to oppose it; he implored Lincoln to veto the bill if it passed both houses. His efforts were in vain. His influence could not be felt. It was true, as he had declared, that no political party could unite upon it. True it was, also, that two years of congressional conflict, plus numerous modifications and amendments, preceded its final passage. However, it triumphed at last, in spite of Greeley's opposition. He fumed and fretted when Lincoln signed the bill, turning the full force of his fomenting editorial fury upon the President's back. Lincoln, however, with customary suavity disregarded Greeley's barrages. Whether or not he had promised the editor the Postmaster-Generalship is not certain; whether or not he intended to keep that promise, if made, is not certain. Nevertheless, it is certain that, at this time, Greeley's attacks seemed to fall upon deaf ears in the White House. Lincoln remained undisturbed and unmoved. The Freedmen's Bureau began to exist and operate, while Greeley's critical condemnations slowly subsided.[54]

It was at this juncture, too, that Lincoln delivered his now famous second inaugural address—March 4, 1865. Greeley, although he was hostile to Lincoln's policies at the time, was struck by the simplicity and the straightforwardness of the document. In spite of the fact that he had not dictated its words or outlined what it should portend, despite the fact that he had had no foreknowledge of its somber content, Greeley praised the message sincerely. He was working on his history of the war at this time, and he decided to close the second volume of his work with this second inaugural address, prefaced by these words:

> Mr. Lincoln's Address, on his second inauguration as President, may fitly close this final chapter of our political history. In its profoundly religious spirit, its tenderness, its undesigned solemnity, in view of the triumphs already achieved and the still more conclusive triumphs rationally anticipated and now just at hand, the reader will discern the . . . shadow of impending death.[55]

To the editor, these words of the second inaugural seemed,

strangely enough, the most fitting, drawing from him undue
sentences of commendation:

> . . . It may seem strange that any men should dare to
> ask a just God's assistance in wringing their bread from
> the sweat of other men's faces. But let us judge not,
> that we be not judged. . . . With malice toward none,
> with charity for all, with firmness in the right as God
> gives us to see the right, let us strive to finish the work
> we are in, to bind up the nation's wounds, to care for
> him who shall have borne the battle and for his widow
> and his orphan, to do all which may achieve and cherish
> a just and a lasting peace among ourselves and with all
> nations.[56]

This was not a radical speech; it was the utterance of a mild-
mannered, kindhearted, honest, pitying, moderate humanitarian.
Why did Greeley the radical underline these words with such
tenderness? The answer lies only in his complex and contradictory personality, for shortly after he had praised this speech as
a great utterance, he was again engaged in deception and intrigue against the man who had made it. In this same month
of March, there appeared in the press, in England, the letter
which the editor had written to Lincoln the summer before concerning the bankrupt and bleeding, prostrate and dying America, a nation which desired peace but which was kept at war by
its leader. This letter may have appeared in print by mischance,
but in all probability Greeley supervised its publication abroad
through Moncure Daniel Conway or some other friend in the
British Isles.[57]

The publication of this notorious letter aroused a storm of
protest against Greeley within the close administration ranks.
On April 1, in his usual vitriolic mood with reference to Greeley
and Greeley's activities, Gideon Welles confided to his diary:

> Greeley's letter of last summer to the President, urging
> peace for our "bleeding, bankrupt, ruined country" has
> been published in England. This was the letter which
> led to the Niagara conference. I advised its publication

and the whole correspondence at the time, but the President was unwilling just then, unless Greeley would consent to omit the passage concerning our ruined country, but to this Greeley would not consent, and in that exhibited weakness, for it was the most offensive and objectionable part of his letter. . . . I should have preferred its appearance at home in the first instance [rather than in England]. Poor Greeley is nearly played out. He has a morbid appetite for notoriety. Wishes to be noted and forward in all shows. Four years ago was zealous—or willing—to let the States secede if they wished. Six months later was vociferating, "On to Richmond." Has been scolding and urging forward hostile operations. Suddenly is for peace, and ready to pay the Rebels four hundred millions or more to get it, he being allowed to figure in it. He craves public attention. Does not exhibit a high regard for principle. I doubt his honesty about as much as his consistency. It is put on for effect. He is a greedy office-hunter.[58]

Welles, Seward, and most of the other Cabinet members constantly advised Lincoln to avoid all contact with Greeley, to refuse his advice, to disregard his editorial influence. Therefore, if Lincoln were still considering Greeley for a Cabinet post, he must have readily seen that to appoint the editor would merely precipitate a Cabinet crisis, causing an influx of wholesale resignations to his desk. At any rate, he made no comment upon the publication of the letter.

Greeley had gone to Washington several times to see Lincoln during the course of the war. After the appearance of the letter in English print, he went down to the capital again. He talked with the President in early April, but what the two men said to each other is not recorded. Whether or not Lincoln re-promised Greeley the Cabinet post cannot be ascertained. However, when the editor returned from Washington, he wrote an editorial in which he spoke in kindly terms of Lincoln's careworn, line-weary face.[59]

But Greeley soon changed his approach again, writing, at about the time Lee surrendered to Grant, these officious and contentious editorial lines:

> I am sure Jesus of Nazareth is not truly represented in this spirit [of hatred for the South and for the Negro]. . . . As for me, I want as many rebels as possible to live and see the South rejuvenated and transformed by the influence of free labor. I should deem it a calamity to have Jefferson Davis die. . . . I have not usually believed that we should win, because I could not believe that we deserved to win. We are a pro-slavery people today. In the great city of Philadelphia, which gave Lincoln nearly 10,000 majority in 1860 and again in 1864, a black Union soldier is not allowed to ride in their streetcars; I tried to pilot through a most respectable colored clergyman, but was obliged to give it up. By all ordinary rules, we ought to have been beaten in this fight and the more consistent and straightforward worshippers of Satan triumph.[60]

If Lincoln read this statement at all, as he probably did not, he would have continued to despair of Greeley's intelligence, sincerity, honesty, and ability. But Lincoln had other problems. On April 9, 1865, Appomattox Court House witnessed the surrender of Robert E. Lee to U. S. Grant. The war was at an end, and Lincoln hoped to inaugurate his lenient reconstruction policy. Perhaps he hoped to secure Greeley's assistance in this endeavor, since he had not "had the editor with him" during the prolonged struggle. Yet he probably realized that, with Greeley's inconsistent nature more pronounced than ever now, it was a hopeless task to expect any firm aid from Greeley and the *Tribune* for any program.

Then tragedy struck, wiping away a life and with it the hope of a New York editor for a Cabinet post and a voice in reconstruction policies and in the second-term decisions of Lincoln's administration. On Friday night, April 14, John Wilkes Booth shot Abraham Lincoln.

Yet the loss the nation had sustained was not immediately apparent. Certainly it was not to Greeley.

On the day of Lincoln's assassination, Greeley considered the President's promise of a Cabinet post, if it had been made, to be a lie; he wrote a caustically critical editorial, condemning the President of every possible failure in bringing the war to a close and in establishing peace. This editorial was to appear in the *Tribune* on the morning of April 15. However, when the type-setters learned that Lincoln had been shot, they held up the editorial, and it never appeared in print. Greeley, who had not been consulted on the matter, seemed to regret the fact that his work had not been shown to the people anyway. Lincoln was not his friend; Lincoln had not taken his advice.

So, at last, the pathway to peace had been found, not by Greeley but by Lincoln. The nation had found peace at Appomattox, and Lincoln had found peace at Ford's Theater. Greeley alone remained at war with himself, confused, afraid, uncertain.[61]

CHAPTER TEN

Aftermath

Before the war, Greeley's *Weekly Tribune* had a subscription list of 25,000 families in Ohio, 16,500 in Illinois, 5,500 even in California. More than any other single agency, the New York *Tribune* set the Republican Party upon its feet in 1856, and made possible Lincoln's election in 1860. But unfortunately, during the Civil War, the *Tribune* possessed neither wisdom, vision, nor stability. With proper guidance and understanding it could have been Lincoln's greatest asset. Before the war was over, however, it had turned into a national liability. With vacillation, hysteria, intemperance of counsel, wrongheadedness, the *Tribune* gave evidence that it had become bigger than its creator, and that the circumstances and events of war had become too great for the comprehension of its creator, too great for the *Tribune* to understand.

Nevertheless, Horace Greeley stands forth as perhaps America's greatest journalist. His kindness, his admirable characteristics, his indifference to monetary gains, his devotion to a trying wife, his godliness, his ceaseless industry—these things made him great: so great that at times he almost ruled the nation.[1] This, he would certainly have liked to do.

One man he did not rule, however. That man was Abra-

ham Lincoln. Although the editor had gone to Washington to
see Lincoln several times, on only two specific occasions had
the President requested Greeley to call on him. Once in 1864,
in connection with the Niagara peace conference, Lincoln had
written Greeley asking for an interview, and Greeley had refused. However, on the other occasion, in 1862, the erratic editor had accepted. According to the reported conversation at this
meeting, Lincoln said, "You complain of me. What have I done,
or omitted to do, which has provoked the hostility of the
Tribune?"

Greeley replied, hastily, "You should issue a proclamation
abolishing slavery."

To this Lincoln retorted affably, "Suppose I do that. There
are now twenty thousand muskets on the shoulders of Kentuck-
ians, who are bravely fighting our battles. Every one of them will
be thrown down or carried over to the rebels."

"Let them do it," Greeley answered, acidly. "The cause of
the Union will be stronger if Kentucky should secede with the
rest than it is now."

"Oh, I can't think that!" Lincoln rejoined, with sadness, and
the interview came to an end.[2]

Greeley's hostility to Lincoln seems to have been chiefly motivated by fears and suspicions that the President was guided and
controlled exclusively by William H. Seward and Thurlow Weed.
The radical Jacobins and the strong antislavery abolitionists
were incessantly condemning Lincoln upon this point; and Greeley, soon after Lincoln's election and the appointment of Seward as Secretary of State, began to include the President in his
ancient and bitter feud with the former senator from the State
of New York.[3]

As for Lincoln, he treasured Greeley's letters. If they did not
lighten his burden, at least they gave him a considerable number of enjoyable and worth-while chuckles. On April 30, 1864,
John Hay confided in his diary:

He [Lincoln] thought of, and found, and gave me to
decipher, Greeley's letter to him of 29 July, 1861. This

most remarkable letter still retains for me its wonderful interest as the most insane specimen of pusillanimity that I have ever read. When I finished reading [the letter aloud to Lincoln], Nicolay said, "That would be nuts to the *Herald;* Bennett would willingly give $10,000 for that." To which the President, tying red tape around the package, answered, "I need $10,000 very much, but he can't have it for many times that." [4]

While Lincoln chuckled over Greeley's hysterical missives, the editor prepared more letters and editorials of condemnation for the President until the war ended. Then Greeley sighed and wrote, with pathetic passion:

What should have been a short, sharp struggle was unnecessarily expanded into a long, desultory one; those whose blundering incapacity or lack of purpose was responsible for the ills, united in throwing the blame on the faithful few who had counseled justly, but whose urgent remonstrances had never been heeded. Weary months of halting, timid, nerveless warfare naturally followed; men talked reproachfully of Grant's losses in taking Richmond, forgetting that his predecessors had lost more in not taking it. In war—energy, prompt and vigorous action—is the true economizer of suffering, of devastation, and of life. [5]

So the general at the head of the *Tribune* columns spoke, but Lincoln did not heed. The war lasted four years and was won. And after the war had ended, Greeley proclaimed himself in favor of forgiving everyone, especially Jefferson Davis, whose bail-bond he eagerly signed. Sometimes he had pleaded with Lincoln, sometimes bullied him, sometimes rejected him as a "poor creature," and always the *Tribune* had been an enormous power in the country, forcing Lincoln to consider the editor when he disagreed with him, but not to yield to him.

Greeley was flighty and inconsistent; Lincoln was statesmanlike and opportunistic. And yet, under Greeley's erratic nature lay a fundamental patriotic feeling, a high-mindedness which, from time to time, revealed itself to Lincoln. But without overt revelation, the President knew that it was there; it was for this reason that he regretted Greeley's prodigal waywardness. Lincoln knew that Greeley possessed courage, that it was of the passive sort—that of the tongue and not of the fist. Lincoln had longed for an opportunity to adapt that courage to his own needs. Greeley, because he yearned so desperately for public office, because Lincoln refused him that office, would not give the President that opportunity.[6]

However, had Lincoln lived, the two men might have agreed, at least for a time, upon reconstruction policies. For in 1865, when Lee surrendered, Greeley openly declared himself not for antagonism in peace but for healing influences which could spring alone from a fraternal unity. He did not hesitate. From the outset he knew that he would be under heavy attack; but once again he believed that he was right—and that belief was all that Greeley ever needed for action. With Lincoln leading the people toward reconciliation, the editor saw an opportunity to take war's hatred out of the nation's future, thus strengthening it to resume its interrupted progress toward a great destiny.[7]

He forgot that his savage war cries, his fraternizations with the radicals, his attacks upon Lincoln's moderate policies, had helped to engender the hatred which the North felt toward the South. And he called his new idealistic creed "magnanimity in triumph." He expressed it in an editorial under that title, and he hoped that it would appeal to many within the Union. It aroused much praise, but more criticism. Pleading against reprisals and for unity was an upstream job, as Woodrow Wilson learned after Word War I. It meant a campaign of education sparked by the *Tribune*—not one like the spirited movement the New York journal had led through the 1850's, but a sober appeal for amnesty, for universal suffrage, and for a genuine resumption of national citizenship. It had to be an appeal to both sections, urging them "to clasp hands across the bloody chasm." Neither section was ready for such an appeal in 1865; that chasm was too wide, too bloody, and too freshly made. It was much too bloody for any hands to stretch across it in 1865, reaching from either side, and remain unstained and unchallenged. Lincoln might possibly have done so, and, for once, he and Greeley stood in perfect accord. But Lincoln died, and Greeley, trying in vain to carry on the work of moderation, joined Andrew Johnson in the failure column. Truly, in this one noble endeavor, Greeley vainly tried, and for his effort, he paid the heavy price that every pleader against victory's instant passion, born of war, must always pay. His price included humiliation, failure, defeat, death.[8]

Two opposing currents of opinion flowed through the North in regard to reconstruction. They blossomed into life and swelled into passionate streams of force during the few days between Lee's surrender and Lincoln's assassination. As usual, Horace Greeley and Henry J. Raymond were their clashing spokesmen. Contrary to customary practice, however, Greeley stood on Lincoln's side, encouraging him to stand firm in his policy toward the South. Then Lincoln died. And, on April 17, the *Tribune* sadly proclaimed that the bullet which killed Lincoln on April 15 ended all temperate discussions of forgiveness. Now, in a worthy cause, Greeley needed Lincoln, needed the man whom he had opposed throughout the war. But it was too late; Lincoln was gone.[9]

Almost without support, Greeley became one of the North's most unpopular men. Sales of his paper dropped off markedly. On April 16, a leading citizen of New York commented tersely but with great truth: "Horace Greeley, the advocate of pacification and amnesty, is as unpopular as General Lee. . . . I directed my waiter to stop the *Tribune*." [10] Again Greeley despaired, as he, strangely consistent for once, continued to pursue his policy—Lincoln's policy.

Perhaps the editor enjoyed swimming against the tide. He almost always did. His lack of judgment may be seen not only in his political utterances but also in his personal estimates, his prudence, and his business endeavors. Often the victim of harebrained schemes, he lost heavily in most of his financial ventures, ultimately largely losing his percentage of ownership in his own paper. Eager for new ideas, he lacked a proper estimate of their real worth. His instability and ardor were not dissimilar to the same traits seen in Owen Lovejoy and John Brown—men whom Greeley trusted, loved, and idolized, as he never did Lincoln. His visionary schemes are put forward only to fail of fulfillment; and such was the case with his reconstruction formula, because he invariably employed an antagonistic approach, angering more would-be followers than he converted. All during the war, all during his life, he stood in sharp contrast to Lincoln, whose sober efforts were put in motion slowly, cautiously, carefully, so that they worked toward the intended goal with apparent ease and with almost imperceptible motion.[11]

But Greeley did not see these characteristics in Lincoln. In writing of the President and his demise, he declared unfalteringly:

> There are those who say that Mr. Lincoln was fortunate in his death as in his life: I judge otherwise. I hold him most inapt for the leadership of a people involved in desperate, agonizing war; while I deem few men better fitted to guide a nation's destinies in time of peace. Especially do I deem him eminently fitted to soothe, to heal, and to reunite in bonds of true, fraternal affection a people just lapsing into peace after years of distracting, desolating internal strife. His true career was just opening when an assassin's bullet quenched his light of life.[12]

But such judgments of a president are worthless, for Greeley had known Lincoln only as a war president, and he had condemned, almost without exception, all of Lincoln's policies. Not knowing what the man would have done in time of peace, it was useless for him to excuse his efforts to influence the President by supposing that the man had been created to serve the nation after, and not during, the Civil War.

Furthermore, Greeley's editorial entitled "Mr. Lincoln's Fame," which appeared in the *Tribune* a few days after the President's death, reads as though the editor were writing about his own conduct toward Lincoln:

Without the least desire to join in the race of heaping extravagant and preposterous laudations on our dead President as the wisest and greatest man who ever lived, we feel sure that the discerning and considerate of all parties will concur in our judgment that Mr. Lincoln's reputation will stand higher with posterity than with the mass of his contemporaries—that distance, whether in time or space, while dwarfing and obscuring so many, must place him in a fairer light—that future generations will deem him undervalued by those for and with whom he labored, and be puzzled by the bitter fierceness of the personal assaults by which his temper was tested. . . .

He sleeps the sleep of the honored and just, and there are few graves which will be more extensively, persistently visited, or bedewed with the tears of a people's prouder, fonder affection, than that of Abraham Lincoln.[13]

Moreover, according to William McKinley, in an address entitled "Abraham Lincoln, the Great Republican," delivered at the Marquette Club in Chicago, February 12, 1896, Horace Greeley shortly after Lincoln's assassination remarked with apparent sympathy if not real fondness: "I doubt whether man, woman or child, white or black, bond or free, virtuous or vicious, ever accosted, or reached forth a hand to Abraham Lincoln, and detected in his countenance or manner, any repugnance or shrinking from the proffered contact, any assumption of superiority, or betrayal of disdain." [14]

In this same speech, McKinley declared that Greeley, in speaking of the events which led up to and embraced the War between the States, declared firmly: "Other men were helpful and nobly did their part; yet, looking back through the lifting mists of those seven eventful, tragic, trying, glorious years, I clearly discern the one providencial leader, the indispensable hero of the great drama, Abraham Lincoln." [15]

Yet, from the day of Lincoln's election to the day of his death,

he had to face the meddling, shouting, impetuous pronouncements of Greeley's *Tribune,* and still more meddling and personal affronts in the form of the editor's letters and interviews.
Edward Everett Hale relates that, on the day Lincoln was shot,
Greeley had written an editorial which was "a brutal, bitter,
sarcastic personal attack" upon the President. As has been noted,
the managing editor of the *Tribune* withheld it from print, and
was vigorously assailed on the following morning by a broadside
of Greeley's most obnoxious wrath. Whether Lincoln lived or
died, that attack against him should have been printed, cried
the editor. "Erratic" is the only word that fits such a man.

His judgment was always erratic, but the years between 1860
and 1865 were the most erratic of his life. But his opinion of
Lincoln in 1865 may be summed up as a reasonable, discontented expression of the complaints of a large number of very
patriotic and very devoted citizens who did not know what Lincoln was striving to accomplish—what his real purposes and true
abilities were. Therefore, it was not until Lincoln had been
dead for several years that Greeley attained any real conception
of his power, and even then it was not without the old erratic
bias. But by 1872 the editor and would-be president had, even
with this bias, begun to adjust his opinions of the assassinated
leader to the true merits of the man.[16]

Consequently, just before his own death, Greeley could write
about Lincoln with more truth than was always his wont:

> He was not a born king . . . but a child of the people,
> who made himself a great persuader, therefore a leader,
> by dint of firm resolve, patient effort and dogged per-
> severance. He slowly won his way to eminence and fame
> by doing the work that lay next to him—doing it with
> all his growing might—doing it as well as he could, and
> learning by his failure, when failure was encountered,
> how to do it better. . . . He was open to all impressions
> and influences, and gladly profited by the teachings of
> events and circumstances, no matter how adverse or un-

welcome. There was probably no year of his life when
he was not a wiser, cooler and better man than he had
been the year preceding.[17]

This, then, was Abraham Lincoln as Horace Greeley finally
saw him and came to know him. As these facts slowly dawned
upon a still-erratic and a dying, heartbroken Greeley, he saw,
too, why he had failed to influence Lincoln, and how very wise
the sixteenth president had been.

Notes

CHAPTER ONE

1 Jeter Allen Isely, *Horace Greeley and the Republican Party, 1853–1861,* p. 266.

2 Gamaliel Bradford, *As God Made Them,* p. 131.

3 *Ibid.*

4 *Ibid.,* p. 132.

5 As cited *ibid.,* p. 148.

6 *Ibid.,* p. 149.

7 *Ibid.,* pp. 162–63.

8 *Ibid.,* p. 164.

9 Abraham Lincoln made this statement to Governor Bramlette, ex-Senator Dixon, and Editor Hodges, when "they waited on him with Kentucky's remonstrance against the arming of Blacks to put down the Rebellion, and against the Emancipation policy, too tardily adopted by the Union," according to the anxious *Tribune* editor (Horace Greeley, *Recollections of a Busy Life,* p. 281).

10 Greeley, *loc. cit.*

11 J. Parton, *The Life of Horace Greeley,* pp. 434–35.

12 *Ibid.*

13 Joseph Bucklin Bishop, *Notes and Anecdotes of Many Years,* p. 24. Bishop, whose lengthy journalistic career spanned more than three decades, served for many years on the New York *Tribune,* becoming an ardent admirer and an able associate of the editor, Horace Greeley, whom he accurately describes in this memoir of his life.

14 *Ibid.*

15 Henry Luther Stoddard, *Horace Greeley: Printer, Editor, Crusader,* p. 205.

16 Allan Nevins, "Horace Greeley, the Editor and the Man," *Bookman,* LXIV (February, 1927), 740–41.

17 *Ibid.*

18 *Ibid.*

19 Don C. Seitz, *Horace Greeley, Founder of the New York Tribune,* p. 155.

20 *Ibid.,* p. 156. Alvan (sometimes spelled Alvin) Bovay was among the leaders in the formation of the Republican organization at Ripon, Wisconsin, in February, 1854.

21 *Ibid.*

22 Bishop, *op. cit.,* p. 8.

23 *Ibid.,* pp. 9–10.

24 *Ibid.,* pp. 10–11.

25 *Ibid.,* pp. 10–12.
26 *Ibid.,* p. 13.
27 *Ibid.,* p. 15.
28 *Ibid.,* p. 16.
29 *Ibid.,* pp. 17–18.
30 *Ibid.,* p. 19.
31 *Ibid.,* pp. 21–22.
32 *Ibid.,* p. 23.
33 Parton, *op. cit.,* pp. 435–37.
34 *Ibid.,* p. 438.
35 *Ibid.,* pp. 439–40.
36 Irving Stone, *They Also Ran,* p. 2.
37 *Ibid.,* p. 3.
38 *Ibid.,* p. 4.
39 *Ibid.,* p. 18.
40 Bradford, *op. cit.,* pp. 134–35.
41 *Ibid.,* pp. 135–37.
42 *Ibid.,* p. 138.
43 *Ibid.,* pp. 140–41.
44 *Ibid.,* pp. 141–42.
45 *Ibid.,* p. 146.
46 *Ibid.,* pp. 146–47.
47 *Ibid.*
48 *Ibid.,* p. 145.
49 S. Margaret Fuller Ossoli, *Literature and Art,* Introduction, p. i.
50 *Ibid.,* p. ii.
51 *Ibid.,* p. iv.
52 "Voice of the *Tribune,*" *Newsweek,* xxxvi (October 2, 1950), 56.
53 *Ibid.*
54 Parton, *op. cit.,* pp. 434–40.
55 *Ibid.,* p. 441.
56 *Ibid.,* pp. 441–42.
57 *Ibid.,* p. 442.
58 Carl Sandburg, *Storm Over the Land: A Profile of the Civil War,* taken mainly from *Abraham Lincoln: The War Years,* pp. 6–7.
59 *Ibid.*
60 John George Nicolay, *The Outbreak of Rebellion,* p. 46.
61 *Ibid.,* pp. 46–47.
62 *Ibid.,* pp. 47–48. See also Paul M. Angle (ed.), *The Lincoln Reader,* pp. 415–16, for statement by Ward Hill Lamon in regard to concern shown in Washington over Lincoln's mode of dress, habits, speech, etc.
63 Nicolay, *loc. cit.*
64 Sandburg, *op. cit.,* p. 13.
65 *Ibid.*
66 *Ibid.*
67 *Ibid.,* p. 126.
68 *An Autobiography of Abraham Lincoln* (consisting of the personal portions of Lincoln's letters, speeches, and conversations), compiled and annotated by Nathaniel Wright Stephenson, pp. 300–301.

69 *Ibid.* In a later chapter, there follows a discussion of the influence of Greeley upon this marked change in Lincoln's attitude toward McClellan and the conduct of the war.

70 *Ibid.,* p. 301.

71 *Ibid.,* p. 317.

72 *Ibid.*

73 *Ibid.,* p. 336.

74 Sandburg, *op. cit.,* pp. 308-9.

75 *Ibid.,* p. 309.

76 *Ibid.*

77 *Ibid.,* p. 310.

78 *Ibid.,* p. 311.

79 *Ibid.,* pp. 311-12.

80 *Ibid.,* p. 312.

81 *Ibid.*

82 *Ibid.,* pp. 312-13.

83 *Ibid.,* p. 313.

84 *Ibid.,* p. 314.

85 *Ibid.* Not only Greeley's *Tribune* and other New York newspapers, but also prominent Chicago papers, like the *Times,* sarcastically chastized Lincoln.

86 *Ibid.*

87 *Ibid.,* p. 315.

88 *Ibid.*

89 Henry B. Rankin, *Intimate Character Sketches of Abraham Lincoln,* pp. 9-10.

90 *Ibid.,* pp. 10-11.

91 *Ibid.,* p. 23.

92 *Ibid.,* p. 37.

93 Lord Charnwood, *Abraham Lincoln,* pp. 143-44.

94 *Ibid.*

95 *The Hidden Lincoln, From the Letters and Papers of William H. Herndon,* edited by Emanuel Hertz, p. 14.

96 *Ibid.,* p. 94.

97 *Ibid.,* pp. 114-15.

98 Herndon describes one of his disagreements with Greeley concerning what the latter printed in the *Tribune;* it may be read in this same letter (*ibid.,* pp. 114-15).

99 *Lincoln and the Civil War in the Diaries and Letters of John Hay,* selected with an Introduction by Tyler Dennett, p. 56.

100 *Ibid.,* p. 56n.

101 William Harlan Hale, *Horace Greeley, Voice of the People,* p. 211.

102 *Ibid.*

103 *Ibid.,* p. 212.

104 *Ibid.*

105 *Autobiography of Abraham Lincoln,* pp. 57-58.

106 *Ibid.*

107 *Ibid.,* pp. 58-59.

108 Charnwood, *op. cit.,* p. 454.

109 *Ibid.*
110 *Ibid.*, pp. 454–55.
111 *Ibid.*, p. 455.
112 *Ibid.*, pp. 455–56.
113 *Ibid.*
114 *Ibid.*, p. 456.
115 Sandburg, *op. cit.*, pp. 89–90.
116 *Ibid.*, p. 90.
117 *Ibid.*
118 *Ibid.*, pp. 90–91.
119 *Ibid.*, p. 91.
120 *Ibid.*, pp. 91–92.

CHAPTER TWO

1 William Harlan Hale, *Horace Greeley, Voice of the People*, p. 208.
2 *Ibid.*, p. 210.
3 *The Complete Works of Abraham Lincoln*, edited by John G. Nicolay and John Hay, ii, 53–54. Herein Lincoln evidences a little humility in deference to Greeley, and a little sarcasm.
4 L. Pierce Clark, *Lincoln: A Psycho-Biography*, p. 444.
5 *Ibid.*, p. 438.
6 Abraham Lincoln to Charles L. Wilson, Springfield, Illinois, June 1, 1858, Nicolay and Hay, *op. cit.*, ii, 363–64.
7 *Ibid.*
8 *Ibid.*, p. 364.
9 *The Lincoln Papers*, edited by David C. Mearns, i, 223.
10 Hale, *op. cit.*, p. 214. Greeley wrote a treatise entitled *Political Economy;* any references to his opinions in this field may be further amplified from his work.
11 *Ibid.*, pp. 214–15.
12 Nicolay and Hay, *op. cit.*, v, 293. Nicolay and Hay place more emphasis upon the power of this speech than do most other contemporaries; however, Nicolay and Hay are inclined to overevaluate Lincoln and his achievements.
13 French Ensor Chadwick, *Causes of the Civil War, 1859–1861*, p. 102.
14 *Ibid.*
15 *Ibid.*
16 Ida M. Tarbell, *The Life of Abraham Lincoln*, Sangamon Edition, ii, 157–58. As the years passed, Greeley forgot that Lincoln's arguments could be sound, and he thought of him as the mildest and the slowest of all men.
17 Mearns, *op. cit.*, i, 231.
18 Hale, *op. cit.*, p. 202.
19 *Ibid.* Unlike Weed and other political bosses, Greeley did not think that the party was an end in itself; it served merely as a convenient means to an end and could be destroyed, revived, or revamped when necessary.
20 *Ibid.*, pp. 202–3. In this instance, Greeley played the political game with the coolness, the unscrupulousness, and the premeditated manner usually associated with his one-time partner, Thurlow Weed of Albany and New York politics.

21 *Ibid.*, pp. 203–4.

22 *Ibid.*, p. 205.

23 Jeter Allen Isely, *Horace Greeley and the Republican Party, 1853–1861,* p. 70. Isely's book gives a more detailed account of Greeley's political partnership with Weed and Seward than it is possible to give here; for further amplification, see his work.

24 William B. Hesseltine, *Lincoln and the War Governors,* p. 30; Isely, *loc. cit.*

25 Isely, *op. cit.*, p. 71.

26 *Ibid.*, pp. 72–73. Weed was still following these "golden dollars" at Chicago in 1860; and Greeley, knowing this better than anyone else, used his knowledge to defeat Seward's nomination and to place Lincoln at the head of the ticket.

27 *Ibid.*, p. 73.

28 *Ibid.*, pp. 109–10; George Fort Milton, *Conflict: The American Civil War,* pp. 82, 129.

29 Isely, *op. cit.*, pp. 209–10.

30 Hale, *op. cit.*, p. 207.

31 *Ibid.*, p. 208.

32 Allan Nevins, *The Emergence of Lincoln,* II, 233–34.

33 Isely, *op. cit.*, p. 255.

34 Horace Greeley, *Recollections of a Busy Life,* p. 389; Clarence Edward Macartney, *Lincoln and His Cabinet,* p. 67.

35 Isely, *op. cit.*, p. 256.

36 *Ibid.*, p. 259.

37 *Ibid.*, p. 263.

38 *Ibid.*, p. 264.

39 Reinhard H. Luthin, *The First Lincoln Campaign,* pp. 62–63.

40 *Ibid.*, p. 63.

41 *Ibid.*, pp. 63–64.

42 Isely, *op. cit.*, pp. 266–67.

43 *Ibid.*, pp. 266–68.

44 *Ibid.*, pp. 268–70.

45 *Ibid.*, pp. 270–72.

46 Luthin, *op. cit.*, pp. 62–64; Isely, *op. cit.*, pp. 272–74.

47 Chadwick, *op. cit.*, pp. 116–17.

48 Isely, *op. cit.*, pp. 274–75.

49 Edward Chase Kirkland, *The Peacemakers of 1864,* pp. 63–64; Isely, *op. cit.*, p. 276. Certain of a Republican victory in 1860, Greeley had his eye upon a political office, possibly a Cabinet post; and the editor knew that, if Seward were nominated and elected, he would again be shelved.

50 Kirkland, *op. cit.*, pp. 63–64; Isely, *op. cit.*, pp. 277–78.

51 Hale, *op. cit.*, pp. 215–16. There is a possibility, although no evidence is available to substantiate it, that Greeley, hungry for political office, hoped that if he backed Bates wisely enough and successfully enough he might become the Missourian's running mate; then, in the quite possible eventuality of the "old man's" death, Greeley would become president, filling an office he secretly desired to hold.

52 Isely, *op. cit.*, pp. 279–80. See also, Hale, *op. cit.*, pp. 216–17. Although

Greeley on almost every other occasion proved erratic and inconsistent in his policies, in regard to his support of Bates and his antagonism toward Seward his attitude remained adamantly unswerving.

CHAPTER THREE

1 Reinhard H. Luthin, *The First Lincoln Campaign,* pp. 136–37.

2 Harry J. Carman and Reinhard H. Luthin, *Lincoln and the Patronage,* pp. 7ff.

3 William B. Hesseltine, *Lincoln and the War Governors,* p. 54.

4 William Harlan Hale, *Horace Greeley, Voice of the People,* pp. 217–18.

5 Ida M. Tarbell, *The Life of Abraham Lincoln,* ii, 178.

6 L. D. Ingersoll, *The Life of Horace Greeley,* p. 339. Ingersoll witnessed Greeley's actions at Chicago and has apparently recorded them with authentic accuracy and impartiality.

7 From Jesse K. Dubois to Abraham Lincoln, Chicago, May 13, 1860 (punctuation and spelling slightly altered), David C. Mearns (ed.), *The Lincoln Papers,* i, 233. This letter is vitally important. Note the reference to the Indiana delegation, remembering that it was mentioned earlier that Greeley and the Blairs and Schuyler Colfax struggled desperately to send an Indiana delegation to Chicago instructed to vote for Bates, but that the anti-nativist Germans prevented this, so that when the delegation arrived in Chicago, "a portion were for Bates," but the rest would vote for Lincoln. Greeley knew that the conservative people of Indiana would not support Seward and that they would give their electoral votes to the Democrats or more probably to the Bell party, unless a conservative, ultimately Lincoln, could be nominated. Moreover, Indiana, like Illinois, was a pivotal state in the November elections. Note how the Lincoln men, sure of Illinois, were concentrating on Indiana, Pennsylvania, and Ohio. It is also vitally significant that Judge David Davis was, to quote the letter, "furious" because of Greeley's incessant activities in behalf of Bates, whom almost everyone knew was out of the running. Some scholars feel, although such opinions are cautiously expressed, that Greeley's support of Bates was merely a blind to confuse the Seward delegates, while Greeley waited to see which other candidate possessed the best opportunity of defeating Seward. Apparently Davis expected Greeley's assistance as soon as the editor saw that Bates's chance for the nomination was hopeless, but Greeley was more cautious, waiting until he was certain that Lincoln could receive the nomination.

8 Clarence Edward Macartney, *Lincoln and His Cabinet,* pp. 53–54.

9 Luthin, *op. cit.,* p. 137.

10 Jeter Allen Isley, *Horace Greeley and the Republican Party, 1853–1861,* p. 282.

11 Allan Nevins, *The Emergence of Lincoln,* ii, 252.

12 Nevins *(ibid.)* carefully contrasts the attitudes and the policies of Weed and Greeley at Chicago; here, Weed was foolish and Greeley clever. After the war came, however, Weed returned to his coolly calculating position, while Greeley became almost erratically insane in his inconsistent condemnation of the President.

13 Henry Luther Stoddard, *Horace Greeley: Printer, Editor, Crusader,* p. 195.

14 *Ibid.,* pp. 195–96.

15 *Ibid.,* pp. 196–98.

16 Hale, *op. cit.,* pp. 218–20.

17 Stoddard, *op. cit.,* p. 197.

18 *Ibid.,* pp. 198–99.

19 *Ibid.,* p. 199.

20 Carl Russell Fish, *The American Civil War,* p. 8.

21 Stoddard, *op. cit.,* p. 199; William E. Baringer, *Lincoln's Rise to Power,* pp. 227–40.

22 Stoddard, *loc. cit.;* Baringer, *op. cit.,* pp. 240–55.

23 Stoddard, *op. cit.,* p. 200. No records have ever been found to indicate what happened to the "lost" tally sheets at the end of the second day of the convention. Certain it is that something was done with them, and probability suggests that the clever Lincoln managers—in many respects more unscrupulous even than Thurlow Weed—made certain that the sheets for recording the ballots did not appear until the last possible moment, until every effort had been made to bargain Lincoln into the first place on the ticket. Neither is there any record to prove that Greeley was connected with the disappearance of the tally sheets; it is safe to assume, however, that he would have enjoyed playing his part in the maneuver.

24 William E. Barton, *The Life of Abraham Lincoln,* I, 429; Stoddard, *loc. cit.;* Baringer, *op. cit.,* pp. 255–70.

25 Stoddard, *loc. cit.*

26 *Ibid.,* pp. 201–2; L. Pierce Clark, *Lincoln: A Psycho-Biography,* pp. 456–57.

27 Ingersoll, *op. cit.,* p. 340.

28 Ingersoll, who was at the convention, in the Wigwam and in Tremont House, believes that Greeley was not deceived, but that he pretended pessimism to make Weed overconfident (*ibid.,* p. 341). No other sources, primary or secondary, wholly agree with Ingersoll in this view.

29 Hale, *op cit.,* p. 222; Baringer, *op. cit.,* pp. 270–75.

30 Stoddard, *op. cit.,* p. 202; Clark, *op. cit.,* pp. 456–57.

31 Stoddard, *op. cit.,* pp. 202–3.

32 Hale, *op. cit.,* p. 223; Baringer, *op. cit.,* pp. 275–80.

33 Isely, *op. cit.,* p. 283; Tarbell, *op. cit.,* II, 187.

34 Isely, *loc. cit.*

35 Horace Greeley, *Recollections of a Busy Life,* pp. 390–91.

36 Francis Nicoll Zabriskie, *Horace Greeley, the Editor,* pp. 227–28.

37 *Ibid.,* pp. 229–30.

38 Don C. Seitz, *Horace Greeley, Founder of the New York Tribune,* p. 168.

39 *Ibid.,* pp. 182–83.

40 *Ibid.,* pp. 183–84.

41 *Ibid.*

42 As Henry J. Raymond quickly pointed out, both publicly to his readers and privately to his friends, this official and public honey-talk of Greeley's absolutely contradicted his bitter, sad, and virile letter of November 11, 1854.

Certain it is, whether one supported Seward as did Raymond, or whether one endeavors to be the objective examiner of historical facts, Greeley told "the big lie" in this sugary public statement; in fact, the entire tone of the piece was fallacious. Seward was no friend of Greeley's, and Greeley was no friend of Seward's. Even before the political partnership collapsed, Greeley held on to it reluctantly, and then only for the sake of Weed and for his own selfish purposes, and not because of any loyalty he had ever felt for William H. Seward. Both Greeley's public and private utterances, some of which have been quoted earlier, indicate that Greeley despised, if he did not altogether hate, Seward. Furthermore, during the years of the American Civil War, Greeley, privately and publicly, proved in instance after instance that Seward was perhaps his favorite enemy.

Not as a "sneaking eavesdropper," not as a "scavenger of private letters," but as a student of history one may see at a glance that Greeley had, or thought that he had, dozens of reasons for bearing a personal hostility toward Seward. Furthermore, Greeley was certain that Seward had never treated him with either kindness or courtesy, saying that the latter never asked advice of anyone as an equal, especially disregarding Greeley's oracular commands. Moreover, Greeley considered Seward's "obliging manner" to be thoroughly obnoxious, and he could not lose Seward's friendship, for he did not possess it. In addition, it can be questioned whether or not Greeley placed party loyalty and principles above his personal animosity to Seward. (Seitz, *op. cit.*, p. 184.)

Perhaps one cannot question Greeley's sincerity in supporting Bates and later Lincoln for the nomination; however, one must, in all fairness and objectivity, question Greeley's motives in doing so.

43 Isely, *op. cit.*, pp. 285–86.

44 *Ibid.*

45 *Ibid.*, pp. 287–88.

46 Nevins, *op. cit.*, ii, 252–53.

47 In February, 1861, when Republicans in Congress were concerned over the possible secession of the "border slave states," Greeley declared that, in organizing the territories of Nevada, Colorado, and Dakota without clauses proscribing slavery therein, the Republicans were following their platform of 1860 to the letter. At this time, Stephen A. Douglas taunted his opponents with the charge of accepting his principle of "popular sovereignty"; and he was, in marked degree, correct in his charges. Such a partial acceptance of the Douglas principle was directly due to Greeley's desperate efforts to conciliate the South, as he played his phenomenal part in framing the platform on which Lincoln ran in 1860. (Isely, *op. cit.*, pp. 288–89.)

48 Greeley employed this same attitude, took this identical position, when he sponsored the Crittenden-Montgomery substitute, when he supported the re-election of Douglas to the United States Senate, and when he favored the absorption of the remaining New York Know Nothings into the Republican Party in 1858 (Isley, *op. cit.*, p. 289).

49 *Ibid.*, p. 290. Greeley desired neither Seward's candidacy nor Seward's policies in the platform.

50 *Ibid.* These three economic matters were fundamental in Greeley's

consideration; they were no less important to him than the naming of a proper candidate.

51 *Ibid.,* pp. 290–93.

52 Horace Greeley, *Overland Journey From New York to San Francisco,* pp. 368–73.

53 Isely, *op. cit.,* p. 293.

54 Stoddard, *op. cit.,* p. 204.

55 Hale, *op. cit.,* p. 224.

56 *Ibid.*

57 Isely, *op. cit.,* p. 284.

58 *Ibid.*

59 John T. Morse, Jr., *Abraham Lincoln,* I, 167–72; Isely, *op. cit.,* pp. 284–85.

60 Roy P. Basler, *The Lincoln Legend,* pp. 64–65.

CHAPTER FOUR

1 James Garfield Randall, *The Civil War and Reconstruction,* p. 92.

2 William E. Baringer, *Lincoln's Rise to Power,* p. 315.

3 Horace Greeley, *American Conflict,* I, 319–22.

4 *Ibid.,* pp. 322–23. Note the resemblance to the established position of Stephen A. Douglas on this point.

5 *Ibid.,* pp. 323–24.

6 Greeley wrote that the Bell-Everett party had a distinct, well-established organization within every slave state except South Carolina, that this party polled 40 per cent of the votes in the South, that had it acted immediately after Lincoln's election, declaring itself for holding the nation together at all hazards, it could have prevented secession (*ibid.,* pp. 324–27).

7 *Ibid.,* pp. 326–27. Greeley played an important role in the Lincoln struggle to carry the state of New York.

8 Reinhard H. Luthin, *The First Lincoln Campaign,* p. 210. It is significant that Lincoln wrote to Weed and not to Greeley; during the campaign, as in later years, it appears that Lincoln trusted the sagacity of Weed more than he did the inconsistent advice of Greeley.

9 *Ibid.*

10 *Ibid.,* pp. 210–11.

11 L. D. Ingersoll, *The Life of Horace Greeley,* pp. 353–54.

12 Jeter Allen Isely, *Horace Greeley and the Republican Party, 1853–1861,* pp. 197–98; Luthin, *op. cit.,* p. 177.

13 Isely, *op. cit.,* pp. 291–92.

14 Luthin, *op. cit.,* p. 177.

15 *Ibid.*

16 Isely, *op. cit.,* p. 292.

17 Ida M. Tarbell, *The Life of Abraham Lincoln,* II, 207.

18 Isely, *op. cit.,* p. 295.

19 *Ibid.*

20 Tarbell, *op. cit.,* II, 208–9.

21 Isely, *op. cit.,* pp. 293–94.

22 Henry Luther Stoddard, *Horace Greeley: Printer, Editor, Crusader,* p. 310.

23 William B. Hesseltine, *Lincoln and the War Governors,* pp. 65–66.

24 Isely, *op. cit.,* pp. 294–95.

25 *Ibid.,* p. 296.

26 *Ibid.,* pp. 296–97.

27 *Ibid.,* p. 297.

28 Luthin, *op. cit.,* p. 192.

29 Isely, *op. cit.,* p. 298. This statement evidences, in a small measure, the ignorance which Greeley possessed as regards conditions and feelings in the South; he felt that the threats of disunion meant nothing and that, were Lincoln elected, the South would accept the fact, and the entire nation would profit by it. Wise as he was in regard to the power of his propaganda throughout the North, he was totally unaware of southern propaganda and of the psychological tension which had been created—a tension which Lincoln's election was to force into active secession. Greeley even wrote that the truly democratic papers of both North and South admitted that the measures proposed by the Republican Party would bring about freedom to large numbers of slaves. He did not see those papers which declared that the Republican proposals would be ruinous to the South, that only on a basis of slavery could the two races live together in peace. Furthermore, these papers informed their readers that emancipation had ruined the British West Indies and had brought the blacks and whites there into a disastrous state of social, economic, and professional competition. Without understanding the charges made against the Republican Party, Greeley only indirectly answered them throughout the campaign, disavowing any feeling of radicalism, disclaiming any idea that Lincoln would bring about immediate emancipation. The Republicans did not desire the amalgamation of the races, although the *Tribune* did wish that the "blacks might become citizens." Greeley added that civil rights must be proffered slowly, with the ex-slaves learning to enjoy their own homes and learning to spend the just return of their own labor. Then they could be taught to save and to improve their economic status, to vote, hold office, and be equal with the whites. It would be a long process, declared Greeley, still not understanding southern fears, the signs of secession.

30 *Ibid.,* pp. 299–300.

31 Luthin, *op. cit.,* pp. 192–93.

32 Isley, *op. cit.,* pp. 301–2.

33 *Ibid.,* p. 302.

34 Ingersoll, *op. cit.,* p. 355.

35 Isely, *op. cit.,* pp. 303–4.

36 *Ibid.,* p. 304.

37 *Ibid.,* p. 305.

38 Don C. Seitz, *Horace Greeley, Founder of the New York Tribune,* p. 185; Francis Nicoll Zabriskie, *Horace Greeley, the Editor,* pp. 228–32.

39 Ingersoll, *op. cit.,* pp. 355–56.

40 *Ibid.*

41 Stoddard, *op. cit.,* pp. 207–8.

42 *Ibid.*

43 Isely, *op. cit.,* p. 305.

44 L. Pierce Clark, *Lincoln: A Psycho-Biography,* pp. 255–56.

CHAPTER FIVE

1 Emil Ludwig, *Abraham Lincoln: The Full Life Story of Our Martyred President,* pp. 238–39.

2 Allan Nevins, *The Emergence of Lincoln,* II, 395.

3 *Ibid.,* p. 365.

4 John W. Burgess, *The Civil War and the Constitution, 1859–1865,* I, 145–46.

5 *Ibid.* In excusing himself for this position three years later, Greeley declared that he had been endeavoring to conciliate the South; actually, he did not believe that secession was about to become a reality.

6 *Ibid.*

7 Preston King to John Bigelow, November 12, 1860; John Bigelow, *Retrospections of an Active Life,* I, 316.

8 *Ibid.*

9 Jeter Allen Isely, *Horace Greeley and the Republican Party, 1853–1861,* pp. 305–6.

10 *Ibid.,* p. 306. Without doubt, Greeley's philosophy lacks logic on almost every point; Lincoln saw how foolish the position appeared to thinking men, how welcome it would be to certain abolitionists, and how useful it might be to the South itself. Yet he refused to speak, heeding the advice in Bryant's letter and the words of other advisers. Why should a section be allowed to secede, when a state was forbidden to do so? Why must coercion be anathema? These were questions to which Lincoln must devote ample time and thought, and he began to resent Greeley's hasty attitude and to fear the adverse effect which the *Tribune* might have upon his administration.

11 John A. Logan, *The Great Conspiracy: Its Origin and History* (a contemporary report), p. 109; James Garfield Randall, *The Civil War and Reconstruction,* pp. 322–23, 323n.

12 Isely, *op. cit.,* p. 306.

13 Kenneth C. Wheare, *Abraham Lincoln and the United States,* p. 160; Isely, *op. cit.,* pp. 307, 328.

14 *The Life of Thurlow Weed, Including His Autobiography and a Memoir,* II, 489. In the above letter, written by Weed to Thomas C. Acton, October 10, 1870, one may see that Weed, from 1860 onward, endeavored, in every possible way, to discredit and disgrace Greeley; in this effort, he was often assisted by Greeley's inconsistency and blunderings.

15 John T. Morse, Jr., *Abraham Lincoln,* I, 191–92; Fred Albert Shannon, *The Organization and Administration of the Union Army, 1861–1865,* I, 301; James Garfield Randall, *Lincoln, the Liberal Statesman,* p. 96.

16 French Ensor Chadwick, *Causes of the Civil War, 1859–1861,* pp. 164–65; William B. Hesseltine, *Lincoln and the War Governors,* p. 95; Clarence Edward Macartney, *Lincoln and His Cabinet,* pp. 8, 116; Wood Gray, *The Hidden Civil War,* p. 34; Albert Bushnell Hart, *Salmon Portland Chase,* p. 199; Edward Conrad Smith, *The Borderland in the Civil War,* pp. 77–78.

17 *The Diary of George Templeton Strong,* edited by Allan Nevins and

Milton Halsey Thomas, III, 76. Greeley and Weed differed markedly on their attitudes toward secession, just as they did on all other points of political policy.

18 Morse, *op. cit.*, I, 192.

19 *Ibid.*, pp. 192–93. It may be seen from these scanty public quotations that Greeley's position, from the time of Lincoln's election to the day of his inauguration, did not change in any noticeable degree.

20 *Ibid.*, p. 193.

21 Smith, *op. cit.*, pp. 77–78.

22 Greeley's third point in this lengthy, rambling, sometimes almost illogical letter seems to indicate that, under certain conditions, he would tolerate the idea of coercion against the seceding states. However, he never advocated such a policy publicly; he blamed the South for conspiring to initiate the war, and he wished it ended quickly, hoping not to coerce the South and save the Union but merely to eradicate slavery from any and every section of the American continent.

23 *The Lincoln Papers*, edited by David C. Mearns, II, 349–50; Henry Luther Stoddard, *Horace Greeley: Printer, Editor, Crusader*, p. 209; Robert S. Harper, *Lincoln and the Press*, p. 102.

24 Chadwick, *op. cit.*, p. 177.

25 *Ibid.*

26 Mearns, *op. cit.*, II, 354–55.

27 Arthur Charles Cole, *The Irrepressible Conflict, 1850–1865*, p. 304.

28 Greeley even accused the South of having a "Potsdam Conference" like that of World War I, in which the Kaiser, according to fable, planned mobilization to serve his own vested interests (Burton J. Hendrick, *Statesmen of the Lost Cause*, pp. 86–87).

29 General John B. Gordon, *Reminiscences of the Civil War*, pp. 21–22.

30 John Shipley Tilley, *Lincoln Takes Command*, pp. xix–xx.

31 Editorial 150, Louisville (Kentucky) *Daily Journal*, January 31, 1861, *Southern Editorials on Secession*, prepared by the American Historical Association, edited by Dwight Lowell Dumond, pp. 434–38. Although this editorial contains certain fallacious statements concerning the innocence of the South in provoking the secession crisis, despite the fact that this editorial is excessively lengthy, it has been included, almost in full, because it serves to sum up candidly and concisely the errors in some of Greeley's newspaper statements and the fallacies in parts of his refutable logic in regard to the secession question and the means of resolving it.

32 Kenneth M. Stampp, *And the War Came*, p. 22. This excellent, authoritative, recent study further amplifies the statements set forth above in the editorial from the Louisville *Daily Journal*.

33 New York *Daily Tribune*, November 26, 1860, as cited in Stampp, *op. cit.*, pp. 23–24.

34 New York *Daily Tribune*, February 2, 1861, as cited in Stampp, *op. cit.*, pp. 23–25.

35 New York *Daily Tribune*, March 19, 1861, as cited in Stampp, *op. cit.*, pp. 24–25.

36 Stampp, *loc. cit.*

37 Ida M. Tarbell, *The Life of Abraham Lincoln*, III, 14–15.

38 Burton J. Hendrick, *Lincoln's War Cabinet*, p. 104.

39 Carl Sandburg, *Abraham Lincoln: The War Years*, I, 91–92; Barney to Bryant, January 17, 1861, as cited in Donnal V. Smith, *Chase and Civil War Politics*, p. 26.

40 Mearns, *op. cit.*, II, 425–26.

41 *The Complete Works of Abraham Lincoln*, edited by John G. Nicolay and John Hay, VI, 104.

42 Allan Nevins, *The Emergence of Lincoln*, II, 445–46; *The Life of Thurlow Weed, Including His Autobiography and a Memoir*, II, 325.

43 Nevins, *loc. cit.; The Life of Thurlow Weed*, II, 325.

44 Frederic Bancroft, *The Life of William Henry Seward*, II, 41–42.

45 *Ibid.*

46 Albany *Evening Journal*, February 25, 1861; Bancroft, *loc. cit.*

47 At this moment, because of Buchanan's hesitancy, the whole Blair family was radical in the truest spirit of Jacksonian fervor.

48 Nevins, *op. cit.*, II, 452. Greeley, in this statement, implies that the Weed-Seward contingent of the party sought to sway Lincoln in their direction by "flattering" his wife. Apparently this appalled Greeley.

49 Both Colfax and Caleb Smith resided in Indiana, and only one representative of that state could serve in the Cabinet.

50 Harry J. Carman and Reinhard H. Luthin, *Lincoln and the Patronage*, p. 37; *The Diary of Gideon Welles*, II, 391.

51 Mrs. Rhoda E. White to Abraham Lincoln, December 15, 1860; Mearns, *op. cit.*, II, 341–42.

52 Carl Sandburg, *Abraham Lincoln: The War Years*, II, 464.

53 Carman and Luthin, *op. cit.*, pp. 59–60.

54 *Ibid.*, p. 60.

55 *Ibid.*, pp. 60–61.

56 Robert S. Harper, *Lincoln and the Press*, pp. 77–78.

57 *Ibid.*, p. 78.

58 Clarence Edward Macartney, *Lincoln and His Cabinet*, p. 9; Francis Nicoll Zabriskie, *Horace Greeley, the Editor*, p. 251; Sandburg, *Abraham Lincoln: The War Years*, I, 62.

59 Tarbell, *The Life of Abraham Lincoln*, III, 36; Sandburg, *op. cit.*, I, 51.

60 Carman and Luthin, *op. cit.*, pp. 61–62.

61 *Ibid.* Actually, Chase was far more responsible for securing the appointment of Barney than was Greeley; however, the latter, always inclined to overrate his importance, partially attributed the result to his own conversation with Lincoln while the latter was en route to Washington for the inauguration.

62 T. Harry Williams, *Lincoln and the Radicals*, pp. 21–22.

63 *Ibid.*

64 *The Diary of George Templeton Strong*, edited by Allan Nevins and Milton Halsey Thomas, III, 102–3.

65 Carman and Luthin, *op. cit.*, p. 64; for further amplification, see *The Diary and Correspondence of Salmon P. Chase*, for March 27, 1861.

66 Carman and Luthin, *op. cit.*, p. 64.

67 Lincoln to Chase, May 8, 1861, Carman and Luthin, *op. cit.*, p. 64; for further details see Nicolay and Hay, *op. cit.*, under this date.

68 Nevins, *op. cit.*, ii, 452–54.
69 Henry Luther Stoddard, *Horace Greeley: Printer, Editor, Crusader,* pp. 210–11.
70 *Ibid.*, pp. 211–12.
71 Isely, *op. cit.*, p. 329.
72 Stoddard, *op. cit.*, pp. 211–12.

CHAPTER SIX

1 Wood Gray, *The Hidden Civil War,* p. 49.
2 Fred Albert Shannon, *The Organization and Administration of the Union Army, 1861–1865,* i, 48.
3 Horace Greeley, *The American Conflict,* i, 355–56.
4 Horace Greeley, *Recollections of a Busy Life,* pp. 402–3.
5 Jeter Allen Isely, *Horace Greeley and the Republican Party, 1853–1861,* p. 330; Gray, *op. cit.,* p. 49. Greeley apparently forgot or denied the fact that his *Tribune* had led the way in creating the southern opinion that the North was willing to submit peacefully to secession.
6 Isely, *op. cit.,* p. 330.
7 *Ibid.,* p. 331.
8 Gray, *loc. cit.*
9 *The American Iliad,* edited by Otto Eisenschiml and Ralph Newman, pp. 28–29. This colorless comment on the first act of hostility between North and South indicates a measure of sarcasm on Greeley's part. He had advised Lincoln to pursue some vigorous action; many students of history feel, without source materials to prove their opinions, that Lincoln provoked the southern attack. Greeley should have been happy if he believed that Lincoln had purposely ended the suspense. However, Greeley had not directed the operation, and he remained in his state of voluble frustration.
10 *The Diary of George Templeton Strong,* iii, 120–21. The "Willy Duncan" to whom Strong refers was William B. Duncan, a conservative Democratic merchant, who, in 1860, had been one of the business leaders that tried to fuse the Douglas, Bell, and Breckinridge parties to defeat Lincoln and thus "save the Union." The fact that Duncan, who deprecated the coming of the war, associated Greeley with the President and with Seward in his "hanging recommendation" would seem to indicate that the *Tribune* editor had no connection with those New York City merchants who desired that the city secede with the South or take other drastic action to prevent the Civil War. This was essentially a Democratic, or a "fusion," movement, and Greeley, despite the advertisements he may have lost, generally opposed it.
11 Isely, *op. cit.,* p. 332.
12 Benjamin P. Thomas, *Abraham Lincoln,* p. 259.
13 Robert S. Harper, *Lincoln and the Press,* p. 100.
14 George William Brown, *Baltimore and the Nineteenth of April, 1861,* pp. 76–77. This is a contemporary account by the chief judge of the "supreme bench of Baltimore," G. W. Brown, who was also mayor of the city in 1861, who resented Greeley's belligerent border-state policy, as did Lincoln.
15 *Ibid.*
16 *The Diary of Gideon Welles,* i, 50–51.

17 *Ibid.*

18 *Ibid.*, p. 51.

19 Horace Greeley to Abraham Lincoln, May 19, 1861, *The Lincoln Papers*, compiled by David C. Mearns, ii, 611.

20 Moncure Daniel Conway, *Autobiography, Memories, and Experiences*, i, 332; Margaret Leech, *Reveille in Washington, 1860–1865*, p. 86.

21 Conway, *op. cit.*, i, 331.

22 Greeley, *Recollections of a Busy Life*, pp. 402–3.

23 George Fort Milton, *Conflict: The American Civil War*, pp. 49–51.

24 *Ibid.*, pp. 50–51.

25 William Harlan Hale, *Horace Greeley, Voice of the People*, p. 246; *The Life of Thurlow Weed, Including His Autobiography and a Memoir*, ii, 336, 490, 496.

26 Greeley, *loc. cit.*; William E. Barton, *The Life of Abraham Lincoln*, ii, 73.

27 Isley, *op. cit.*, p. 332.

28 New York *Daily Tribune*, July 23–July 25, 1861; letter from Horace Greeley to B. Brockway, August 14, 1861, in the Greeley Manuscripts, as cited in T. Harry Williams, *Lincoln and the Radicals*, p. 31.

29 T. Harry Williams, *loc. cit.*

30 Barton, *op. cit.*, ii, 73–75; Thomas, *op. cit.*, p. 273; Harper, *op. cit.*, pp. 104–6.

31 Clarence Edward Macartney, *Highways and Byways of the Civil War*, p. 17; Carl Sandburg, *Abraham Lincoln: The War Years*, i, 305–6.

32 Macartney, *op. cit.*, pp. 17–18; Sandburg, *loc. cit.*

33 Conway, *op. cit.*, i, 336. Greeley does not mention Lincoln in this letter, nor is there any allusion to the fact that the President has not responded to his urgent missive. However, the editor still expresses an implied criticism of the chief executive in no uncertain terms. To him, Lincoln is still not, and may never be, a great man.

34 Shannon, *op. cit.*, i, 185–86.

35 *Ibid.*, p. 186.

36 Harry J. Carman and Reinhard H. Luthin, *Lincoln and the Patronage*, pp. 150–51.

37 *Ibid.*

38 T. Harry Williams, *op. cit.*, p. 38.

39 Kenneth P. Williams, *Lincoln Finds a General*, iii, 33–35.

40 *Ibid.*

41 *Ibid.*, pp. 34–35.

42 *Ibid.*

43 New York *Daily Tribune*, May 9, 1861; Shannon, *op. cit.*, i, 221–22.

44 Shannon, *loc. cit.*

45 Thomas, *op. cit.*, p. 278.

46 New York *Daily Tribune*, October 13, 1861; William B. Hesseltine, *Lincoln and the War Governors*, pp. 230–31.

47 Kenneth P. Williams, *op. cit.*, iii, 103.

48 *Ibid.*

49 T. Harry Williams, *op. cit.*, p. 42.

50 Sandburg, *op. cit.*, i, 401–3.

51 *The Complete Works of Abraham Lincoln,* edited by John G. Nicolay and John Hay, xi, 120–22. This letter tends to indicate that Lincoln had, by the autumn of 1861, determined not that Greeley should influence him but that he should influence Greeley. The letter itself indicates that Greeley suggested the arrangement, but there is no other proof of it.

52 Emil Ludwig, *Abraham Lincoln,* translated by Eden and Cedar Paul, p. 297.

CHAPTER SEVEN

1 Kenneth P. Williams, *Lincoln Finds a General,* iii, 154.

2 *Ibid.* Momentarily, Greeley forgot his support of John C. Fremont and his proclamation, gloating over Lincoln's praise of him in the letter to Robert J. Walker and supporting presidential policies.

3 *Ibid.*

4 *Ibid.*

5 Harry J. Carman and Reinhard H. Luthin, *Lincoln and the Patronage,* pp. 110–11.

6 *Ibid.*

7 Greeley to Chase, February 10, 1864, as cited in Carman and Luthin, *loc. cit.* Wakeman's appointment was confirmed by the Senate in March, and the following June he initiated a thorough purge of the remaining Democrats from the nation's largest post office. Suggestions that key men in the office be spared in the interests of efficiency fell on deaf ears; political reward rather than fitness for service prevailed.

8 *The Life of Thurlow Weed, Including His Autobiography and a Memoir,* the memoir being compiled by Weed's grandson, Thurlow Weed Barnes, ii, 287–88.

9 T. Harry Williams, *Lincoln and the Radicals,* p. 54.

10 *Ibid.* See also, Benjamin P. Thomas, *Abraham Lincoln,* p. 289.

11 Kenneth P. Williams, *op. cit.,* iii, 484.

12 *Ibid.*

13 William B. Hesseltine, *Lincoln and the War Governors,* pp. 233–34.

14 Kenneth P. Williams, *op. cit.,* iii, 484.

15 Carl Sandburg, *Abraham Lincoln: The War Years,* i, 401. Lincoln appears to have employed real sarcasm here, for Greeley's lecture was a direct frontal attack upon the President's primary principles and policies.

16 *Ibid.*

17 Donnal V. Smith, *Chase and Civil War Politics,* p. 53.

18 Lincoln to Greeley, March 24, 1862, as cited in Sandburg, *op. cit.,* i, 564–66. Apparently, both Greeley and Lincoln engaged in the same sort of trickery—that is, both men wrote letters intended for each other to mutual acquaintances, instructing those acquaintances to show the letters to the true recipient. As Lincoln had written to Robert J. Walker a letter meant for Greeley, now Greeley had written to Schuyler Colfax a letter which the latter had been instructed to show to Lincoln, with the hope that it might speed action toward emancipation.

19 *Ibid.,* p. 566.

20 T. Harry Williams, *op. cit.,* p. 162.

21 *Ibid.*, p. 171; Frederic Bancroft, *The Life of William Henry Seward*, II, 358.

22 New York *Daily Tribune*, July 10–11, 1862; Hesseltine, *op. cit.*, p. 202.

23 Sandburg, *op. cit.*, I, 559–60.

24 *Ibid.*, p. 560.

25 Carl Russell Fish, *The American Civil War*, pp. 121, 324; Henry Luther Stoddard, *Horace Greeley: Printer, Editor, Crusader*, pp. 220–21.

26 Albert Gallatin Riddle, *Recollections of War Times, 1860–1865*, p. 204; Horace Greeley, *The American Conflict*, II, 249–50; George Fort Milton, *Conflict: The American Civil War*, p. 228; Francis Nicoll Zabriskie, *Horace Greeley, the Editor*, pp. 243–44.

27 Rossiter Johnson, *A Short History of the War of Secession, 1861–1865*, pp. 212–13; Clarence Edward Macartney, *Lincoln and His Cabinet*, p. 236; Hesseltine, *op. cit.*, pp. 250–51.

28 Ida M. Tarbell, *The Life of Abraham Lincoln*, III, 182.

29 James Ford Rhodes, *History of the Civil War, 1861–1865*, pp. 154–55; *The Complete Works of Abraham Lincoln*, edited by John G. Nicolay and John Hay, XI, xi–xii.

30 Tarbell, *op. cit.*, III, 182; Rhodes, *op. cit.*, pp. 154–55; Sandburg, *Abraham Lincoln: The War Years*, I, 567; James Garfield Randall, *The Civil War and Reconstruction*, pp. 485–86; *The Diary of Gideon Welles*, I, 70; Ephraim Douglass Adams, *Great Britain and the American Civil War*, II, 92–93; John T. Morse, Jr., *Abraham Lincoln*, II, 105–6, 108–9; Kenneth C. Wheare, *Abraham Lincoln and the United States*, pp. 240–41; John A. Logan, *The Great Conspiracy: Its Origin and History*, pp. 432–34.

31 Johnson, *op. cit.*, p. 213; Hesseltine, *op. cit.*, pp. 250–51; Macartney, *Lincoln and His Cabinet*, p. 236.

32 *The Complete Works of Abraham Lincoln*, edited by John G. Nicolay and John Hay, VIII, 15–16; Burton J. Hendrick, *Lincoln's War Cabinet*, pp. 350–54; Benjamin P. Thomas, *Abraham Lincoln*, pp. 342, 409; Robert S. Harper, *Lincoln and the Press*, pp. 172–73.

33 Rhodes, *op. cit.*, pp. 154–55.

34 William E. Barton, *The Life of Abraham Lincoln*, II, 140; George Fort Milton, *Abraham Lincoln and the Fifth Column*, p. 99.

35 Donnal V. Smith, *Chase and Civil War Politics*, pp. 44–45; Roy P. Basler, *The Lincoln Legend*, p. 211.

36 Kenneth C. Wheare, *Abraham Lincoln and the United States*, p. 244.

37 *Ibid.*

38 Burton J. Hendrick, *Lincoln's War Cabinet*, p. 292.

39 George Fort Milton, *Abraham Lincoln and the Fifth Column*, p. 109.

40 Hesseltine, *op. cit.*, pp. 281–82.

41 *Ibid.*, pp. 282–84.

42 Kenneth P. Williams, *op. cit.*, III, 212–13.

43 *Ibid.*, p. 231.

44 New York *Daily Tribune*, February 13, 1862; Kenneth P. Williams, *loc. cit.*

45 Burton J. Hendrick, *Lincoln's War Cabinet*, p. 295.

46 Kenneth P. Williams, *op. cit.*, III, 231.

47 *Ibid.*, pp. 438–39.

48 *Ibid.*

49 T. Harry Williams, *op. cit.,* pp. 114–15. Although for eighty years the world's best military minds have been unable to solve the problem of the quandary of George B. McClellan—his plans, his hesitations, his purposes, his changes of plans, his 1862 Peninsula campaign, his personal arrogance and public ambitions—the anti-Lincoln radicals solved these unanswerables immediately: the man's heart was not in the war; he did not wish the North to win or, at least, not to win quickly or decisively. Horace Greeley thundered almost daily in the *Tribune* that the ambitious general was determined to prolong the strife in order to be elected President. His real design, according to this Jacobin editor, was to restore the southern dynasty that had ruled the nation before 1860, and to re-establish on an impregnable basis its system of slave labor. Not many critics of McClellan today accept this explanation, but there proved to be a multitude who, in 1862, believed it implicitly. (Burton J. Hendrick, *Lincoln's War Cabinet,* p. 288.) Perhaps Greeley did not directly influence Lincoln in his decision to dismiss McClellan; however, indirectly, through guiding public opinion away from the eager young McClellan, Greeley did have some influence upon the President's decision. Nevertheless, in view of McClellan's 1864 popularity, plus the fact that Lincoln, in choosing and in dismissing other generals, did not bow to Greeley's erratic will, one may say that the editor's influence remained slight.

50 Sandburg, *Abraham Lincoln: The War Years,* I, 604.

51 T. Harry Williams, *op. cit.,* p. 190.

52 *Ibid.,* p. 195.

53 *Ibid.*

54 Harry J. Carman and Reinhard H. Luthin, *Lincoln and the Patronage,* p. 121.

55 T. Harry Williams, *op. cit.,* p. 207.

56 Hendrick, *Lincoln's War Cabinet,* pp. 325–27.

57 *Ibid.*

58 T. Harry Williams, *op. cit.,* p. 219.

59 Kenneth P. Williams, *op. cit.,* II, 504.

60 *Ibid.,* p. 505.

61 *Ibid.*

62 Donnal V. Smith, *Chase and Civil War Politics,* p. 61; see also, *Memoirs and Letters of John R. Adams* and the Cincinnati *Commercial,* both under date of January 2, 1863.

63 *Diary of Ephraim Cutler,* December 16, 1862, as cited in Donnal V. Smith, *op. cit.,* p. 61.

64 Donnal V. Smith, *op. cit.,* p. 61; J. R. Gilmore, *Personal Recollections of Abraham Lincoln and the Civil War,* p. 75.

65 T. Harry Williams, *op. cit.,* p. 272.

66 *Ibid.,* p. 273.

67 *Ibid.,* p. 285.

68 Bruce Catton, *Glory Road,* p. 230.

69 *Ibid.*

70 *Ibid.*

CHAPTER EIGHT

1 Carl Sandburg, *Abraham Lincoln: The War Years,* III, 249; William Eleroy Curtis, *The True Abraham Lincoln,* p. 284.

2 Sandburg, *loc. cit.;* Curtis, *loc. cit.*

3 *The Lincoln Papers,* compiled by David C. Mearns, I, 41; Benjamin P. Thomas, *Abraham Lincoln,* p. 466.

4 Carl Russell Fish, *The American Civil War,* p. 345.

5 Donnal V. Smith, *Chase and Civil War Politics,* pp. 62–64; *The Complete Works of Abraham Lincoln,* edited by John G. Nicolay and John Hay, VI, 268.

6 Donnal V. Smith, *loc. cit.*

7 Frederic Bancroft, *The Life of William Henry Seward,* II, 370.

8 *The Writings of Abraham Lincoln,* Constitutional Edition, edited by Arthur Brooks Lapsley, VIII, 354.

9 *Ibid.*

10 Wood Gray, *The Hidden Civil War,* p. 128; *The Diary of George Templeton Strong,* edited by Allan Nevins and Milton Halsey Thomas, III, 285–86.

11 Gray, *loc. cit.*

12 James Ford Rhodes, *History of the Civil War, 1861–1865,* p. 201; John T. Morse, Jr., *Abraham Lincoln,* II, 175; Gray, *op. cit.,* p. 128; Sandburg, *op. cit.,* II, 66–67.

13 Ephraim Douglass Adams, *Great Britain and the American Civil War,* II, 75–76.

14 Ida M. Tarbell, *The Life of Abraham Lincoln,* IV, 2.

15 *Ibid.,* p. 3. See also, James R. Gilmore, *Personal Recollections of Abraham Lincoln,* for complete details.

16 Clarence Edward Macartney, *Lincoln and His Cabinet,* p. 249; Sandburg, *op. cit.,* II, 195–96, 421; Tarbell, *op. cit.,* IV, 3.

17 Tarbell, *loc. cit.*

18 *Ibid.*

19 New York *Daily Tribune,* July 4, 1862, as cited in Fred Albert Shannon, *The Organization and Administration of the Union Army, 1861–1865,* I, 274–75.

20 James Garfield Randall, *The Civil War and Reconstruction,* p. 607.

21 Shannon, *op. cit.,* I, 299–300.

22 *Ibid.,* p. 300.

23 Randall, *op. cit.,* p. 607.

24 Horace Greeley to Edwin M. Stanton, June 12, 1863, as cited in James Garfield Randall, *Constitutional Problems Under Lincoln,* p. 268n.

25 William B. Hesseltine, *Lincoln and the War Governors,* p. 292; Randall, *Constitutional Problems Under Lincoln,* p. 268.

26 Randall, *loc. cit.*

27 George Fort Milton, *Abraham Lincoln and the Fifth Column,* pp. 137–38.

28 T. Harry Williams, *Lincoln and the Radicals,* pp. 293–94.

29 *Ibid.,* pp. 295–96.

30 James Kendall Hosmer, *The Outcome of the Civil War, 1863–1865,*

p. 135; Kenneth C. Wheare, *Abraham Lincoln and the United States,* p. 261.
31 Hosmer, *op. cit.,* pp. 135–38; Wheare, *op. cit.,* p. 261; Benjamin P. Thomas, *Abraham Lincoln,* p. 408.
32 Hosmer, *loc. cit.;* Thomas, *loc. cit.;* Wheare, *loc. cit.*
33 Thomas, *loc. cit.;* Hosmer, *loc. cit.;* Wheare, *loc. cit.*
34 Macartney, *Lincoln and His Cabinet,* p. 250.
35 *Ibid.*
36 Burton J. Hendrick, *Lincoln's War Cabinet,* p. 387.
37 Macartney, *Lincoln and His Cabinet,* p. 250.
38 T. Harry Williams, *Lincoln and the Radicals,* p. 303; Harry J. Carman and Reinhard H. Luthin, *Lincoln and the Patronage,* pp. 231, 242–44; William B. Hesseltine, *Lincoln and the War Governors,* p. 353; Albert Bushnell Hart, *Salmon Portland Chase,* p. 309; William Harlan Hale, *Horace Greeley, Voice of the People,* p. 279.
39 Donnal V. Smith, *Chase and Civil War Politics,* p. 86; T. Harry Williams, *op. cit.,* p. 307; Hale, *loc. cit.;* Hart, *loc. cit.;* Carman and Luthin, *op. cit.,* pp. 231, 242–44; Hesseltine, *loc. cit.*
40 Donnal V. Smith, *loc. cit.;* T. Harry Williams, *op. cit.,* p. 309; Hale, *loc. cit.;* Hart, *loc. cit.;* Hesseltine, *loc. cit.;* Carman and Luthin, *loc. cit.*
41 Judge James W. White to Horace Greeley, February 13, 1864, as cited in Donnal V. Smith, *Chase and Civil War Politics,* pp. 112–13. It is significant that Greeley refused this handsome offer, for this same judge's wife, Mrs. Rhoda E. White, was the foremost pleader to Lincoln, in 1860–61, begging that Greeley be given a Cabinet post. Perhaps Greeley, who carried personal grudges, disliked the Whites for their failure. At any rate, he would work with them no more.
42 Carl Sandburg, *Abraham Lincoln: The War Years,* II, 569–70, 643–45. In turning away from Lincoln and toward Chase as his presidential candidate, Greeley attempted to assassinate Lincoln in print as he had Seward in 1859–60.
43 *Ibid.,* pp. 570, 643–45.
44 *Ibid.*
45 Donnal V. Smith, *Chase and Civil War Politics,* pp. 116–20.
46 Burton J. Hendrick, *Lincoln's War Cabinet,* p. 406; Donnal V. Smith, *op. cit.,* p. 42.
47 Hendrick, *loc. cit.;* Donnal V. Smith, *loc. cit.*
48 T. Harry Williams, *op. cit.,* p. 312; Donnal V. Smith, *op. cit.,* p. 86; Carman and Luthin, *op. cit.,* pp. 231, 242–44; Hesseltine, *op. cit.,* p. 353; Hale, *op. cit.,* p. 279; Hart, *op. cit., Salmon Portland Chase,* p. 309.
49 T. Harry Williams, *op. cit.,* pp. 311–13; Edward Chase Kirkland, *The Peacemakers of 1864,* pp. 100–105; L. Pierce Clark, *Lincoln: A Psycho-Biography,* pp. 456–57; Thomas, *Abraham Lincoln,* pp. 416–17; Donnal V. Smith, *op. cit.,* p. 128.
50 T. Harry Williams, *op. cit.,* pp. 311–13; Donnal V. Smith, *op. cit.,* p. 128; Carman and Luthin, *op. cit.,* p. 247; Thomas, *op. cit.,* pp. 416–17, 441–42; Kirkland, *op. cit.,* pp. 100–105; L. Pierce Clark, *op. cit.,* pp. 456–57.
51 *The Diary of Gideon Welles,* I, 440. Welles had no sympathy either for Greeley or for the editor's views; he strived constantly to prevent Greeley from influencing Lincoln.

[52] *Ibid.,* pp. 476–77.

[53] *Ibid.,* II, 7.

[54] *Ibid.,* entry for Friday, April 15, 1864, II, 11–12.

[55] T. Harry Williams, *op. cit.,* p. 314; Carman and Luthin, *op. cit.,* p. 247; Kirkland, *op. cit.,* pp. 100–105; Donnal V. Smith, *op. cit.,* p. 128; Clark, *op. cit.,* pp. 456–57; Thomas, *op. cit.,* pp. 416–17, 441–42.

[56] John T. Morse, Jr., *Abraham Lincoln,* II, 260–62.

[57] Francis B. Carpenter, *Six Months at the White House With Abraham Lincoln,* pp. 152–53.

[58] Sandburg, *Abraham Lincoln: The War Years,* III, 420–21.

[59] Carman and Luthin, *op. cit.,* pp. 262–63.

[60] Hendrick, *Lincoln's War Cabinet,* pp. 438–39.

[61] Tarbell, *The Life of Abraham Lincoln,* IV, 30–31.

[62] *Ibid.*

[63] *Ibid.*

[64] *Ibid.*

[65] *The Writings of Abraham Lincoln,* Constitutional Edition, edited by Arthur Brooks Lapsley, VIII, 397; Frederic Bancroft, *The Life of William Henry Seward,* II, 409; Henry Luther Stoddard, *Horace Greeley: Printer, Editor, Crusader,* p. 226. To the South, unable to read Greeley's violent attacks upon Lincoln, it appeared logical that Greeley had much influence on the President. This fallacious assumption brought much embarrassment to the Confederate emissaries at Niagara.

[66] Randall, *The Civil War and Reconstruction,* p. 615; E. Merton Coulter, *The Confederate States of America, 1861–1865,* p. 548; Charles H. Wesley, *The Collapse of the Confederacy,* p. 97; George Fort Milton, *Conflict: The American Civil War,* pp. 353–54; Morse, *Abraham Lincoln,* II, 267–71.

[67] Lapsley, *op. cit.,* VIII, 397–99; Wesley, *op. cit.,* p. 97; Bancroft, *op. cit.,* II, 409; Stoddard, *op. cit.,* p. 226.

[68] Lapsley, *loc. cit.;* Bancroft, *loc. cit.;* Stoddard, *loc. cit.*

[69] Carl Russell Fish, *The American Civil War,* p. 352; Wood Gray, *The Hidden Civil War,* p. 167.

[70] Donnal V. Smith, *op. cit.,* p. 143; Fish, *loc. cit.*

CHAPTER NINE

[1] Edward Chase Kirkland, *The Peacemakers of 1864,* pp. 51–59. See also Emil Ludwig, *Abraham Lincoln,* p. 408; *The Diary of George Templeton Strong,* edited by Allan Nevins and Milton Halsey Thomas, III, 473n.

[2] Kirkland, *op. cit.,* pp. 60–64; Strong, *loc. cit.;* Ludwig, *loc. cit.*

[3] Strong, *loc. cit.;* Kirkland, *loc. cit.;* Ludwig, *loc. cit.*

[4] Kirkland, *op. cit.,* pp. 64–66; Strong, *loc. cit.;* Ludwig, *loc. cit.*

[5] Strong, *loc. cit.;* Kirkland, *loc. cit.;* Ludwig, *loc. cit.*

[6] Kirkland, *op. cit.,* pp. 66–67; Strong, *loc. cit.;* Ludwig, *loc. cit.*

[7] Kirkland, *loc. cit.;* Strong, *loc. cit.;* Ludwig, *loc. cit.*

[8] Kirkland, *op. cit.,* pp. 67–68; George Fort Milton, *Abraham Lincoln and the Fifth Column,* p. 215.

[9] Ida M. Tarbell, *The Life of Abraham Lincoln,* IV, 31–32; Francis Nicoll

Zabriskie, *Horace Greeley, the Editor,* pp. 246–50; William Harlan Hale, *Horace Greeley, Voice of the People,* pp. 280–85.

10 *The Complete Works of Abraham Lincoln,* edited by John G. Nicolay and John Hay, x, 154; *The Writings of Abraham Lincoln,* Constitutional Edition, edited by Arthur Brooks Lapsley, vii, 170–71. Although practically every authority considers that Greeley was actually duped by Jewett and the southern schemers, some will admit, as the present writer believes, that the editor employed this peace mission to embarrass Lincoln. The President, moreover, who by this time no longer trusted Greeley, held the same belief and sought to embarrass the editor and thus to remove him, as a dead political albatross, from about his neck, at least during the remainder of the presidential campaign.

11 Tarbell, *loc. cit.;* Hale, *loc. cit.;* Zabriskie, *loc. cit.*

12 Nicolay and Hay, *op. cit.,* x, 158–59; Lapsley, *op. cit.,* vii, 174.

13 Nicolay and Hay, *op. cit.,* x, 159.

14 Tarbell, *loc. cit.;* Hale, *loc. cit.;* Zabriskie, *loc. cit.*

15 T. Harry Williams, *Lincoln and the Radicals,* pp. 322–23; William E. Barton, *The Life of Abraham Lincoln,* ii, 294ff. See also, L. Pierce Clark, *Lincoln: A Psycho-Biography,* pp. 463–68, for a psychological interpretation of the Niagara peace conference.

16 *The Diary of Gideon Welles,* ii, 83; Robert S. Harper, *Lincoln and the Press,* pp. 311–13; Benjamin P. Thomas, *Abraham Lincoln,* pp. 436, 438.

17 The entire correspondence was not published until 1890, when Nicolay and Hay published it.

18 Nicolay and Hay, *op. cit.,* x, 182; Lapsley, *op. cit.,* vii, 186; Carl Sandburg, *Abraham Lincoln: The War Years,* iii, 157–58, 162, 210–11.

19 Entry for Saturday, August 6, 1864, *The Diary of Gideon Welles,* ii, 94.

20 Entry for Tuesday, August 9, 1864, *The Diary of Gideon Welles,* ii, 99.

21 Nicolay and Hay, *op. cit.,* x, 184–85; Sandburg, *loc. cit.*

22 Nicolay and Hay, *loc. cit.;* Sandburg, *loc. cit.*

23 James Ford Rhodes, *History of the Civil War, 1861–1865,* pp. 333–34; Benson J. Lossing, *Pictorial History of the Civil War in the United States of America,* iii, 446–47.

24 This reference is to the newspaper stories regarding the Niagara peace conference which "leaked" out in the northern press; it is not a reference to the Lincoln-Greeley correspondence, which had not yet been published.

25 Judah P. Benjamin to James M. Mason, August 25, 1864; *A Compilation of Messages and Papers of the Confederacy,* edited by James D. Richardson, ii, 670.

26 Entry for Wednesday, August 17, 1864, *The Diary of Gideon Welles,* ii, 109–10.

27 Rhodes, *op. cit.,* pp. 333–34.

28 Entry for Friday, August 19, 1864, *The Diary of Gideon Welles,* ii, 111–12; Carl Sandburg, *Storm Over the Land,* p. 92.

29 Ida M. Tarbell, *The Life of Abraham Lincoln,* iv, 33.

30 L. Pierce Clark, *Lincoln: A Psycho-Biography,* p. 468.

31 Donnal V. Smith, *Chase and Civil War Politics,* pp. 146, 148.

32 Entry for Tuesday, July 26, 1864, *The Diary of Gideon Welles,* ii, 87.

[33] Entry for Saturday, August 13, 1864, *The Diary of Gideon Welles,* II, 104.

[34] Entry for Wednesday, August 31, 1864, *The Diary of Gideon Welles,* II, 130.

[35] Burton J. Hendrick, *Lincoln's War Cabinet,* pp. 453–55; James Garfield Randall, *Lincoln, the Liberal Statesman,* pp. 80–81.

[36] Randall, *loc. cit.;* Hendrick, *loc. cit.*

[37] Randall, *loc. cit.*

[38] Hendrick, *loc. cit.;* Randall, *loc. cit.*

[39] T. Harry Williams, *Lincoln and the Radicals,* pp. 324, 326; Wood Gray, *The Hidden Civil War,* p. 190; Edward Chase Kirkland, *The Peacemakers of 1864,* pp. 138–46.

[40] T. Harry Williams, *loc. cit.;* Kirkland, *loc. cit.;* Gray, *loc. cit.*

[41] T. Harry Williams, *op. cit.,* pp. 326, 328–30; Kirkland, *loc. cit.;* Gray, *loc. cit.;* Benjamin P. Thomas, *Abraham Lincoln,* p. 447; Hendrick, *Lincoln's War Cabinet,* p. 456.

[42] T. Harry Williams, *loc. cit.;* Gray, *loc. cit.;* Thomas, *loc. cit.;* Kirkland, *loc. cit.;* Hendrick, *loc. cit.*

[43] Don C. Seitz, *Horace Greeley, Founder of the New York Tribune,* p. 267.

[44] This editorial appeared in the *Tribune* on the sixth of September, and may have been the result of Sherman's victory, although a possibility exists that it was inspired by Hoskins, who may or may not have gone to Washington to see Lincoln.

[45] Seitz, *op. cit.,* pp. 268–70; Sandburg, *Abraham Lincoln: The War Years,* III, 249; Robert S. Harper, *Lincoln and the Press,* p. 347. All three of these sources took their information from the only original source for this story, an article by D. S. Alexander, which appeared in the Lyons (New York) *Republican,* for August 3, 1921. There is no other substantiation, by Greeley or Lincoln or anyone associated with them. Carl Sandburg points out one discrepancy, the fact that Lincoln never shaved himself. However, there might have been one exception; and Lincoln might have promised the Postmaster-Generalship to Greeley. However, when one remembers that, only a few days before, Lincoln had talked to his Cabinet about the untrustworthiness of that "old shoe" Greeley, it seems unlikely that he would have done so. Nevertheless, he may have decided again to fight fire with fire, promising Greeley an office to obtain his support, either in sincerity or otherwise. However, if he did, such action was unprecedented.

[46] Seitz, *op. cit.,* p. 270; Harper, *loc. cit.;* Sandburg, *loc. cit.*

[47] Seitz, *loc. cit.;* Harper, *loc. cit.;* Sandburg, *loc. cit.*

[48] Harper, *op. cit.,* p. 315.

[49] T. Harry Williams, *Lincoln and the Radicals,* pp. 350–51; Horace Greeley, *The American Conflict,* II, 673.

[50] T. Harry Williams, *loc. cit.;* Greeley, *loc. cit.* Once again Greeley was misinterpreting political signs and making political forecasts which could not come to fruition.

[51] Entry for Friday, January 6, 1865, *The Diary of Gideon Welles,* II, 222.

[52] Enry for Saturday, January 14, 1865, *The Diary of Gideon Welles,* II, 223–24. Welles found in his vocabulary no kind words for Greeley; therefore, he is inclined to minimize the editor's generosity and unselfishness, when

those characteristics do appear. However, he does here correctly analyze Greeley's support of Butler and his failure to deter Lincoln from yielding to Grant's wishes in dismissing the general.

53 Paul Skeels Peirce, *The Freedmen's Bureau,* p. 44.

54 *Ibid.*

55 Greeley, *The American Conflict,* II, 676–77.

56 *Ibid.*

57 Sandburg, *Abraham Lincoln: The War Years,* IV, 254–55. There is no record anywhere that Greeley ordered the foreign publication of this letter. However, it seems reasonable that only he could have released it and that, hence, he knew of the affair—an incident which embarrassed Lincoln by placing him in a bad position in the eyes of the British and the French.

58 Entry for Saturday, April 1, 1865, *The Diary of Gideon Welles,* II, 271–72.

59 William Harlan Hale, *Horace Greeley, Voice of the People,* pp. 292–93.

60 Jeter Allen Isely, *Horace Greeley and the Republican Party, 1853–1861,* p. 933.

61 Hale, *loc. cit.*

CHAPTER TEN

1 Allan Nevins, "Horace Greeley, the Editor and the Man," *Bookman,* LXIV (February, 1927), 741–42.

2 Carl Sandburg, *Abraham Lincoln: The War Years,* III, 421.

3 *Ibid.*

4 From John Hay's *Diary,* as cited in William E. Barton, *The Life of Abraham Lincoln,* II, 299.

5 Horace Greeley, *Recollections of a Busy Life,* p. 403.

6 Gamaliel Bradford, *As God Made Them,* pp. 150–51.

7 Henry Luther Stoddard, *Horace Greeley: Printer, Editor, Crusader,* p. 229.

8 *Ibid.*

9 *Ibid.*

10 *The Diary of George Templeton Strong,* edited by Allan Nevins and Milton Halsey Thomas, III, 586.

11 L. Pierce Clark, *Lincoln: A Psycho-Biography,* p. 468.

12 Greeley, *Recollections of a Busy Life,* p. 404.

13 New York *Daily Tribune,* April 19, 1865, as cited in Robert S. Harper, *Lincoln and the Press,* p. 356; Francis Nicoll Zabriskie, *Horace Greeley, the Editor,* pp. 251–54.

14 *The Complete Works of Abraham Lincoln,* edited by John G. Nicolay and John Hay, V, vi. Greeley possessed no real fondness, no great admiration for Lincoln. At times his heart may have contained such thoughts of praise, but not often.

15 *Ibid.,* p. xxvi. Greeley spoke these words in 1872, seven years after the end of the war. By this time he was better able to appreciate Lincoln's true character and worth.

16 Roy P. Basler, *The Lincoln Legend,* pp. 65–67.

17 Benjamin P. Thomas, *Abraham Lincoln,* pp. 497–98.

Bibliography

PRIMARY SOURCES

COLLECTED WORKS

Angle, Paul M. (ed.), *New Letters and Papers of Lincoln*. Boston: Houghton Mifflin Company, 1930.

Autobiography of Abraham Lincoln, An, compiled and annotated by Nathaniel Wright Stephenson. Indianapolis: Bobbs-Merrill Company, 1926.

Basler, Roy P. (ed.), *The Collected Works of Abraham Lincoln,* 8 vols. New Brunswick, N.J.: Rutgers University Press, 1953.

Brooks, Phillips, *Addresses.* New York: Frederick A. Stokes Company, 1899.

Gross, Anthony (ed.), *Lincoln's Own Stories.* Garden City, N.Y.: Garden City Publishing Company, 1926.

Hertz, Emanuel (ed.), *The Hidden Lincoln, From the Letters and Papers of William H. Herndon.* New York: Viking Press, 1938.

Howells, William Dean, and John R. Hayes (eds.), *Lives and Speeches of Abraham Lincoln and Hannibal Hamlin.* Columbus: Follett, Foster & Company, 1860.

Lapsley, Arthur Brooks (ed.), *The Writings of Abraham Lincoln,* Constitutional Edition, 8 vols. New York: G. P. Putnam's Sons, 1905.

Lincoln and the Civil War in the Diaries and Letters of John Hay, selected and with an Introduction by Tyler Dennett. New York: Dodd, Mead & Company, 1939.

Mearns, David Chambers (ed.), *The Lincoln Papers,* with an Introduction by Carl Sandburg, 2 vols. Garden City, N.Y.: Doubleday & Company, 1948.

Nicolay, John G., and John Hay (eds.), *The Complete Works of Abraham Lincoln,* 12 vols. Cumberland Gap, Tenn.: Lincoln Memorial University, 1894.

Richardson, James D. (ed.), *A Compilation of the Messages and Papers of the Confederacy, Including the Diplomatic Correspondence, 1861–1865,* 2 vols. Nashville: United States Publishing Company, 1905.

Stern, Philip Van Doren (ed.), *The Life and Writings of Abraham Lincoln.* New York: Random House, 1940.

Uncollected Works of Abraham Lincoln, assembled and annotated by Rufus Rockwell Wilson, vols. I and II. Elmira, N.Y.: Primavera Press, 1947.

AUTOBIOGRAPHIES, DIARIES, AND MEMOIRS

Angle, Paul M. (ed.), *The Lincoln Reader.* New Brunswick, N.J.: Rutgers University Press, 1947.

Bigelow, John, *Retrospections of an Active Life,* 3 vols. New York: Baker & Taylor Company, 1909.

Bishop, Joseph Bucklin, *Notes and Anecdotes of Many Years.* New York: Charles Scribner's Sons, 1925.

Conway, Moncure Daniel, *Autobiography, Memories, and Experiences,* 2 vols. Boston: Houghton Mifflin Company, 1904.

Diary of Gideon Welles, The, with an introduction by John T. Morse, Jr., 3 vols. Boston: Houghton Mifflin Company, 1911.

Gordon, General John B., *Reminiscences of the Civil War.* New York: Charles Scribner's Sons, 1905.

Greeley, Horace, *Overland Journey From New York to San Francisco.* New York: C. M. Saxton, Barker & Company, 1860.

———, *Recollections of a Busy Life,* New York: Tribune Association, 1873.

Nevins, Allan, and Milton Halsey Thomas (eds.), *The Diary of George Templeton Strong,* 4 vols. New York: Macmillan Company, 1952.

Rankin, Henry B., *Intimate Character Sketches of Abraham Lincoln.* Philadelphia: J. B. Lippincott Company, 1924.

Rice, Allen Thorndike (ed.), *Reminiscences of Abraham Lin-*

coln *by Distinguished Men of His Time.* New York: Harper & Brothers, 1909.

Riddle, Albert Gallatin, *Recollections of War Times, 1860– 1865.* New York: Knickerbocker Press, 1895.

Weed, Harriet A., and Thurlow Weed Barnes (eds.), *The Life of Thurlow Weed, Including His Autobiography and a Memoir,* 2 vols. Boston: Houghton Mifflin Company, 1884.

CONTEMPORARY ACCOUNTS

Brown, George William, *Baltimore and the Nineteenth of April, 1861.* Baltimore: N. Murray, Publication Agent, Johns Hopkins University, 1887.

Carpenter, Francis Bicknell, *Six Months at the White House With Abraham Lincoln.* New York: Hurd & Houghton, 1866.

Dumond, Dwight Lowell (ed.), *Southern Editorials on Secession.* New York: Century Company, 1931.

Eisenschiml, Otto, and Ralph Newman (eds.), *The American Iliad: The Epic Story of the Civil War, as narrated by Eyewitnesses and Contemporaries.* New York: Bobbs-Merrill Company, 1947.

Giddings, Joshua R., *History of the Rebellion: Its Authors and Causes.* New York: Follett, Foster & Company, 1864.

Greeley, Horace, *The American Conflict,* 2 vols. Hartford: O. D. Case & Company, 1864, 1866.

———, *Essays Designed to Elucidate the Science of Political Economy.* Philadelphia: Porter & Coates, 1869.

Greeley, Horace, and others, *The Great Industries of the United States.* Hartford: Burr & Hyde, 1872.

Grout, Josiah, *A Lincoln Book: A Soldier's Tribute to His Chief.* Rutland, Vt.: Tuttle Company, 1925.

Ingersoll, L. D., *The Life of Horace Greeley.* Philadelphia: John E. Potter & Company, 1874.

Logan, John A., *The Great Conspiracy: Its Origin and History.* New York: A. R. Hart & Company, 1886.

Ossoli, S. Margaret Fuller, *Literature and Art,* New York: Flowers & Wells, 1852.

Parton, J., *The Life of Horace Greeley*. New York: Mason Brothers, 1855.

Political Text Book for 1860, compiled by Horace Greeley and John F. Cleveland. New York: Tribune Association, 1860.

Tribune Almanac and Political Register, The. New York: G. Dearborn & Company, 1838.

Zabriskie, Francis Nicoll, *Horace Greeley, the Editor.* New York: Funk & Wagnalls, 1890.

SECONDARY SOURCES

MAGAZINE ARTICLES

"Horace Greeley to Dr. Shaw," *Saturday Review of Literature,* XXVI (May 1, 1943), 13.

Nevins, Allan, "Horace Greeley, the Editor and the Man," *Bookman,* LXIV (February, 1927), 740–42.

"Voice of the *Tribune,*" *Newsweek,* XXXVI (October 2, 1950), 56.

GENERAL WORKS AND MONOGRAPHS

Adams, Ephraim Douglass, *Great Britain and the American Civil War,* 2 vols. New York: Longmans, Green & Company, 1925.

Angle, Paul M., *Here I Have Lived: A History of Lincoln's Springfield, 1821–1865.* New Brunswick, N.J.: Rutgers University Press, 1935.

Baringer, William Eldon, *Lincoln's Rise to Power.* Boston: Little, Brown & Company, 1937.

Basler, Roy P., *The Lincoln Legend,* Boston: Houghton Mifflin Company, 1935.

Burgess, John W., *The Civil War and the Constitution, 1859–1865,* 2 vols. New York: Charles Scribner's Sons, 1901.

Carman, Harry J., and Rinehard H. Luthin, *Lincoln and the Patronage,* New York: Columbia University Press, 1943.

Catton, Bruce, *Glory Road.* Garden City, N.Y.: Doubleday & Company, 1952.

——, *Mr. Lincoln's Army,* Garden City, N.Y.: Doubleday & Company, 1951.

Chadwick, French Ensor, *Causes of the Civil War, 1859–1861*, vol. xix of *The American Nation*, edited by Albert Bushnell Hart (27 vols.). New York: Harper & Brothers, 1907.

Cole, Arthur Charles, *The Irrepressible Conflict, 1850–1865*, vol. vii of *A History of American Life*, edited by Dixon Ryan Fox and Arthur M. Schlesinger. New York: Macmillan Company, 1934.

Coulter, E. Merton, *The Confederate States of America, 1861–1865*, vol. vii of *A History of the South*, edited by Wendell Holmes Stephens and E. Merton Coulter. Baton Rouge: Louisiana State University Press, 1950.

Craven, Avery, *The Coming of the Civil War*. New York: Charles Scribner's Sons, 1942.

Fish, Carl Russell, *The American Civil War*. New York: Longmans, Green & Company, 1937.

Gray, Wood, *The Hidden Civil War*. New York: Viking Press, 1942.

Harper, Robert S., *Lincoln and the Press*. New York: McGraw-Hill Book Company, 1951.

Hendrick, Burton J., *Lincoln's War Cabinet*. Boston: Little, Brown & Company, 1946.

——, *Statesmen of the Lost Cause*. Boston: Little, Brown & Company, 1939.

Hesseltine, William B., *Lincoln and the War Governors*. New York: Alfred A. Knopf, 1948.

Hosmer, James Kendall, *The Outcome of the Civil War, 1863–1865*, vol. xxi of *The American Nation: A History*, edited by Albert Bushnell Hart. New York: Harper & Brothers, 1907.

Isely, Jeter Allen, *Horace Greeley and the Republican Party, 1853–1861*. Princeton, N.J.: Princeton University Press, 1947.

Johnson, Rossiter, *A Short History of the War of Secession, 1861–1865*. Boston: Ticknor & Company, 1888.

Kirkland, Edward Chase, *The Peacemakers of 1864*. New York: Macmillan Company, 1927.

Leech, Margaret, *Reveille in Washington, 1860–1865*. New York: Harper & Brothers, 1941.

Lincoln Bibliography, 1839–1939, compiled by Jay Monaghan, 2 vols. Springfield: Illinois State Historical Library, 1943.

Lincoln Library, The. Buffalo, N.Y.: Frontier Press Company, 1950.

Lossing, Benson J., *Pictorial History of the Civil War in the United States of America,* 3 vols. Hartford: T. Belknap, 1868.

Luthin, Reinhard H., *The First Lincoln Campaign.* Cambridge, Mass.: Harvard University Press, 1944.

Macartney, Clarence Edward, *Highways and Byways of the Civil War,* Pittsburgh: Gibson Press, 1938.

——, *Lincoln and His Cabinet.* New York: Charles Scribner's Sons, 1931.

McClure, Alexander Kelly, *Lincoln's Yarns and Stories.* Chicago: J. C. Winston Company, 1904.

Milton, George Fort, *Abraham Lincoln and the Fifth Column.* New York: Vanguard Press, 1942.

——, *Conflict: The American Civil War.* New York: Coward-McCann, 1941.

Monaghan, Jay, *Diplomat in Carpet Slippers.* New York: Bobbs-Merrill Company, 1945.

Nevins, Allan, *The Emergence of Lincoln,* 2 vols. New York: Charles Scribner's Sons, 1950.

Nichols, Ray Franklin, *The Disruption of American Democracy.* New York: Macmillan Company, 1948.

Nicolay, John George, *The Outbreak of Rebellion.* New York: Charles Scribner's Sons, 1901.

Nicolay, John George, and John Hay, *Abraham Lincoln: A History,* 10 vols. New York: Century Company, 1917.

Peirce, Paul Skeels, *The Freedmen's Bureau.* Iowa City: University of Iowa Press, 1904.

Potter, David Morris, *Lincoln and His Party in the Secession Crisis.* New Haven: Yale University Press, 1942.

Randall, James Garfield, *The Civil War and Reconstruction.* New York: D. C. Heath and Company, 1937.

——, *Constitutional Problems Under Lincoln.* New York: D. Appleton and Company, 1926.

———, *Lincoln and the South.* Baton Rouge: Louisiana State University Press, 1946.

———, *Lincoln, the Liberal Statesman.* New York: Dodd, Mead & Company, 1947.

Riddle, Donald W., *Lincoln Runs for Congress.* New Brunswick, N.J.: Rutgers University Press, 1948.

Rhodes, James Ford, *History of the Civil War, 1861–1865.* New York: Macmillan Company, 1917.

———, *History of the Civil War,* 8 vols. New York: Macmillan Company, 1914.

Sandburg, Carl, *Storm Over the Land: A Profile of the Civil War,* taken mainly from *Abraham Lincoln: The War Years.* New York: Harcourt, Brace & Company, 1942.

Shannon, Fred Albert, *The Organization and Administration of the Union Army, 1861–1865,* 2 vols. Cleveland: Arthur H. Clark Company, 1928.

Smith, Donnal V., *Chase and Civil War Politics,* reprinted from the *Ohio Archaeological and Historical Quarterly,* July and October, 1930. Columbus, Ohio: Heer Printing Company, 1931.

Smith, Edward Conrad, *The Borderland in the Civil War.* New York: Macmillan Company, 1927.

Stampp, Kenneth M., *And the War Came: The North and the Secession Crisis, 1860–1861.* Baton Rouge: Louisiana State University Press, 1950.

Stephenson, Nathaniel Wright, *Abraham Lincoln and the Union.* New Haven: Yale University Press, 1918.

Stone, Irving, *They Also Ran.* New York: Doubleday, Doran & Company, 1944.

Tilley, John Shipley, *Lincoln Takes Command.* Chapel Hill: University of North Carolina Press, 1941.

Villard, Henry, *Lincoln on the Eve of '61.* New York: Alfred A. Knopf, 1941.

Wesley, Charles H., *The Collapse of the Confederacy.* Washington, D.C.: Associated Publishers, 1937.

Wheare, Kenneth Clinton, *Abraham Lincoln and the United States.* London: English University Press, 1948.

Williams, Kenneth P., *Lincoln Finds a General,* 3 vols. New York: Macmillan Company, 1952.

Williams, Thomas Harry, *Lincoln and His Generals.* New York: Alfred A. Knopf, 1952.

———, *Lincoln and the Radicals.* Madison: University of Wisconsin Press, 1941.

BIOGRAPHICAL WORKS

Arnold, Isaac N., *The Life of Abraham Lincoln.* Chicago: Jansen, McClurg & Company, 1885.

Baldwin, James, *Four Great Americans.* Chicago: Werner School Book Company, 1897.

Bancroft, Frederic, *The Life of William Henry Seward,* 2 vols. New York: Harper & Brothers, 1900.

Barton, William E., *Abraham Lincoln and Walt Whitman.* Indianapolis: Bobbs-Merrill Company, 1928.

———, *The Life of Abraham Lincoln,* 2 vols. Indianapolis: Bobbs-Merrill Company, 1925.

Beveridge, Albert J., *Abraham Lincoln, 1809–1858,* 2 vols. Boston: Houghton Mifflin Company, 1928.

Bradford, Gamaliel, *As God Made Them.* Boston: Houghton Mifflin Company, 1929.

Charnwood, Godfrey Rathbone Benson, Lord, *Abraham Lincoln.* New York: Henry Holt & Company, 1917.

Clark, L. Pierce, *Lincoln: A Psycho-Biography.* New York: Charles Scribner's Sons, 1933.

Curtis, William Eleroy, *The True Abraham Lincoln.* Philadelphia: J. B. Lippincott Company, 1903.

Dodd, William Edward, *Lincoln or Lee.* New York: Century Company, 1928.

Donald, David Herbert, *Lincoln's Herndon.* New York: Alfred A. Knopf, 1948.

Fahrney, Ralph Ray, *Horace Greeley and the Tribune in the Civil War.* Cedar Rapids, Iowa: Torch Press, 1936.

Hale, William Harlan, *Horace Greeley, Voice of the People.* New York: Harper & Brothers, 1950.

Hart, Albert Bushnell, *Salmon Portland Chase*. Boston: Houghton Mifflin Company, 1909 (?).

Ketcham, Henry, *The Life of Abraham Lincoln*. New York: A. L. Burt, 1901.

Korngold, Ralph, *Two Friends of Man: The Story of William Lloyd Garrison and Wendell Phillips, and Their Relationship With Abraham Lincoln*. Boston: Little, Brown & Company, 1950.

Linn, William Alexander, *Horace Greeley, Founder of the New York Tribune*. New York: D. Appleton & Company, 1903.

Lothrop, Thornton Kirkland, *William Henry Seward*. Boston: Houghton Mifflin Company, 1909 (?).

Ludwig, Emil, *Abraham Lincoln: The Full Life Story of Our Martyred President,* translated by Eden and Cedar Paul. New York: Liveright Publishing Corporation, 1930.

————, *Lincoln,* translated from the German by Eden and Cedar Paul. Boston: Little, Brown & Company, 1930.

Morse, John T. Jr., *Abraham Lincoln,* 2 vols. Boston: Houghton Mifflin Company, 1893.

Newton, Joseph Fort, *Lincoln and Herndon*. Cedar Rapids, Iowa: Torch Press, 1910.

Randall, James Garfield, *Lincoln, the President,* 3 vols. New York: Dodd, Mead & Company, 1945.

Sandburg, Carl, *Abraham Lincoln: The Prairie Years,* First Edition, 2 vols. New York: Harcourt, Brace & Company, 1926.

————, *Abraham Lincoln: The War Years,* 4 vols. New York: Harcourt, Brace & Company, 1939.

Seitz, Don C., *Horace Greeley, Founder of the New York Tribune*. Indianapolis: Bobbs-Merrill Company, 1926.

Shaw, Albert, *Abraham Lincoln*. New York: Review of Reviews Corporation, 1929.

Stoddard, Henry Luther, *Horace Greeley: Printer, Editor, Crusader*. New York: G. P. Putnam's Sons, 1946.

Tarbell, Ida M., *The Life of Abraham Lincoln,* 4 vols. New York: Lincoln History Society, 1924.

Thomas, Benjamin Platt, *Abraham Lincoln*. New York: Alfred A. Knopf, 1952.

Thomas, Benjamin Platt, *Portrait for Posterity*. New Brunswick, N.J.: Rutgers University Press, 1947.

Wagenknecht, Edward Charles, *Abraham Lincoln: His Life, Work, and Character*. New York: Creative Age Press, 1947.

Warren, Raymond, *The Prairie President: Living Through the Years with Lincoln, 1809–1861*. Chicago: Reilly & Lee Company, 1930.